THE BOOK
of LETTERS

THE BOOK
of LETTERS

150 Years of

Private Canadian

Correspondence

COMPILED *and* EDITED *by*

PAUL *and* AUDREY GRESCOE

Macfarlane Walter & Ross
Toronto

Macfarlane Walter & Ross
An Affiliate of McClelland & Stewart Ltd.
37A Hazelton Avenue
Toronto, Canada M5R 2E3
www.mwandr.com

National Library of Canada Cataloguing in Publication

Main entry under title:

The book of letters : 150 years of private Canadian correspondence /
[edited by] Paul and Audrey Grescoe.

Includes index.
ISBN 1-55199-104-7

1. Canadian letters (English) 2. Canada – History. 3. Canada – Biography.
I. Grescoe, Paul, 1939- II. Grescoe, Audrey

FC25.B65 2002   971   C2002-902837-X
F1005.B65 2002

Macfarlane Walter & Ross gratefully acknowledges support for its publishing program from the Canada Council for the Arts, the Ontario Arts Council, and the Government of Canada through the Book Publishing Industry Development Program.

Printed and bound in Canada

This book is printed on acid-free paper that is 100% ancient-forest-friendly (100% post-consumer recycled).

For all who wrote the past,
and especially for Lara and Taras,
who are writing the future.

Contents

INTRODUCTION
The Letters that Link Us 1

THE MAKING OF CANADA
"Please God, we shall get a living" 6

LOVE AND FRIENDSHIP
"I shall write a little of my love to you" 124

THE ART OF THE ORDINARY
"No time for repining" 207

IDEAS AND IDEALS
"What of the Soul of Canada?" 272

ACKNOWLEDGMENTS 323

BIBLIOGRAPHY 329

INDEX OF LETTER WRITERS 332

INTRODUCTION

The Letters that Link Us

"Harry, my boy, never write a letter if you can help it, and never destroy one." Canada's first prime minister, Sir John A. Macdonald, offered that advice to a colleague in the House of Commons. Although many Canadians have ignored the first half of his admonition, many others have heeded the second half. They have cherished correspondence from relatives and friends, often for decades, even as the letters grow brittle and crack along their folds. Reading them now is like eavesdropping on one side of an intimate conversation.

Sometimes, as parents and grandparents die, their offspring give their once-private mail to public archives, where it will be preserved as evidence of another time and place. Letters are far more immediate, dramatic, and personal than any historian's account. In their passion and eloquence, they testify to Canadians' deep feelings about war and other calamities, their doubts and fears about their society, their hope and love for their families.

Unlike e-mail, which is informal and often hurriedly typed, letters written in longhand (that old-fashioned phrase) suggest thoughtfulness – both in the time expended in putting pen to paper and in the deeper thinking this act can prompt. Messages sent via the Internet also lack the physical clues we find in handwritten letters. They have no inkblots, no words blurred by tears, no lines rising in excitement, no disintegration of penmanship as the writer's hand is gradually crippled by arthritis. They don't carry a faint scent, telling us what perfume a sister was wearing or whether a father has resumed smoking (a woman writing family in England from her 1880s Ontario homestead asked for more letters and added: "Tell Father to give them all a good smoke, as, as soon as we opened the last one, we smelt Father's pipe and passed it around so we all had a whiff"). Even typed letters convey something of the writer's state of mind: the quality of paper, the impression made by the keys, the x-ed-out words, the individuality of the signature. And the packaging itself is important: as Nick Bantock (creator of the Griffin and Sabine series, in which fictional letters are enclosed in envelopes within the books) put it: "One of the key pleasures of receiving a letter is the act of holding and entering an envelope – a sort of cross between Christmas and sex."

For most Canadians, the telephone long ago replaced the letter as the primary means of communication. But as Christopher Dafoe, a columnist for *The Winnipeg Free Press*, noted: "Telephone calls cannot be tied up with string and kept in a bottom drawer for future reference. Unlike a letter, a phone call has no afterlife. It is as evanescent as a natter over the back fence or a conversation conducted across a body of open water with semaphore flags."

This is the first general collection of English-language letters that Canadians have written to one another. As our starting point we chose 1851, the year a young Scottish immigrant named Sandford Fleming designed Canada's first postage stamp, the Three-Penny Beaver; our cut-off date is that globe-jangling year, 2001. Along the way we found fascinating Canadiana in public archives, libraries, and antiquarian bookstores. But what we hope distinguishes this collection is the fruit of our widespread call for letters from the public. Magazine and newspaper articles and letters to the editor elicited contributions from across the country.

Bryan Goodyer wrote from North Vancouver: "Enclosed is a copy of the last known letter from France of my uncle, Robert Henry Goodyer, who was killed in action in Holland within 2 months of having written it. As far as I can remember, no one in the family . . . ever spoke of Uncle Bob from that day to this . . . What was he like? What were his hopes and dreams? The letter gives few clues, suggesting only that he was a fun-loving guy, a good friend and a loyal soldier, who paid the ultimate price to ensure our freedom from tyranny."

Pauline Rowe of Winnipeg offered a love letter sent by her great-grandfather, a country doctor, to his intended in 1862. "It gives me goosebumps to read it," she wrote, "and imagine him sitting at a table, under an oil lamp, nibbed pen in hand, pouring out his feelings to his 'dear Maggie.' He even includes a prescription for a remedy for her recent fever."

Almost all the letters on these pages were composed by Canadians. A few were written by outsiders commenting on Canadian people, places, or events. The letters are presented in English, though some were written in other languages, mainly French. A collection of French-language correspondence, *Chers Nous Autres* ("Dear Us"), edited by Robert Blondin and Gilles LaMontagne, was published in 1978. We have had some of these translated and, with the editors' permission, included them.

Is there anything uniquely Canadian about Canadian correspondence? Well, yes and no. There is nothing singular about the kinds of feelings these correspondents express, the range of stories they tell. As the Quebec comedian Yvon Deschamps put it, "This is the paradox about life – that every individual is different. But together we're all alike." Yet nuances exist. Letters written in French are often more passionate than those written in English. Even when describing desperate situations, many English-speaking letter-writers show a certain reserve. This matter-of-factness somehow intensifies the experiences they're recounting.

Some of the most stirring correspondence comes from the wars of the past century. We found so much in public and private archives that we have limited the selections in this book to a sampling from the First and Second World Wars. One such letter was sent to us by the niece of a twenty-one-year-old flying officer in the Royal Canadian Air Force who was making forays over Germany in the second year of the Second World War. In her note Mary Jane Cowan says: "Those of my generation think of letter writing as a lost art. As a tutor and teacher, I spend much of my time encouraging students to explore and enjoy the written word. In reading these passages in Donald's letter, I find I am amazed at the ability of this 'ordinary' young man to convey his memories and feelings about his family and his home in such an evocative way." Is there a more enduring vehicle for the expression of such sentiment than the humble letter?

For practical reasons, we have not tried to reproduce actual letters. Often we had to work with less-than-clear photocopies of original correspondence. In some cases the letter-writers' handwriting was nearly illegible. Occasionally, we failed to figure out a word; in that case, we either take an educated guess, enclosing the likely word in [brackets], or indicate a missing word with a question mark in brackets [?]. To maintain each letter's integrity, we have not corrected the writer's spelling and grammatical errors unless we thought those errors might confuse the reader. In those cases, we have made corrections or provided short explanatory notes [in brackets]. We've preserved personal eccentricities as well as peculiarities of punctuation – for example, the habits of avoiding commas, using dashes rather than full stops, or starting a sentence with a lower-case letter. We sometimes omit sentences, or paragraphs, that seem less relevant or less interesting than the rest of the letter. We signal such omissions with ellipses (. . .).

We've done our best to obtain permission to reproduce all the letters in this book. Errors or omissions brought to our attention will be corrected in future printings.

Finally, we invite readers to submit copies of letters written by Canadians, or covering Canadian topics, for possible inclusion in two forthcoming volumes. *The Book of War Letters: Two Centuries of Private Canadian Correspondence*, to be published in 2003, will cover conflicts in which Canadians served – from the War of 1812 through the North-West Rebellion, the Boer War, and the Spanish

Civil War, to the First and Second World Wars, Korea, Vietnam, Bosnia, and Afghanistan. *The Book of Love Letters*, scheduled for 2004, will contain correspondence of romance and friendship. If you have such letters or know of any that seem suitable, please send copies (which cannot be returned), along with background material and contact information, including a mailing address, an e-mail address, and/or a daytime telephone number. If a letter you submit is chosen for inclusion in either book, we will contact you for formal permission to publish it.

Paul and Audrey Grescoe
R.R. 1, I-33
Bowen Island, B.C.
V0N 1G0

THE MAKING OF CANADA

"Please God, we shall get a living"

Letters can be first drafts of history. Over time, they become intriguing primary sources for those who would like to know how this country came to be. In 1851, when the first of the letters in this section were written, Canada was not yet a nation. There was a Province of Canada, with fewer than two million people scattered across Canada West (Ontario) and Canada East (Quebec). In what's now called western Canada, there were no towns to speak of, only forts and trading posts. Not for another sixteen years would Confederation unite Ontario and Quebec with the Maritime colonies of New Brunswick and Nova Scotia to create the Dominion of Canada.

Yet the consuming issues of the day were remarkably similar to the concerns that still preoccupy Canadians. Even in 1851 the topic most prominent in the columns of newspapers and magazines was the Canadas' relationship with their swaggering, intrusive neighbour. The talk was of reciprocity, an early version of free trade. *The Globe*, founded seven years earlier by George Brown, was editorializing: "The great advantage of the measure"– the passing of the reciprocity bill being considered by the United States in early 1851 – "we conceive to lie in the freedom which it will give to trade – the facility it will give us for going into the American as freely as into the English market to make our purchases of manufactured goods, and foreign merchandize; and especially, in the removal of all pretence of grumbling at the commercial position of our country." The grumbles, of course, go on.

Outnumbered more than ten to one by Americans even then, pre-Confederation Canadians were eager to grow, in population and in geography. *The Journal & Express* of Hamilton, Canada West, urged the government to enlist British aid to advertise the Province of Canada's attractions overseas to foster immigration, particularly from Germany. (In 2002 Ottawa pledged to encourage more immigration, arguing that Canada's population growth had fallen to an all-time low.) Meanwhile, amid advertisements for phrenologists and purveyors of "the noble medicine" sarsaparilla, the January 25, 1851, edition of *The Globe* spoke of "the construction of a Rail road from Halifax to the Pacific, as a great national undertaking, social and commercial." Over the next half-century, of course, the national railway would be realized.

By the late 19th century some of the most exciting developments in the new nation were happening on the left side of the map: the Canadian Pacific Railway, the creation of the North-West Mounted Police, the fine-tuning of the 49th Parallel, and the influx of immigrants to the Klondike, the prairies, and the West Coast. Not that the East was asleep. Even then, whites were contending with aggrieved natives in Oka, Quebec. Homesteaders were finding fresh land in Ontario, and swarms of newcomers – some of them British orphans – were arriving in eastern ports as well.

The image that recurs in these letters is of Canada as a place to come to, a place where – as an Englishwoman wrote while homesteading in 1883 – "please God, we shall get a living." What follows is a brief, selective, often eccentric history of Canada, written by some of the people who helped create the nation over the past 150 years.

THE FACTOR'S WIFE

Letitia Hargrave was the well-born wife of James Hargrave, chief factor of the main Hudson's Bay Company (HBC) post of York Factory, near the bay that gave the great fur-trading enterprise its name. By 1851 Manitoba's oldest settlement – a small cluster of white wooden buildings surrounded by fog- and snow-bound barrens – was in decline. Letitia, like her husband a Scot, was a finishing-school graduate now raising four children among natives and rough traders. In these letters to her travelling husband shortly before she left York Factory after eleven years, she commented on a doctor's wife named Mrs. Wills ("the Doctress"), who had complained to an HBC governor's wife, Mrs. Colvile (whose name Letitia spelled as "Colville").

York Factory 10th August 1851

My dearest Hargrave

. . . Before Mr Ballenden left York he gave Willie [Letitia's brother] a hint & some thing more that Mrs Wills had not flattered any of us here in her communications to Mrs Colville, & mentioned one thing wch has finished the little deviless in my opinion. She abused the cooking. Mrs C. said she found it better than any where else in the country. Oh said the Doctress, it is I assure you perfectly changed since y^u came, every thing is very different – I vowed that across her threshold I should never step, & she has become dignified since she got a house of her own, & has only returned my visits, so that we meet on the platform where I flatter myself I combine graciousness & majesty in my demeanor. Ballenden wound up his harangue by calling her a malevolent lying bad woman . . .

York Factory 12, Aug^st 1851

My dearest Hargrave

. . . We had 50 Salmon from Churchill. They were not exactly 1st chop, or Garson damaged them. George Lootit is pointed in his attentions to Mary [a servant] & has even got the length of intimating that it is his intention of leaving off smoking & taking a wife. Their flirtations being carried on with open doors between the nursery & me & Mary's not finding it necessary to mitigate her naturally loud voice I have the benefit of their conversations wch on Mary's side consist entirely of invections agst Orkney men & Indian women varied by abuse of old Garson in wch his assistant & successor cordially joins –

Soon after writing this letter Letitia and her family, including baby Dugald ("Buffy") and Mary, embarked on a visit to London aboard a vessel that offered her some civilized delights – and some lonely sailors who became surprising babysitters.

38 Finsbury Square Octr 5th [1851]

My dearest Hargrave

We are all here after a smart but rough passage. We came on board at York on Sunday the 7th Sept^r & left the ship on Friday the 3rd Oct^r . . .

Captⁿ Pullen is married & has 2 children he has not seen his wife for 4 years, & attached himself particularly to Master Dugald whom he carried up & down the companion much to Mary's relief & the Baby's safety . . .

I must now do justice to poor Captⁿ Herd. He gave Miss Mills & me the 2 large cabins in the after part. Mary had the 3rd & he coolly put his chronometers into the 4th thereby excluding Miss Mowat or Mrs James who had theirs in the gun room. He also gave us a hot supper every night & a bottle of champagne every day in <u>private</u> after dinner . . . & Buffy was on his knee when idle, during the whole voyage . . .

Y^{rs} m^o affec^{ly}

L Hargrave

Letitia accompanied her husband to the HBC post of Sault Ste. Marie in Canada West (present-day Ontario). She died three years later, during a cholera epidemic; little Buffy died soon after. An era was ending: in 1870 – exactly two centuries after Britain had granted it a vast territory stretching from northern Quebec to southern Alberta – the HBC grudgingly sold most of the land to the new nation of Canada.

SLAVE AND MASTER

Henry Bibb, son of a black mother and a white father, ran away from six successive owners in the southern United States. In 1850, with the passage of the U.S. Fugitive Slave Law, Bibb fled to Canada West, where slavery had declined after 1793 and was abolished in 1833. He was among an estimated thirty thousand slaves who escaped through the loose network of sympathizers and safe houses that made up the Underground Railroad. In exile Bibb began publishing an influential newspaper, Voice of the Fugitive, *and wrote repeatedly to one of his former masters.*

Windsor, Sept. 23, 1852

MR. ALBERT G. SIBLEY

Sir,

It has now been about sixteen years since we saw each other face to face, and at which time you doubtless considered me inferior to yourself, as you then held me as an article of property, and sold me as such; but my mind soon after became insubordinate to the ungodly relation of master and slave, and the work of self-emancipation commenced and I was made free.

I have long felt inclined to open a correspondence with you upon the subject, but have refrained from doing so, until now, for two reasons; first, I knew not your post office address; and secondly, you then held in bondage several of my mother's children, of which you robbed her when you left the State of Kentucky in 1836. But as those obstacles are now both removed out of the way, I can venture to address you.

For more than twenty years you have been a member of the Methodist Episcopal Church – a class leader and an exhorter of that denomination, professing to take the <u>Bible</u>, as your standard of christian duty. But sir, know ye not that in the light of this book, you have been acting the hypocrite all this while! I feel called upon as a christian to call your attention to a few facts with a regard to it. But before doing so, I am happy to inform you that my brothers, John, Lewis, and Granville, whose legs brought them from your plantation, are now all at my house in Canada with our dear mother, free and doing well on British soil: so you need not give yourself any trouble about advertising or looking for them. They have all served you as slaves for 21 to 30 years without compensation, and have now commenced to act for themselves. Is this incompatible with the character of a Bible christian? . . .

October 7, 1852

MR. ALBERT G. SIBLEY
SIR

At the close of my last I promised to call your attention to this subject again – and in doing so my object is not merely to convince you that I have acquired the art of communicating my thoughts intelligibly on paper to be read by tyrants, notwithstanding they with yourself have done their best to keep me in perpetual bondage and ignorance – but it is to warn you of the great danger to which you are exposed while standing in the attitude of an incorrigible slave-holder . . . I mean that you shall know that there is a law which is more binding upon the consciences of slaves than that of Congress, or any other human enactment – and I mean that you shall know that all of your slaves have escaped to Canada, where they are just as free as yourself, and that we have not forgotten the cruel treatment which we received at your hands while in a state of slavery . . .

. . . let me ask who is it that takes care of the slave holders and their families? . . . I answer that it is the slaves that perform this labor, and yet they or their children are not permitted to enjoy any of the benefits of these Institutions: your former slaves are now British subjects, are about trying the <u>dangerous experiment</u> of taking care of themselves – which has so far proved to be a very successful one. Their services are worth to them here upon average one dollar per day – they are also attending a night School for the purpose of learning to read and write . . .

P.S. If you do not answer this soon you may expect to hear from me again.

December 2, 1852

MR. ALBERT G. SIBLEY:

SIR,

I have now waited patiently for your answer to my letters of interrogation respecting your <u>slave holding</u>, <u>christian selling</u>, and <u>sheep stealing</u> character, and at the same time allowing your name to be enrolled on the class books of the M.E. Church, as leader among that body of professional christians – I confess I have been a little disappointed at your very singular defence, which has been only an unbroken silence . . .

But there is another demand now pressing upon my time so that I must necessarily be short. In conclusion let me inform you that Canada is a great country – Great in its extensive Territory, comprising about 346,362 square miles, being about six times, the size of England and Wales – It is also great in its agricultural, commercial and mineral resources. The soil and climate of Canada West is now universally acknowledged to compare favorably with the most fruitful portions of North America, and is well adapted for the rearing of ladies and gentlemen, christians, and philanthropists of the first order. But the best of all, it is under an anti-slavery Government, which affords an effectual refuge for the American slaves: it is the home of Granville, John and Lewis, who fled from your custody in search of liberty, about four months ago. They are all here, each one, thank God is now the owner of his own farm within eight miles of a large city. Should you or any of the slave population in that vicinity feel disposed to visit us, I will instruct you in my next letter how to enter on the underground rail road; that is if I don't hear from you soon: and I shall by the grace of God, ever remain true to the cause of downtrodden humanity.

H. Bibb

There's no indication that Albert Sibley ever replied to his former chattel, who died less than two years after writing this letter.

THE UNION OF ALL

In 1864 delegates from Nova Scotia, New Brunswick, and Prince Edward Island had decided to meet in Charlottetown to discuss Maritime union. They were astonished by a request from leaders in the Province of Canada, including John A. Macdonald, to discuss a more ambitious scheme: a confederation with the Province of Canada (later to become Ontario and Quebec). Among the observers of the Charlottetown Conference was Sarah Stretch Harris, newly arrived from England, who wrote her mother-in-law about her teenaged son Robert's role in entertaining the politicians.

September 13, 1864

Dear Mother,

. . . There have been very important meetings and consultations during the past week in Charlottetown. A large number of the leading members of the Canadian, New Brunswick and Nova Scotia governments came over to confer with the Island government on the union of all under a British Viceroy. When they first arrived the majority of the people here were opposed to it, but in a few days the opinion became very general that the Union would be desirable. A grand Banquet was given to the delegates in the Colonial Building. Robert was there with the Band. He says it was a great feast. One of the gentlemen told him to fill his pockets, so the following morning he had a store of good things to distribute around the house. He is going again with the Band this evening; they are engaged for a moonlight excursion up the river, and tomorrow they are to go over to Pictou in the Princess of Wales . . .

I remain,

your loving daughter,

Sarah Harris

Agreeing that a British North American union made sense, the delegates opened the door for a further conference in Quebec, which led to the creation of the Dominion of Canada. In 1884 amateur flautist Robert Harris painted the famous portrait of the Fathers of Confederation, which was lost in the 1916 fire that destroyed one of the Parliament buildings in Ottawa (see pages 47–48).

A NEAR-DEATH EXPERIENCE

In late 1866 **John A. Macdonald,** *the Conservative Party leader in the Province of Canada's coalition government, was staying at the Westminster Palace Hotel while attending the London Conference to finish drafting an act to finally unite the British colonies in North America as the Dominion of Canada. Along with George-Étienne Cartier and Alexander Galt, Macdonald, a widower, was meeting with Henry Carnarvon, the earl shepherding the act through the British Parliament. As he confessed to his spinster sister in Kingston, Canada West, the hard-drinking Macdonald almost did himself in.*

London Dec. 27, 1866

My dear Louisa

I sailed from New York on 14 Novr. There have been bi-weekly steamers ever since and yet I have not had a word from Heathfield [the home he rented for Louisa in Kingston], altho there have been 10 regular mails since I sailed. This is not right, had it not been for some business letters from Shannon, I would have been without any news from Kingston.

We have got on very satisfactorily with our work so far, & confidently expect a successful issue to our labours. When I am to return however, it is as yet impossible to say.

For fear that an alarming story may reach you, I may as well tell it you as it occurred. Cartier, Galt & myself returned from Lord Carnarvon's place in the country late at night. I went to bed but commenced reading the newspapers of the day, after my usual fashion. I fell asleep & was awakened by intense heat. I found my bed, bed clothes & curtains all on fire.

I didn't lose my presence of mind, pulled down the curtains with my hands, extinguished them with the water in my room. The pillow was burnt under my head and bolster as well. All the bed clothes were blazing. I dragged them all off on the floor & knowing the action of feathers on flame, I ripped open bolster and pillows and poured an avalanche of feathers on the blazing mass, & then stamped out the fire with my hands & feet. Lest the hair mattress might be burning internally I then went to Cartier's bedroom, & with his assistance carried all the water in three adjoining rooms into mine, & finally extinguished all appearance of fire. We made no alarm & only Cartier, Galt & myself knew of the accident. After it was all over, it was then discovered that I had been on fire. My shirt was burnt on my back & my hair, forehead & hands scorched. Had I not worn a very thick flannel shirt under my nightshirt, I would have been burnt to death, as it was my escape was miraculous.

It was found that my right shoulder blade was much scorched, so I got it dressed and thought no more of it. In a day or two, however I found that it would not do and have been under the Doctor's hands for a week. The wound at one time took an ugly look. I was kept in bed for three days & have not left the House these eight days. I shall take a drive today, if the doctor allows it when he calls to look at my back. So much for that story. I had a merry Xmas alone in my own room and my dinner of tea & toast & drank all your healths in bohea [black tea] though you didn't deserve it. I was to have gone to Evan Macpherson's to dinner, if I did not go down to William Clark, but I could do neither. The town is quite empty and I have no news to tell.

I shall know tomorrow whether I can have anything like a holiday, before the British Parliament meets.

Love to Hugh, Mag^t & the Parson & believe me,

affectionately yours

John A. Macdonald

I got all kinds of praises for the presence of mind and admonitions ag^t reading in bed. I still read however. Tell the Professor to write what he wants me to get for him. Prepay all letters

J.A.MD.

Macdonald stayed in London until after March 29, 1867, when Queen Victoria signed into law the British North America Act. While awaiting passage of the legislation in London, he met an old flame, Susan Agnes Bernard, and courted and wed her there.

LEPERS OF A NEW KIND

Father Albert Lacombe, a Quebec-born priest who had some native blood, was a confidant of Macdonald and three other prime ministers. He became an Oblate missionary and peace-promoting adviser to Cree, Blackfoot, and Assiniboine tribes and the Metis in the West between 1849 and 1872. The native peoples called him "The Man of the Good Heart" for the care he offered them during the scourges of smallpox brought by white men. In this letter, translated from French, he graphically reported to his friend Bishop Alexandre-Antonin Taché on an epidemic that killed scores of Cree along the North Saskatchewan River.

L.J.C. et M.I.
Mission de St. Paul des Cris
12 September 1870

S.G. Mgr Taché
Monseigneur,

. . . Day and night I was constantly occupied, barely had time to say mass. I had to instruct and baptize dying infidels, confess and anoint our neophytes at the point of death, minister to the different wants, give a drink to one and food to another, kindle the fire during the cold nights. This dreadful epidemic has taken all compassion from the hearts of the Indians. These lepers of a new kind are removed at a distance from the others and sheltered with branches. There they witness the decomposition and putrefaction of their bodies several days before death . . .

The patient is at first very feverish, the skin becomes red and covered with pimples, these blotches in a few days form scabs filled with infectious matter. Then the flesh begins to decompose and falls off in fragments. Worms swim in the parts most affected. Inflammation of the throat impedes all passage for meat or drink. While enduring the torments of this cruel agony the sufferer stops breathing, alone in a poor shed with no other help than what I can offer. The hideous corpse must be buried, a grave must be dug and the body borne to the burial ground. All this falls on me and I am alone with Indians disheartened and so terrified that they hardly dare approach even their own relatives. God alone knows what I have had to endure merely to prevent these mortal remains being devoured by dogs . . .

Of Your GRACE
the affectionate and devoted
missionary
Alb. Lacombe ptre
OMI

P.S. Pardon me, Monseigneur, if I take the liberty to ask you to send to us, at the first opportunity, a dozen boxes of the Ayer pills [a general-purpose patent medicine] and charge it to our account.
A.L.

FOUNDING VANCOUVER

While Father Lacombe was ministering to dying natives in Alberta, a new settlement was being created on the West Coast. The original townsite of Vancouver, surveyed in 1870, was called Granville, after a British colonial secretary. Less formally it was Gastown, after one of its first settlers, **John – Gassy Jack – Deighton.** *In 1867 the loquacious gold prospector, customs agent, and steamboat pilot had rolled several barrels of whisky onto the shore of what is now the city's downtown waterfront and convinced sawmill workers to erect the Globe Saloon in a single day. Deighton boasted of his successes to his brother Tom in England.*

Granville,
Burrard Inlet – B.C.
June 28. 1870

Dear Brother

You may imagine my surprise when I got your letter not having one so long. You see by the head of this letter where I live has got a name it has been laid out as a town site since I wrote home last. I was the first settler here three years ago I have purchased the largest and it proves by luck to be the best but I can assure you it was a loansome place when I came here first surrounded by Indians I dare not look out doors after dark there was a friend of mine about a mile distant found with his head cut in two the Indian was caught and hung this place is a lumber country we have two Saw Mills here but only one is running at present owing to the Lumber Market being low but both Mills will run shortly. I have done well since I came here, Tom, and I have seen hard times too. I find a man has few friends when he is sick and no means. I was three years and a half sick and most of the time on crutches and four months in my bed. I run in debt Two thousand dollars and business in New Westminster fell off so I could not make a living I started with all my traps and six dollars and me sick came to this place I was here one year and a half before anyone found out I was making money finally it was found out and then a rush. Hotels

Saloons Stores &c everybody was going to make a pile and run me out but they did not succeed for I have done the most of the business all the time I have got a good house and garden plenty of chickens and have an Indian boy to cook. I paid all my debts do not owe a cent and have a little cash besides . . .

Tom I wish you was out of that Country and here you could make an easy living with little work if things start up here again I might send for you and Emma . . . By the time you get this you will have got the Salmon. It is Salmon be[l]lies you will have to soak them before cooking you will find them nice Tom I have given you a long twister [?] with my kind of love to you and Emma

I remain your

Affectionate Brother

John Deighton.

By 1874 Tom and his wife were in Vancouver running his brother's new hotel, Deighton House. Gassy Jack, now ailing, soon had a falling-out with Emma over his young son: "She hated the litle Earl of Granville, you know, and she spread the rumor that I didn't have the tackle to father him, and that his mother Madeline had laid with someone else to get pregnant." Tom and Emma moved to Victoria; Jack died the following year.

Meanwhile, Henry Glynne Fiennes Clinton, an Anglican priest from England, had been tending to his flock in Granville. And as he explained in this letter to a relative back home, he preferred the town's original name to the one it received on becoming a city in 1886.

Vancouver City
British Columbia
April 3, 1886

My dear Lucilla
I got your letter all right yesterday, thank you for it. I left New Westminster about the middle of December to take up my abode among the people of Granville, where I have been working all along,

but used to come over for the Sundays. Lately we have changed our name from the pleasing one of Granville, for this bombastic swaggering title of Vancouver – It is called this because it is to be the terminus of the great Canadian Pacific Railway. The CPR are so fond of high sounding names that Granville did not suit them so they changed it to another which will create much confusion as there is besides Vancouver Island two other places in the States, one quite near, also called Vancouver. However all the swagger in the world will not build houses, and if they don't mend soon they will have this place a city of shanties, without water, roads or drains . . . The roads are quite impassable from the mud holes till this week when a bit of glorious weather has improved matters, though still leaving some awful mudholes, so bad that even a short legged man on horseback can hardly keep his feet out of the mud . . .

Y^{rs} in affection:

H.G. Fiennes Clinton

ALL THEY SURVEY

Cities were springing up in the West well before the international boundary between the United States and the Dominion of Canada had been entirely demarcated along the 49th Parallel. American and British officials oversaw the boundary survey. In the survey's second phase, from Lake of the Woods in northwestern Ontario west across the prairies, **Captain Samuel Anderson,** *a thirty-three-year-old Royal Engineer from England, was the chief astronomer. To determine latitude Anderson used a telescope to focus on numerous stars over several nights. He wrote to his sister about his trials, including an encounter with unexpected guests.*

Pembina Manitoba, Dominion of Canada 8 Dec. 1872
My dearest Janet,
My last family letter was despatched from the Lake of the Woods on the 2 Nov. and tho' I have sent several short letters home since that

date I have still to give you a detailed account of what I have been
doing during the past month . . .

Fortunately at this time I heard that there was a gang of Indians
lately employed on the Government road between the Lake of the
Woods and Fort Garry [Winnipeg] and now paid off, so I sent for
them and in about 5 days they arrived, 7 of them, but imagine my
consternation when they appeared bringing all their camp, their
wives and children and old people. There were 6 women and about
12 children, and several old men . . . I set these men to work at once
carrying pork and flour down the cutting, and in two successive
days they made two trips, and transported sufficient food to last for
15 days . . .

The women employed themselves in cutting fire wood which they
stored at the tent door in great heaps and made themselves very comfortable. At this time I engaged a small boy, an Indian, to carry letters
from my own camp to the camp down the cutting and in this way I
got intelligence every second day of the progress of the work, and
I was able to send my own men any little comforts from time to time
that were obtainable . . .

At last after cutting thro' a belt of bushes, there was the open
Lake beyond. Half ice and half snow the southerly winds had caused
such a surf, that at last it froze in heaps . . . It was blowing a gale of
wind, the day we reached this spot, and the appearance of the whole
party journeying over this frozen district muffled up in blankets and
furs reminded me of Arctic explorations. We cut a hole with axes in
the ice and set up a long pole which we had brought along for the
purpose, put a flag on it and left it, for the information of our sur-
veying parties, who will be visiting this spot at Christmas time.

I should like the old Plenipotentiaries who decided this Boundary
Line by Treaty in 1818 to be resuscitated for a short time in order to
come and live at this spot. They would probably have then decided
to fix it in some other locality, instead of a swamp, where it will be
difficult to find a spot for setting up a permanent mark. Finding that
our line ran into the Lake, and ended in the Lake I was saved all
further trouble, so after been nearly blown off our feet by the wind

in this exposed locality, the whole party beat a retreat and reached
the camp at nightfall . . .

> I must now conclude, with best love,
> I remain
> Your ever affect. brother
> Sam Anderson

*Anderson and his colleagues, travelling west from Manitoba to the
Rockies and back again, completed the survey near the end of 1874.
Following in their footsteps were the first 318 scarlet-garbed
members of the newly created North-West Mounted Police, who rode
across the prairies along trails blazed by the surveyors.*

TRIALS OF STRENGTH

*Richard Barrington Nevitt was among the Mounties making the
Great March West to bring order to a territory overrun by unscrupu-
lous whisky traders and restless Indians and Metis. At fourteen,
during the American Civil War, Nevitt had fled his native Georgia to
avoid being drafted in the failing Confederate army. After schooling
in Quebec he earned a bachelor's degree in medicine in Toronto and
became assistant surgeon to the North-West Mounted Police. In
October 1874 he reached Fort McLeod, the Mounties' first permanent outpost, where he stayed for two and a half years. He recounted
his adventures in letters to his fiancée, Elizabeth Eleanor Beaty.*

Jany 3rd, 1875, Sunday

Dear Lizzie,

I had no time to write you before. On New Years day we were very
busy with the races and trials of strength and feats of agility. I ran in
the smoking race and did not win it and also starred in the mile race
but found it too cold on my face and so at the end of the quarter I
stopped . . . Denny [a fellow officer] had started down to Fort Kipp
the evening before to get our letters and bring them up as soon as

possible. He did not make his appearance tho' until dark this evening (Jan^y ^{1st}) and when he came he brought sad tidings. Wilson and Baxter, two men stationed at Fort Kipp, who had come up to camp on leave and started for Kipp again in the afternoon about three o'clock, had not yet arrived or at least Wilson had been on the prairie half frozen and Baxter not found at all. Their horses had however both come in. While I was preparing to go down to see if I could do anything for him an Indian came in with a letter stating that Wilson was dead. However the Col. told me to go on and perhaps Baxter might be found and possibly I might be able to help him.

So I got this Indian to go down with me and wrapping up well I got on the Col.'s horse and started. It was now quite dark and blowing pretty cold, cloudy so that we could see no stars and blowing pretty cold, whew! it was cold. I was told not to spare horse flesh and we cantered down 17 miles without drawing rein. We spoke not a word but three times; once when his horse got on some glare ice and slipped, I told him to take care. He laughed, and we proceeded on our way. Again he made some sign to me by which I understood the river was off to the left, and a third time he pointed to the north and made some signs and then whipped up his horse to full speed. I did the same and we flew along; within a minute such a storm of wind and snow broke upon us. Everything became dark and the cold was intensified to a terrible degree. I was afraid I would lose my guide and spurred up and altho' I could hear him I could not see anything. My foot touched his and still I could not see him. Finally we both got so cold that almost intuitively we both got down and began to run. About 8:30 we saw sparks from the chimney of the fort and in a minute or two were within the inclosure. How thankful I was to again be in safety I cannot tell you. Imagine it yourself – I was determined to go there even if I had to go alone as at first I thought I was to. I had your little book along and it seemed to me as tho' I could feel it warming my heart; it appeared to fill me with a blessed assurance of safety such as I had never before felt except that time on the prairie alone.

I was sorry to hear that Baxter had not yet been found. We set the Indians after him, promising rewards should they find him alive or dead. In the morning, an Indian came in to say he had found Baxter, dead, about six miles from the fort.

We then started off, bearing on a sleigh the body of Wilson, and about six miles from the fort and a mile off the road we found the body of the unfortunate man. He was put in the sleigh and about three o'clock we arrived in Fort McLeod . . .

I hope that I will never again have such a ride. There was something terribly exciting about the ride – the cold wind whistling around us, the bounding of the willing animal beneath me, the strange dreary silence, the dense obscurity, the sad news and the idea that perhaps I would never reach the end alive – all contributed to make the journey exciting and one to be long remembered . . . I expect that I will never be called on again to have such a ride so, old woman, don't be anxious about me. I am all right and even had I started alone I feel assured that I would have reached Fort Kipp in safety.

There is talk of sending in a mail from here in a few days. I do not know of any other opportunity just yet. This was not such a large mail as I expected it would have been, but all things in this country are magnified to an extraordinary extent.

Barrie

Nevitt and Beaty married when Nevitt returned to Toronto, where he obtained his medical degree and eventually became dean of Women's Medical College and a founder of St. Michael's Hospital.

WORDS OF HOPE

Between 1869 and 1896 a suffragette in England named Maria Rye brought five thousand orphans from British workhouses to a supposedly better life in Canada. These were the first of more than eighty thousand "home children" that well-meaning Britons sent from the slums of the Old Country, mostly to labour on Canadian farms, until the beginning of the Great Depression. As young as eight, they were *often beaten and worked to exhaustion, unloved and passed from family to family. One was **Mary Ford**, who, rejected by several foster parents, wound up as a domestic servant in Hamilton, Ontario. This letter to a brother in London is the last remaining trace of her.*

[Hamilton, 1873]

Dear Edward:

I take the greatest pleasure in writing to you these few lines, as I suppose you have long been expecting a letter from me, but you must please pardon my neglect; give my best to darling Willie, and tell him that I feel very anxious about him; I hope that both of you may see better days to come; I hope my dear sister Jane has been to see you, and I hope, dear, that you are improving in your lessons, as I feel very anxious about you. I have been very sick for a long time as the winter has been very cold, but summer has been very warm, and I hope in time to come that I may be able to take you both out of the poorhouse . . .

My pen is bad, my ink is pale,

My love for you will never fail . . .

your affectionate sister

Mary

THE FIRST OKA CRISIS

It sounds horribly familiar: the natives of Oka, Quebec, at war with the surrounding whites. But this was 1875, more than a century and a half after Sulpician priests had promised the Mohawks the deed to four hundred square kilometres of land around Lac des Deux-Montagnes if they would leave the island of Montreal. The Mohawks never did get the deed, and the priests kept selling off the land to French-Canadian settlers. In protest the natives converted from Catholicism to Protestantism, and in 1877 they chopped down trees to replace the pasture gates and posts that Catholic natives had destroyed. The Mohawks' plight was detailed two years later to the British colonial secretary in this letter from F.W. Chesson of the Aborigines Protection Society, a London-based lobby group of evangelical Christians.

17 King William Street Strand W.C.

July 11th 1877.

To The Right Honorable

The Earl of Carnarvon

Her Majestys Principal Secy of State

for the Colonies.

My Lord,

I beg to inform your Lordship that the Committee of the Aborigines Protection Society have now received full details of the alleged Indian disturbance at Oka near Montreal. They are glad to learn the disturbances have been exaggerated, but at the same time they regret to find that a state of things by no means favourable to the maintenance of order exists among these Indians, and also that since the Committee addressed Your Lordship on the subject nearly two years ago, no progress appears to have been made towards the satisfactory settlement of the dispute between the Indians and the Authorities of the Roman Catholic Seminary of Montreal as to the ownership of the lands upon which the latter accuse the former of trespassing.

It appears that early in the month of June a number of policemen entered the houses of the Protestant Indians at Oka with the intention of arresting 48 members of the tribe on a charge of illegally and maliciously cutting down certain trees on land claimed by the Seminary . . .

The arrests it seems were attempted by a large police force in the dead of the night. The majority of the Indians, including the Chief Joseph, however, succeeded in escaping into the woods and only eight of those for whose apprehension warrants had been issued were actually captured . . .

One thing appears clear to those who have examined this subject. The Seminary never would have attempted to dispossess the Indians of the privileges of commonality which they had enjoyed for a hundred years if they had not embraced Protestantism. This fact will not be denied although it reflects little credit upon the just or charitable feeling of those who have thus acted towards a dependant race . . .

The Committee think that this is a matter in which the Imperial government – the natural protector of the aboriginal subjects of the Crown – is eminently entitled to employ its influence for the purpose of obtaining a just and amicable settlement of a difficulty which, if it remain unsettled, may lead to bloodshed . . .

I have &c:

F.W. Chesson

An assistant to Lord Carnarvon replied that a court case had already settled the issue in the seminary's favour and that Her Majesty's government could not interfere in the matter. The predicted bloodshed finally occurred 115 years after this first Oka crisis, when Mohawks, reduced to four square kilometres of property, protested the municipality's enlargement of a golf course on land they considered sacred. They were met by the armed Sûreté du Québec and later by Canadian soldiers in tanks and helicopters. A Sûreté corporal died in a brief gunfight as the natives stood off the troops through the summer of 1990. By the end of the standoff, they again lost their right to disputed land.

HOMESTEAD PRIDE

Ontario in the 1870s was rapidly being settled and its land broken for farming. The soil was good – the province has half of Canada's best farmland – and often even very young child labourers in a family were engaged in tilling it, as **F.W. Whelihan** *noted in this testimonial he sent to Massey Manufacturing, forerunner of the famous Massey Ferguson company.*

[Thornhill Place, Ontario, August 24, 1877]
Massey Manufacturing Company
Newcastle, Ontario
Gentlemen: I purchased one of your Sharp's Horse Rakes from your agent. I am very much pleased with it. A boy six years old, with a pony, raked 45 acres of hay and about 30 acres of stubble, and the little fellow feels proud of his pony and Sulky Rake.

F.W. Whelihan

HOMESTEAD PERIL

Anna Leveridge had lived comfortably in a big house in Britain before the man in her life led her to the Ontario backwoods. David, an estate manager, had sailed for Canada to flee debtor's prison without knowing his thirty-seven-year-old wife was pregnant with their seventh child. A desperate Anna finally joined him in the summer of 1883. After staying in Millbridge, Hastings County, until the onset of winter, the family decided to homestead on land David had acquired about fifty kilometres away. In this undated fragment, she told her family in England about their two-day trip through the snow. Her account ended abruptly, without her usual "Your loving Anna."

Faraday Post Office/Faraday/Hastings Co/Ontario/Canada [1883]
My dearest Mother and all,
I dare say you will have wondered at my silence, but I have had a muddling time and I thought that I would not write till I was settled. Again, you will see by the heading of this letter that we are away from Millbridge. We are got to Wollaston, 28 or 30 miles from there. David has bought a hundred acres of land and built a shanty on it, in which we have just come to live . . .

There is 4 or 5 acres chopped, and everyone says the land is good. So I hope, please God, we shall get a living, if it is a rough one . . .

You will want to know all about our journey. It was quite an undertaking this time of the year with all the little children, but, thank God, we are got here all right. It is awfully cold; and the shanty, being new and green, is not as warm as it will be. We are obliged to keep good fires, but firing is cheap, and it lies around the house.

We left Millbridge on the Thursday after Christmas, started with part of our things, the beds and stove, etc., about 8 in the morning. We were packed in a sleigh, which is like a long wooden box set on runners instead of wheels, the horses with bells. We glided over the snow, up hill and down dale, sometimes nearly out on one side, sometimes nearly out on the other. I had to put all the children's warm clothing on and wrap blankets round them, but it was not as sharp then as it is now.

When we were got a short distance away from home, nearly up to Mr. Russell's, the sleigh broke down. One of the runners broke. So out we all had to get, and tramp through the snow to Mr. Russell's, while the young man went five miles back to fetch another sleigh. I was thankful it did not happen when we were out on the road away from any habitation, we must have perished of cold; it delayed us three hours, so we did not get to our journey's end that day but had to take lodgings.

The people treated us kindly, and I might have got rid of Gertie [the Leveridges' lovable daughter] there. Next morning we started off again. It was bitterly cold. I had all I could do to keep myself and the children warm. Awful hilly roads; one hill was so steep we had to get out and walk. Sometimes the horses came down the hills sliding. I felt very frightened, but we got safely to our destination, which was at the home of a Mr. Hewton, who offered to take us in for 2 or 3 days till our place was aired out.

So we took them by storm, myself and seven children, 1 dog and 1 cat, besides beds and bedclothes. They are young people. She put me in the mind of sister Gertie. She is only 20, and was married when she was 16, 2 little children. We stayed there a week, only one room to live in. I shall be a long time getting used to such ways; however, I was forced to put the best face I could on the matter. They did not mind it.

When David and the young man got down to the shanty, they found the stove broken all to pieces. So David had to go back again and buy –

The Leveridges began farming, grew orchards, built a new house, and had an eighth child. They later went to live with the grown-up Gertie near Trenton, Ontario, until Anna's death in 1928 and David's in 1930. One son took over the family farm but was killed during the First World War.

NATIONAL NIGHTMARE

It was the longest transcontinental railway in North America and one of the world's great engineering feats. The Canadian Pacific Railway (CPR) helped make a nation from a loose collection of scattered settlements, many of them tempting targets for an American takeover. Its fifty-four months of construction during the early 1880s was freighted with delays, disaster, and death. James Ross, the CPR's manager of construction through the Rockies, wrote regularly to brief his boss, the American railwayman William Van Horne. Here Ross described an abject failure of labour relations in which the legendary Mountie Sam Steele came to the rescue.

CANADIAN PACIFIC RAILWAY CO.
MOUNTAIN DIVISION
OFFICE OF MANAGER OF CONSTRUCTION

April 8, 1885

W. Van Horne Esq
Vice President –
Dear Sir:
. . . I have been so engaged this week with the strike that I have not had much time to take up other business. While I knew it was necessary

to pay the men this and next week for January and February, I had no idea that we would be met by them with such a determined stand as we have had to encounter . . .

After I received the first notice of a general strike, they telegraphed me they had checked the men interfering with those willing to work. Afterwards I received another that the rioters had gained a victory and were marching in force. I immediately got out and met them at End Track; at the first, fired by their zeal, they had closed all saloons, and were protecting all property, but during the night the whiskey men succeeded in supplying the ringleaders with liquor, and on Saturday we had a riot.

The Police could do nothing, and matters looked very serious, the men being well armed and firing indiscriminately.

I went amongst them and said that I would guarantee them nothing as to their pay until I knew that I had the money; that I would feed them at End of Track that day, but if they did not leave by night, I would charge every man fifty cents a meal and not pay a dollar until every man was in his camp, and also hold them as a body responsible for any damage to the Company's property, and should expect each gang to go to work as they were paid for January and February. This had the effect of driving the majority back to their camps, but they all stood out on having every man paid before any work was started, and nothing to be charged for board.

I led them to understand we were prepared for a fight on these points. In the meantime, I asked Captain Steele, who was unfortunately ill in bed, to gather all his men at end of track, to be prepared for a fight, and to swear all our men in as specials. On Sunday and Monday, I borrowed every dollar I could get, giving my personal cheque when nothing else would answer; I have reserved some money expecting trouble.

Yesterday (Tuesday) after our track layers were paid off, I sent them out and the Paymaster went to Mountain Creek, with an escort, on the understanding I would meet them there in the morning; the devils knew it was the track and Mountain Creek bridge I wanted going, if the grading did stop. 150 men met the track laying gang and drove them back here, with the police. I then took charge myself, and told Captain Steele I intended laying the track, and expected him to protect me by reading the Riot Act, and if necessary firing into the crowd, who were led by a desperate character, a former contractor, whom I had turned off. I told our men I would be the first to commence work, and did not want them to risk their lives. We succeeded this time, arrested the ring leaders and the Police shot one man who interfered with the arrest . . .

I may be accused of using harsh measures, but you must take into consideration the country we are in, surrounded by desperate fugitives from justice, and 1,500 men willing to work, with 1,000 who will not let them . . . It would never do here to show the white feather; as when the men were paid, they might demand $2.50 per day, and we would have no control over them during the remainder of this job . . .

Yours faithfully,
James Ross.

CHIEF TO CHIEFNESS

Van Horne had shrewdly cultivated **Crowfoot**, *the peace-promoting chief of the Blackfoot, in an attempt to avoid conflict during the railway's construction. The native leader would come to rue his co-operation when CPR trains drove buffalo herds into less accessible areas and sparks from locomotives caused grass fires on reserves – but in this message Crowfoot thanked Van Horne for giving him a perpetual rail pass.*

[about 1887]

Great Chief of the Railway:

I salute you, O Chief, O Great.
I am pleased with railway key,
Opening road free to me.

The chains and rich coverings of
your name, its wonderful power
to open the road, shows the greatness
of your Chiefness.

I have done.
His
Crow (X) Foot
Mark

SPIKING A RUMOUR

*In 1885 Donald Smith, one of the original investors in the CPR,
presided at Craigellachie, in British Columbia's Monashee Mountains,
to drive the last spike linking the tracks from the west and the east –
six years ahead of schedule. Forty years later controversy arose over
whether that spike had been made of gold and extracted to make sou-
venir jewellery. To settle the matter, a CPR official exchanged letters
with Henry J. Cambie, a Canadian government engineer who had
overseen the construction of the challenging Fraser Canyon stretch of
the line.*

[November 1925]

E. Alexander Esq
Secretary CPR
Montreal
My dear Sir
I have yours of 16th Inst. in reference to the "driving of the last
Spike" at Craigellachie on November 7th 1885.

As you remark I was present on that occasion and can be seen in
the photograph of that ceremony with my face, apparently, close to
Lord Strathcona's left ear.

I had at that time a long red beard, which in the picture is partly
hidden, by the waterboy's head.

You can state, on my authority, that the spike used was a common track spike, and was not withdrawn at that time, at all events.

The description given in your letter of its being cut up &c. makes a pretty story, but I never heard it before – and don't believe a word of it.

H.J. Cambie

THE PRICE OF GOLD

Québécois adventurer **Charles-Henri Langlois** *was one of the 100,000 or more people from all over the world who came to the Klondike in Canada's Yukon during the gaudiest gold rush in history. Beginning in 1897, gold seekers fled a global depression in search of fortune. The "instant city" of Dawson, at times thirty thousand strong, was the hub of the action, though it was ebbing when Langlois wrote home (in French) two years after the rush began.*

Dawson City 5 June 1899

My dear parents and friends,

I did not receive your two letters until 28 May. I thought we would get mail at the mouth of the MacWestion [McQuesten River], but the recorder [of claims] had left for Dawson at the beginning of winter, so the letters stayed at Stewart until spring, except for a few that some prospectors brought up to their friends.

I trust that these explanations cause you to forgive my long silence. I've heard some talk about the poor administration of the Klondike, which you mention in your first letter. But I believe that the problems were somewhat exaggerated. We don't have to pay five bucks to get our letters, it's just people who want their mail on a Sunday who have to pay something, and that's only .50 a letter. Anyway, that's all over now. We have a new administration, and nobody has any complaints except a few grumblers.

Laura, you tell me you have a bicycle. I am very happy to learn that. Bicycling is very good exercise as well as a diversion, especially for someone in your type of occupation. I plan to buy one myself, if I return home with any gold. I am not upset to learn that the spanish have been defeated by the americans and that they've had to give up the Island of Cuba. There's another bit of the Americas, pulled free from the europeans. They still have plenty. Tell Uncle Léonard for me that I am shattered to learn that my checkers champion has been defeated, but even so, his fate has not quite reduced me to tears.

I am sorry indeed to learn that Uncle Cézaire was ill this winter and I hope that he will soon recover his health. Speaking of that, there has been a great deal of sickness up here this winter. Especially at Stewart: some 3/4 of the people there have been ill, with scurvy, pneumonia or one of the other diseases that are common here.

At the moment, my news is not very good. First, I have to acknowledge that my claim, which I thought so rich, is virtually worthless. The bit of gold in the creek is all on the surface, not in the bedrock, so it would be a waste of time to wash the two or three hundred pans that you would find. Once we saw that the creek would not be profitable, some of the group decided they were not going to waste their winter here so they took to the ice and headed for Dawson, and that's no joke I can tell you when the thermometer is reading more than 50 degrees below zero. My young companion, Gagnon, went with one of the first groups to set out. It took him 27 days to get there. He froze his foot during the trip and it still has not healed properly.

I did not risk it. I spent the winter on the useless creek, in good health, but obviously not earning anything either. Even so, I don't regret my decision. Most of the people who went to Dawson barely survived. The claim owners have had their men working for a long time now, so our men had to kick their heels all winter. The ice went out this spring on 20 May. We soon followed it, as you can imagine.

As we came down the Stewart, we were lucky enough to kill a bear, which we sold in Dawson for .50 a lb. Philipp Warron and I were the ones who shot it. We also sold about a hundred fresh fish, at .60 a lb. That was the first fresh fish in Dawson this year.

Work is scarce here this spring and wages are low. I looked for work for a couple of days, but given the kind of money you earn, I have decided to go with four fellows I know back up the Stewart where we will either pan for gold along the river banks, if the water permits, or make a wooden raft to sell in Dawson.

Winter was quite pretty here, we had about 2 feet of snow in the entire winter. The coldest day was 20 February, when the thermometer hit 65 degrees below zero. But the coldest month, in terms of the number of cold days, was November, when the thermometer spent a whole week without ever climbing above minus 50 degrees. The extreme cold is much easier to bear than I had expected. I was out hunting on the mountain peaks when the thermometer in the valley was registering 40 degrees below zero. You can work your claims very easily even on the coldest days of the year, and there wasn't one day this winter that I had to dress as warmly as I used to do in Montreal when I worked on the Express.

We had two corpses to bury this winter. The first was a Mr. Johnson from Saint-Paul Minnesota, dead from scurvy; he left a wife and 3 children. The second, a woman named Heison, also from Saint-Paul Minnesota. She came here with her husband just a few months after their marriage. That poor man has suffered a great deal. First, he had to have a miner amputate 6 of his toes for him and now he is in hospital in Dawson where they are going to have to cut off both his feet. As for me, well as I just said, I was healthy all winter long, and even though I have not made my fortune I'm not discouraged. I am still absolutely convinced that there will be big discoveries up here and that I shall have my own little share. So you must not expect me home for a few years yet, and above all, you can be sure that I will not be driven out.

That is pretty well everything that I have to say to you in this letter. It is almost midnight as I write. It is still as bright as mid-day outside, but even so I am beginning to feel sleepy. I have been writing for 6 hours.

Well then, I shall close and please write me as often as you can and do not fear that you might bore me. I shall be awaiting your letters with impatience.

Charles-Henri Langlois

A CHILLY RECEPTION

*The wave of immigration that washed over the Prairie provinces between 1896 and 1905 was generated largely by one man: the visionary, autocratic **Clifford Sifton**, minister of the interior in the Liberal government of Wilfrid Laurier. He wanted to populate the West, and if the familiar nations of France and Germany couldn't offer many potential immigrants, Austria and Hungary could. They had the largest percentage of farmers of any country in Europe. Sifton tapped this resource, defending the "stalwart peasant in a sheepskin coat," whom his opponents took to calling "the scum of Europe." Sifton owned the influential* Winnipeg Free Press *and expressed his controversial opinions to his highly respected editor, John Wesley Dafoe.*

Personal.

Ottawa, 11th November, 1901.

My Dear Dafoe,

I have yours of the 7th. First respecting the Doukhobors, there is nothing in reality in the charge that special advantages have been given to the Doukhobors. As stated the cost of getting these people to Canada was $7.47 per head. British immigrants cost us vastly more than that; although we do not pay that amount as a bonus the entire expenses of the propaganda in Great Britain have to be taken into consideration. These are the cheapest immigrants that ever came to Canada in large numbers. As to special privileges; the feed, grain, stock and agricultural implements that were furnished were furnished by their friends and not by the Government, except in some trifling cases, and whatever was advanced has been paid back. A reserve was made and a certain time allowed for the performance of homestead duties on condition of the people taking up their residence there and doing substantial improvements. There is not one of these inducements that would not be given in the case of any large body of desirable settlers in any other part of the world. The cry against the Doukhobors and Galicians is the most absolutely ignorant and absurd thing that I have ever known in political life. There is simply no question in regard to the advantage of these people, and I do not think there is anyone in the North West who is so stupid as not to know it – even the Editor of the Telegram.

The policy adopted of exciting racial prejudice is the most contemptible possible policy because it is one that does not depend upon reason. As you know you can excite the prejudice of one nationality against another by simply keeping up an agitation. You can excite the French against the English or the English against the French or the Germans against the English or vice versa. All you have to do is keep hammering away and appealing to their prejudices, and in the course of time you will work up an excitement, but a more ignorant and unpatriotic policy could not be imagined . . .

. . . With kind regards, I am
Yours faithfully,
Clifford Sifton

PROPAGANDA VS. REALITY

*The federal government gave the CPR and other rail companies vast tracts of land as an incentive to build their lines. In the second decade of the 20th century, the companies followed Sifton's drive to attract European farmers with their own attempts to lure homesteaders who would buy land from the railways. A Russian Jew named Abraham Shumiatcher, later to become a lawyer in Alberta, translated letters from immigrants like **Mike Vitzko** for the CPR to publicize.*

May 27th, 1915
Bremen, Sask.

I came to Canada from Hungary in 1903.

I had nothing at that time. My family consisted of 4 boys, and one girl, who married in the old country. We all worked together the first year on the farm.

Some of my family went to work to save some money, and start their work on the farm.

I like to live here, because I like Canada, and would not like to go somewhere else.

I have a house – $600 barn – $200; grainary – $200, all machinery – $500 2 horses – $400; 4 head of cattle – $400; 12 hogs – $30;

The land produces 20 bushels of wheat to an acre; oats – 40–60 bushels; barley – 40–50 bushels; flax – 20–30 bushels. Potatoes, and all vegetables grow well here.

When came to Canada my family consisted of 7 members; myself, my wife, 3 sons, my daughter and her husband, and now have 26 members: 16 grandchildren, 3 daughters in law.

All my children grew fast big and strong.

Have a church, school, priest, town, railroad, station.

I like the Canadian Government and laws; and would not like to go to the old country back. All the members of my family live well.

Mike Vitzko

Some immigrants were not doing as well as the Vitzko family claimed to do. In another letter translated by Shumiatcher, the Russian Pheodor Savelieff, farming in Saskatchewan, explained his plight.

February 18th 1916.

The Canadian Pacific Railway Company,
Calgary, Alberta.
Dear Sir: –

In response to your letter, in which you express your wonder why I am not prompt in making payments on the land while there was an abundant crop on my farm, I may say that you may better send an inspector to me and let him inspect and investigate. He will then find that my crop was frozen. From 60 acres of summerfall I threshed 700 bushels of frozen grain, and how could I then make any payment at all.

Please, do wait till the next crop, when I will pay you immediately as soon as I will sell my first car of wheat. My acreage this year consists of 130 acres of wheat and oats and 30 acres of barley.

I will forward you the money received from the first car of wheat, if God Almighty will bless me with a crop.

Awaiting your early reply in Russian, I remain,

Yours very truly,

Pheodor Savelieff.

NO PORT FOR PUNJABIS

Not all immigrants were welcome in Canada during the first half of the 20th century. Skin colour, as Chinese and Japanese arrivals learned, was always a factor. When the Japanese freighter Komagata Maru *docked on Vancouver's waterfront on May 23, 1914, the 376 Punjabi men on board were refused entry on the specious ground that they hadn't sailed directly from India (a service that no steamship company offered). Throughout their two-month ordeal, the passengers – including* **Bhan Singh** *and* **Pohlo Ram** *– sent letter after letter to the press and government officials. (The letters give the ship's name as* Komogata Maru.*)*

[June 26, 1914]

The Immigration Agent,
Vancouver, B.C.

Sir: –

I have the honour to inform you that there is no supply of water on the board since forty eight hours; therefore we could not cook our food and there is not a single drop of water to drink.

If the water is not supplied within an hour a few passengers will breathe their last, and the result will be very bad.

We have asked Mr. Gurdit Singh many times, but there is no satisfaction.

Kindly make arrangements as soon as possible.

We are,

Yours truly,

Bhan Singh and

Pohlo Ram

for the passengers on s.s. Komogata Maru

Vancouver, B.C., June 26th [1914]

Ottawa File No. 798545 Imm.

W.D. SCOTT, ESQ.,
Superintendent of Immigration,
Ottawa, Ont.

Sir: –

I beg to confirm my night lettergram of the 25th instant, as follows: –

"Following wire sent Governor General Ottawa
tonight signed passengers Komogata Maru, begins:
Many requests to Immigration Department for water
but useless better order to shoot than this miserable death, ends. Gardener Johnson refused supply
water unless paid two dollars a ton; Rahim and
Temple Committee claim to be charterers therefore
are liable. Bhag Singh of Temple Committee taken
on board this afternoon and has now arranged supply
water is possible tonight."

In this connection I may say that Messrs Gardner Johnson & Co. arranged to send out water, a payment having been promised in a day or two by the new alleged charterers, Rahim and Ram Singh.

I find, however this morning, that the water has not yet gone out, and after discussing the matter with Mr. R.L. Reid, we are trying to get the City to take it out, on receiving a letter from Rahim through Messrs Gardner Johnson & Co., to the effect that they – the

Committee – have no money to pay for the water; thus practically admitting that the passengers of the S.S. KOMOGATA MARU, are public charges on the City.

Your obedient servant,

Malcolm J.R. Reid

DOMINION IMMIGRANT AGENT & INSPECTOR

The Komagata Maru's *passengers finally got water but no satisfaction in their attempts to come ashore. When Ottawa ordered them to leave port on July 17, 1914, the Punjabis, most of them Sikhs, took over the vessel. A week later, as soldiers stood guard on the pier and a Canadian warship hove to, the* Komagata Maru *sailed for Calcutta, where suspicious police killed twenty passengers in an exchange of gunfire. Racism was prevalent in Canada well into the Second World War, when humorist and political scientist Stephen Leacock wrote of the 1914 incident, with no irony intended: "Hindu immigration to British Columbia was ingeniously sidetracked by the 'continuous voyage' rule, as smart a piece of legislation as any that disenfranchised negroes in the South."*

BAPTISM BY FIRE

On August 4, 1914, the British Empire, including Canada, declared war on Germany and the Austro-Hungarian Empire. The Canadian regular army numbered only about three thousand men, but by October more than 32,000 – most of them patriotic volunteers – were in England to train and form the 1st Canadian Division. They missed the first mass slaughter of the war (more than 1.6 million combatants on both sides died before Christmas 1914). But in 1915 they were front and centre during the Second Battle of Ypres, named for the Belgian town ("Wipers" in troop slang) in the infamous Ypres Salient, which bulged about six kilometres into German-held territory. Here the enemy unleashed the first effective attack of the war that used chlorine gas – the fatal lung irritant of liquid chlorine in

*shells fired into the trenches. As French Zouave infantrymen fled,
opening a six-kilometre gap in the front line, the 1st Canadian
Division's troops stood firm, using handkerchiefs soaked in their
own urine, which contained ammonia that helped neutralize the
chlorine. One of three brothers in the battle was* **Captain Clarence
McCuaig** *of Montreal, with the 13th Battalion of the Royal Highland
Regiment – the Black Watch – who reported to his mother.*

May 1, 1915

Dearest Mater:

Our recent terrible experience is still so fresh in my memory that I
have not felt able to write to you before. You will have read most of
the details in the papers by this time, and I am not going into grue-
some details any more than I have to, so I shall just give you a brief
account of what we have been through.

Our Battalion was on the extreme left of the British line and
immediately adjoining the French right which was being held by
Algerian troops. On the morning of April 22nd, everything was quiet
and there was no sign of what was to come, except perhaps the
unusual stillness. At four o'clock in the afternoon we were surprised
to see huge clouds of yellowish vapour blowing across from the
German trenches to the portion of the trench held by the Algerians.
A few minutes later the German artillery commenced to shell the
trenches, and for three hours they poured in the most terrible fire
that has probably ever been seen. Then came the attack, and the
remainder of the Algerian[s] who had not either been killed by the
shells or the poisonous vapour left their trenches and ran.

Well, the Germans came right through and poured reinforce-
ments right in behind our own trenches by the thousands. Night came
and still they were pouring through. All our communications by telephone had been cut by the heavy shelling and we could not get word
back to tell them of our great need for help.

Night passed and all the next day without any help. During this
period our trenches were continually shelled and many of our men
killed and wounded. Just as darkness was falling we received orders

to evacuate our trenches and to dig ourselves in at right angles to our old line. Under heavy machine gun fire we left our trenches and dug a long trench down the hill as we had been ordered.

Morning came and found us lying in a narrow earth trench cold and tired. With the dawn, two German aeroplanes came and flew over our new trenches for a few minutes[;] then everything seemed to happen at once.

The German artillery opened fire on us from all directions and simply murdered us. For three hours we lay there under a perfect hell of fire. It was terrible to see our men blown to pieces in groups of four and five at a time. The bravery shown by them will never be forgotten, for not a man left our trench or wanted to go, even though we all knew that it was only a matter of minutes until we were all finished. Then came the order to retire. Out we got under a perfect hell of machine gun bullets, rifle fire and with huge shells bursting all around. The German aeroplanes followed us and directed their guns and their fire was deadly.

All day we retired and occupied different positions, trying to hold the enemy in check and doing our best. At length as night was falling we arrived at the last line of the reserve trenches which were occupied by British Troops. By this time we were almost done, for we had no food or water for three days and were half poisoned with the murderous gas fumes.

Well, since then we have been moved from place to place always under heavy shell fire and continually digging ourselves in for our very lives. The eleven days of continual shelling has nearly broken my nerve, but we hope to be relieved to night and go back for a long rest.

Over half of our regiment is gone and eleven officers, either killed or wounded. Rykert [a brother] held the extreme left of the whole British line and his bravery, courage and coolness will never be forgotten. He is to be mentioned either for the V.C. [Victoria Cross] or D.S.O. [Distinguished Service Order].

I have been doing my best to get some information of him and feel sure that he is only a prisoner as he was last seen just before the Germans surrounded a party of our men and was still unhurt. We all feel confident that nothing has happened to him and before long I am sure that there will be good news. In the meantime you must keep up your courage, dearest Mater, and remember that he acted like a hero, everyone is praising him. Our Brigadier was more effected when he heard that he was missing than I can tell you and he knows and appreciates what he has done.

Eric [another brother] was wounded slightly by a piece of debris when a shell hit our headquarters. He is back in England, I think, and hopes to be well very soon. I am O.K. and thank God for bringing me through safely.

I cannot write any more now.

Ever so much love to all, and keep up your courage,

Clarence.

McCuaig lived through the battle to return home to launch a brokerage firm with his two brothers (Rykert survived the war). He later became governor of the Montreal Stock Exchange.

UNKY-PUNK'S WAR

In 1916 **A.Y. Jackson** *was a thirty-four-year-old artist from Montreal who had trained in Chicago and Paris. He had also been fighting as an enlistee with the Canadian army in Europe for a year. As an uncle – nicknamed Unky-punk – he tried to explain the ugly brutality of battle to a beloved six-year-old niece, Naomi Jackson.*

[About 1916]
457316 Signal Section
60th Can B.n

Dear Naomi

Unky-punk got your letter and enjoyed it very much. you have such a good way of saying just what you think. later on when you grow big. (I was going to say "bid dirl." but thats only baby talk) you are not supposed to say what you think. girls very seldom do anyway. It is nearly one o'clock in the morning. I am sitting up to hear if the telephone has anything to say. there is a war on here. and so they have no bells on the telephones. they just give a quiet little buzz now and then. and someone away off says, "that you A.Y. hows things down there." and I say, "quiet as Toronto on Sunday." and he says "same here, be good." and then I go on writing to you. Its chilly. I have my overcoat on too. later on I am going to make some soup. I have some soup powder and some OXO cubes. I must have slept on them the other day because its all mushed together and I had to scrape OXO off my socks and a whole lot of other things. still I think it will taste nice. soldiers are not particular they are at first, but they lose things. first you lose your fork. and you find out your fingers are just as good. then you lose your spoon, and find out you can get things into your mouth with a knife just as well. if you lose your mess tin you get an empty marmalade tin for a cup. we used to carry heaps of things before we knew what war was. and you remember all the funny things we used to do on the M.A.A. grounds. well you don't do those in real war. you just hide in long ditches. and if you peek over the top you have to be very careful, because there are other long ditches full of Germans trying to see you. if you see a nasty German peeking, you shoot at him with your gun. When it gets dark of course you can look over, but you have to be careful. if he throws something at you, you throw something back. sometimes we throw everything we have at him. that is when he gets nasty, and for awhile it is all smoke and terrible bangs and the air is full of bullets and pieces of iron and dirt and of course someone gets hurt. several soldiers have been hurt that way. but they don't seem to mind. they take the bullets out of them, and give them jelly and nice things to eat and a nice soft bed to lie on. and they soon get well and go back and get some more bullets put in them. Its funny to hear the bullets pass. some of them pass very quietly just a gentle whiz. almost a beg your pardon sound. while others sound very angry. like a mad bumble bee who has been shaken off a flower. and some of them whistle. they come very suddenly and seem to be in a awful hurry to get to where they are going. then some of them go in swarms. these are the machine guns bullets. when you hear them coming you flop on the ground very flat and let them go over you. it doesn't do to interfere with them at all. The first rooster is just crowing; and a kind of cat bird thinks he is singing. no one else does. in a little while the larks will fly away up in the air so they can see the sun before anyone else and welcome in the day with a real bird song. There are a lot of mules close by and so homesick, they don't believe in hiding their feelings either. they just give themselves up to paroxams of woe. your mother will tell you what that means. In a little while the early morning aeroplanes will come buzzing round away up in the air, and as soon as its light the Germans will put up their observation sausages, like this [there's a sketch] with a little basket hanging to it with a man inside. of course we put ours up too, and they stare at each other very stupidly all day long. Now this will have to do for now. its time for that thoup. I showed your letter to Mr. Private Jackson and he appreciated it very much. Now a big hug and lots of kisses.

Ever your affectionate
xxx Unky-punk xxxx

In 1917 Jackson was hired as an artist with the Canadian War Records; he specialized in landscapes before returning to Canada a year later. In 1919 he travelled with Lawren S. Harris (see pages 318–20), J.E.H. Macdonald, and Franz Johnston to the Algoma area of Ontario, to work on paintings that would be exhibited at the first show by the Group of Seven, in 1920.

HOME FRONT DISASTERS

Canadians at home were easy prey for rumours about enemy infiltration of the country – especially when, on the evening of February 3, 1916, a fire of unknown origin destroyed the handsome, Gothic-revival Centre Block of the Parliament Buildings in Ottawa. Although a cigar or cigarette in the Reading Room was the probable cause, The Globe in Toronto said insiders believed "the Hun hath done this *thing" – a rumour that **Maynard Grange**, a young woman still living at home with her well-off parents in Toronto, enlarged on in writing to her brother, who was serving overseas.*

36 Lowther Ave.
Feb. 6th [1916]

Dearest Roch,

. . . I suppose you have heard about the burning of the Parliament buildings in Ottawa it is quite the worst thing that has happened to us here. I will send you a paper about it. The officials deny that it was a German outrage but every one seems sure that it was, especially as a factory in Ottawa and a munitions factory in Hesp[e]ler have since been burned down. Of course everyone is awfully up in arms about the Parliament buildings and there are so many of the French Canadians that are rank traitors that it is hard to tell who did it. Senator Choquette and Armand Lavergne are particularly vile and make the most lying and traitorous speeches on all occasions lately the priests in Quebec have been going about forbidding the women to work for the Red Cross and stopping the men from recruiting. Quite the patriots aren't they? Tommy Church came into Eunices department (the Patriotic Ass!) and showed them a warning he had had from someone saying that the City Hall and other public buildings are to be blown up so that is a nice little excitement for them to look forward to! I feel like Baba reciting a list of Chicago [gangster] atrocities! Having been discreet for a page or two I think I may begin & tell you the latest gossip . . .

Ever your loving sister
Maynard Grange.

THE GLORY OF VIMY

Dr. Harold McGill *was a medical officer in the trenches at the Battle of Vimy Ridge on Easter weekend in 1917. All four Canadian divisions, under Lieutenant General Sir Julian Byng, were assigned to*

*take the eleven-kilometre-long escarpment that rose as high as a fifty-
storey building between two river valleys in northern France. Since
1914 the Germans had commanded the ridge, fortifying it with heavy
armaments and a network of tunnels and dugouts. French and British
troops had failed to dislodge them. McGill, then thirty-eight, had
been doctoring to the Sarcee people on a reserve near Calgary before
going overseas with the 31st Battalion. He recounted the battle to
Emma Griffis, the Calgary nurse he was courting by mail, who had
just arrived in England to work.*

France, April 23, 1917.

Dear Miss Griffis; –

I have your letter of April 13 and am delighted to know that you are
safely on this side of the Atlantic. Did you sleep with a life preserver
on when you were crossing? Your letter reached me the night we
came out of the line and the day following that splendid box of
chocolates arrived. We are all busy eating them up and I simply do
not know how to thank you enough. You have put me everlastingly
in your debt by the very many kindnesses you have done me since I
came to France. Although I may be crude in the expression of my
gratitude it is none the less deep and sincere . . .

The past month has been a very strenuous one for all of us. You
would read all about the big show in the newspapers. The enemy is
now "Over the hills and far away" and we are at present in tents on
a site where it was unsafe to show one's nose above ground 2 weeks
ago. It was by all odds the most spectacular battle I have seen. One of
our officers remarked that a show manager would require to charge
10 dollars a seat to put on as good an exhibition. We moved into our
assembly trenches during the night before and there waited for
morning. It was a moon light night but partially cloudy. We were
shelled on our way in but nobody was hit. We had some breakfast at
4$\frac{30}{}$ A.M. and afterwards waited for zero hour which was 5$\frac{30}{}$ A.M.
It began to drizzle rain just before the fateful hour. Promptly on the
minute the whole sky behind us lit up with a sheet of flame from hundreds of guns, and our barrage opened with a noise like a terrible

peal of thunder. There was a wonderful display of fireworks for miles along the German trenches caused by the bursting of our shells and Fritz's frantic S.O.S. signals. It looked as though the sky were raining fire. It was still too dark for us to see our boys going over the wall.

Our brigade had to wait until the first two lines of German trenches were taken and then push through the first attacking lines to reach the most advanced objective. We had to wait for over 2 hours in the trenches; when the time came the whole battalion got out of the trenches and advanced overland. We sustained some casualties going through the German barrage but not many. After we got over into the captured territory we came up on some high ground and could see for miles to the right. It was a splendid sight. Our barrage was sweeping over the country like a blizzard and close behind it we could see our troops advancing in thousands. The whole country seemed crawling with them and the sight must have put the fear of retribution into the German hearts.

My first R.A.P. [Regimental Aid Post] was a wrecked German concrete machine gun emplacement. I soon afterwards got into an unfinished dugout. When our troops took the village they were attacking and moved up and took over the German aid post. There was one wounded German in it and all sorts of dressings and supplies. We had boiled German potatoes for dinner and they tasted just as good as though they had been obtained through the ordinary channels of commerce. We found a good stove, coke, and in fact all the comforts of home in Fritz's dugout. His blankets came in very useful for the night of the battle was bitterly cold with quite a fall of snow. We had quite a few German wounded through our hands and I am becoming quite used to being addressed as Kamerad.

We had wretched weather for our last tour of duty in the line. It rained nearly all the time and was cold enough for January. Personally I did not suffer much discomfort for I was in comfortable quarters in a cellar recently taken over from Fritz. We had a kitchen range with a small stove in nearly every room into which the cellar had been divided, also easy chairs. The Germans certainly knew how

to make themselves comfortable but of course they simply stole anything they wanted from the civilian population. We shall not be able
to work this system until we get into Germany.

During our last tour in the line the battalion scout officer and an
N.C.C. [Non-Combatant Corps] went out and captured a German
patrol consisting of one officer and a man. They wounded the officer
in the arm and put a bullet through the man's cap before they surrendered. The officer had been in British Columbia and could speak
good English. He belonged to the 8th Prussian Guard. He said, "It
iss a long time since I haf seen ze maple leaf". I told him his men
were getting a good chance to become acquainted with it these days.
He was not a bad sort of a chap though for a Prussian officer.

Give my love to all the Calgary nurses in your party.

Yours ever

Harold McGill

*The opening barrage McGill described was the sound of 983 artillery
pieces and 150 machine guns blazing together, a cacophony so loud
that British Prime Minister David Lloyd George is said to have heard
it on London's Downing Street. It signalled the beginning of the end
for the Germans at Vimy. Over the next five days the Canadians –
four infantry divisions fighting together for the first time – covered
themselves in glory by capturing the ridge. The battle is considered a
touchstone in Canada's evolution as an independent nation.*

CARNAGE AT PASSCHENDAELE

*In October 1917 bull-headed Douglas Haig, British commander in
chief, ordered Canadian troops into the Third Battle of Ypres. British,
Australian, and New Zealand forces had been struggling for three
months to take Passchendaele Ridge, defended by the Germans in
concrete pillboxes and machine gun nests. The Canadian commander,
General Arthur Currie, knew an attack would mean heavy losses.*

*Nevertheless the Canadians were sent in on October 26. In an inferno
of poison gas and shellfire, they advanced over several days, moving
forward slowly behind a creeping artillery barrage.* **George Stratford**
*was one of five Ontario brothers who had signed up for action over-
seas. Three were in the vicinity of Passchendaele.*

November 4th 1917

Dear John:

Your letter of Oct. 18th – Thanks. I've been away on leave and
thereby missed a great big show, thank heavens. I spent most of the
time at Bournemouth just taking it easy, but here I am back again in
the midst of the Flanders mud . . .

I'm about all that's left in the way of officers in this company so
you can imagine we have had a pretty tough time, however we were
right there with the goods as usual.

There is nothing much I can write about as I'm as busy as h —
and will be for some time to come. Now don't forget to sit tight right
where you are as long as you can. Will write again soon. Let me
know if you want anything outside of money, – I'm broke.

Your aff. bro.

George

November 18th [1917]
Fort Garry Horse
France

Darling Mother:

Long before this letter reaches you, you will have heard the news of
dear old Geordie. He was killed on the 17th, which was about two
days after I saw him. I passed him on the road, he was going up the
road and I was coming down. The next day I found out where he
was located and went up and stayed a short time with him. The place
he was hit was only a short distance from there so as soon as I can
get a few days off I will go up and see that his grave is nicely fixed

up, also have a cross with his name on it. Jack has already been over as he is not so far away . . .

Now darling try and not worry too much, surely this war will be over before long . . .

. . . God bless you and help us all.

Your loving son
Joe

November 20th 1917

Dearest Mother,

. . . It seems pretty rotten luck, as Capt. Little put it, that he should go so far and then get it where and when he did. They had been up the line three days and through one of the worst bombardments they had ever experienced and everything went fine and things were comparatively quiet, about an hour before they were to be relieved on their last trip in, in Belgium, George who was evidently in charge of the Company, was up on top arranging guides for the relief, when a whiz-bang came over and got him, and he was killed instantly, which is something to be thankful for, as I would hate to think he had been wounded and probably buried alive in the mud . . .

. . . Don't worry Moth dear and take good care of yourself. With much love to you all

Your loving son
Jack

On November 12, 1917, the Canadians held the ridge and the town of Passchendaele. The cost was horrendous: a quarter of a million German and 300,000 British soldiers died, and General Currie's prediction of sixteen thousand dead and wounded Canadians proved accurate. The Stratfords' great-nephew, Toronto actor R.H. Thomson, learned recently that George had not died instantly: "They were hit by a shell and buried in mud. George clung to life for fifteen minutes. Joe was killed five months later. Jack survived but was

*disabled by the repeated gas attacks he'd fought through. Brother
Harold was sent home from England with tuberculosis without seeing
action. Only Arthur, of them all, returned to Canada in one piece,
but he carried a sniper's bullet near his spine for the rest of his life."
The Stratford sons are memorialized in* The Lost Boys, *a play about
his great-uncles that Thomson both wrote and performs.*

THE WAR HITS HOME

*The horrors of war reached Canadian soil on December 6, 1917,
when the world's greatest man-made explosion to that time rocked
Halifax. Many locals believed the Germans had penetrated the
harbour.* **Alvah Chipman**, *a fifty-year-old insurance company executive visiting from New Brunswick, sent an eyewitness account of the
calamity to his brother.*

[December 13, 1917]

MY DEAR BROTHER – I was at breakfast at the Halifax Hotel at
9.06 a.m., one week ago. There came an explosion which shook the
building severely but did no damage that we could see or feel. In a
few seconds the concussion reached us and the glass in the upper
part of the window went flying across the room. Fortunately, and I
feel selfish in saying it, I am uninjured.

There were perhaps thirty of us together at the time. We made
our way to the door, each of us stopping and looking back with uncertainty or fear towards the harbour wondering where the next shot
would strike. Each of us had in his mind the thought that with their
wonderful skill the Germans had come under our guards at the mouth
of the harbour and in a submarine were having their "fling" at the
town. The sensation was precisely that of a building through which a
shell had passed. Glass was crashing in all directions. The hallway
and lobby were two inches deep in small pieces of thick plate for the
pressure came equally upon each square foot of glass. Through
the swivel doors we stepped with a stoop to sidewalk and street.

Up north was a great white cloud more strange than I had seen before. Later we learned its cause – the explosion of five thousand tons of munitions of greatest power. On either side and as far north as I could see except in windows which had been open at least an inch or two no pane or plate of glass was left intact. Such was the condition throughout three quarters of the City and every building suffered at least from breakage of glass. No materials from the ship came our distance, two miles. A shower of soot was felt. Then there came from every door "a Casualty," that is a person who, though more or less wounded, could walk. There were from fifty to two hundred of these within two blocks of our hotel and thirty of our people were more or less cut on the arms or neck or face.

My first work was to assist in a drug store which immediately became a dressing station. There was shown in the people themselves a sense of a shock but not of fear or confusion and each one did what he could for the other. The offices and stores as soon as their injured had proper assistance were deserted. People went home to find how their folks had fared. Here and there a car could be used. The electrics had stopped with the explosion.

Conveyances generally were given at once to the wounded. Within a few minutes I returned to my room for hat and coat. Nothing was disturbed. My window being open saved it. But across the hall a late sleeper was dressing. He had covered his head and in this way escaped for his room was showered with broken glass.

Then I went out to make my way more than six blocks to our laundry enquiring for friends at several offices on the way. I began to realize the extent of the damage and destruction, meeting everywhere the injured who were being rushed to hospital or taken home for first aid. In the laundry everyone escaped except one woman quite severely cut with glass. I moved up to the Common past the barracks from which a great truck was bringing its first load of wounded men.

These were blue coats – French – who were on shore for a visit. The roof of the Garrison Chapel had lifted up and dropped in. The side of Park Street Church had fallen in. The force was from without and came equally from all sides except in narrow spaces or between a stone building and one of wood.

The great Armoury, costing $180,000 lost glass and window frames to the injury of hundreds of men and its heavy slate roof was broken at the edge. Across the street here was an important corner, Cunard Street crosses Park Street at an angle. A recruiting hut was quickly turned into a relief station and to this and hastily through it came hundreds of cases, while around its sharp corner and across the Common back of it there rushed, as I saw them then and later, hundreds, I think thousands, of conveyances. There were great ferries, automobiles more than I could count, express waggons, delivery waggons, waggons of every kind, carts, slovens [long, low horse-drawn wagons], baby carriages and even stretchers. As I stood for a minute below the corner I saw come around it a delivery boy erect on his seat as at parade, driving an old horse. In his waggons were three or four grocery boxes. A soldier found it difficult to stop him and in answer to his question, "Why don't you stop" he fairly screamed "I have to deliver these just down there." Such was his controlling idea of duty, for he was capless and above his collar his entire head was a mass of blood. I mention the incident because it clearly reveals the spirit of thousands as I saw it on every hand, that fearful day.

There were soldiers and sailors everywhere; no one suffered for lack of attendance. I offered what assistance I could and continued my way towards the scene of the explosion. But I was not to reach this and I am very thankful that it so happened. I was relieved and did not have before my eye the destruction in the area two miles square over which the force of destruction spread.

A herald came running down the street with an order from the Military to rush to the open for the powder magazine at the Dry Dock was in danger and might explode any minute. Then there formed and I became a part of a procession such as the roads of Belgium know so well. The section was a congested one. The destruction on every hand was far greater than down town. Every human being that could walk or could be carried came into the streets throughout the entire city. The great Common was covered with thousands including the lame, the blind, the dead, and dying . . . the quick and the dead – There, within ten or fifteen minutes, were assembled in the cold of a winter's day, with no snow on the ground, a light wind and sunshine. We waited for about two hours in constant apprehension, expecting an explosion that would level the remaining buildings. Fortunately the wind was light and from the south-east, blowing the fire from the city and saving it from complete destruction.

Near me I found a boy from the Naval College in blue uniforms of light weight. He had been badly cut about the head, face and hands. He had walked a mile to the relief station, then as now without hat or overcoat. I gave him my coat and tried to learn his condition. In the four hours that he was in my care he invariably refused to admit that he was badly hurt or in pain or even homesick. He was all of these for in addition to his wounds he was almost in a state of collapse from shock. I made this boy my particular care and if, as I hope, I was the means of helping him to come through then there is something to my credit in day of need.

No central control was established until night. The uninjured were too busy to think of disorder or even of self interest. There was nothing of hysteria or panic. In general the men in khaki and in blue directed transportation and rendered first aid. During the first day there was slight conception of the far reaching effects of the explosion and the demand for skilled assistance. This consciousness came with a rush on the first night and the second day.

Men whom I met were free to express their suspicion as to the cause of it and far and near the words were heard "An enemy hath done this." Suspicion was cast upon the character of so called relief ships as they had come and gone. Rumors as to ships on fire in the harbour and the alien control of this particular relief ship were rife. I talked with an officer of a steamer within a few yards of the [Mont] Blanc. In his mind there was no question but that the relief ship was to blame. He saw her hold to her course in the face of certain destruction. But only a thorough investigation, and such is being held, may fix the blame. Aside from this phase of the question, there was and is in Halifax a striking illustration of the horrors of war. Only war conditions could have wrought such destruction.

There were many very narrow escapes. The ways of mysterious force which covered the city were freakish at least. In the King Edward Hotel a man on the side of his bed dressing saw his door go past him and out the window. Two men, and I talked with the survivor, were standing near the hatch of a ship in the harbour. One said to the other "How strange that looks." He was pointing towards the fire which caused the explosion. In an instant this man was gone leaving no trace. A gun from the ship was found some distance away. A man was carried on a pile of lumber one quarter of a mile and escaped with his life. A ship steward was uninjured but the cleaver with which he was about to cut a quarter of beef was fixed three inches deep in the floor at his feet and the quarter of beef had disappeared. These are mere incidents among the rest of the strange happenings at Halifax.

Broken wires prevented sending out anything until late in the day except that by wireless. St. John was reached by way of Havana and New York. I was assured that I would be in the way and that my undisturbed quarters would be of value so I came away as soon as possible in a special train from the hitherto unused terminals at the south of the city. A friend had offered me a passage to Truro in an automobile which went out with operators and some 2500 messages of the Western Union. I was ready to go on this when the train went out. It was three o'clock when we reached Truro. Few of us had slept a wink. Messages were sent by telegram and telephone from Truro for friends and myself. I gave Mabel [Alvah's wife] her first word saying that I was uninjured. This she could hardly believe and the service was so interrupted that very little could be understood.

I look back upon it with increasing distress. So many are anxious to hear the story that it has become almost a nightmare. This is to lessen the necessity to talk it over in detail. We are deeply thankful to have escaped and our sympathies as never before are enlarged and deepened.

As ever your brother,

A.H. CHIPMAN.

As Chipman guessed, it was a relief ship, the Belgian Imo, *that had collided with the French munitions carrier* Mont-Blanc. *The resulting explosion, a four-metre wave, and fires levelled more than two and a half square kilometres of the city, shattered windows a hundred kilometres away in Truro, killed about sixteen hundred people, and injured nine thousand others in a population of fewer than fifty thousand. Searchers dug up bodies in the wreckage until spring. The* Halifax Herald *said in an editorial, "We know now what war is."*

THE GREAT FLU

*The First World War exported more tragedy to Canada in the year after the Halifax explosion. Troops returning from the European battlefields brought with them a lethal strain of influenza, the Spanish flu. A letter from gunner **Horace Bishop**, serving with Canadian forces in France, sounded an early warning to his family back home.*

France July 1st 18

Dear Mother

It must be nearly time I was writing you. I would have done so before but we have been somewhat occupied & then I had the influenza for a few days. there is quite an epidemic of it in Europe according to the papers . . .

France July 4th 18

Dear Father

. . . I suppose you read in the paper of a lot of influenza. I was sick for a few days with it. except for leaving one a little weak I dont think it has any bad effects . . .

Your affectionate son
Horace.

The Spanish flu swept the world, killing about 21 million people –
about fifty thousand of them Canadians. In this plea to Vancouver's
mayor, Robert Gale, store clerk **Ernest Rea** *described the era's*
working conditions.

139 39 Ave W
Vancouver BC
Oct 22nd 1918.

Mayor Gale,
Dear Sir,
As a clerk in a retail store & on behalf of my fellow workers I appeal
to you to use your influence & that of the City Council to bring
about an earlier closing hour for Retail Stores on Saturdays during
this Epidemic of Spanish Flu.

My working hours are from 8 am to 10 pm on Saturdays. Now
these hours are absurd at any time, but to allow stores open these
long hours during this epidemic is like inviting disaster. Clerks are in
close contact with the public all day long & often coming in actual
contact with those afflicted with the disease.

Saturday nights our bodys are worn out from the strain of the
long day & also from insufficient food. Some of us who live out
a long way have to bring two lunches along for the mid-day & evening
meals. Now I think you will agree that no serious loss of business
can occur to merchants if the closing hour is fixed at 5 30 or 6'oc
while the closing order remains on the city. In any case as citizens we
clerks have a right to fair treatment and first consideration during
this crisis.

Yours truly
Ernest T. Rea

Mayor Gale responded that he would alert provincial authorities
overseeing influenza regulations; "I am, however, thoroughly in sym-
pathy with your suggestion as I believe that any individual when
tired and all-in as the result of a long day's work is then less able to

resist an epidemic of the nature through which we are passing." Less
than a month later, the mayor's office reported 4,039 cases of Spanish
flu and 451 deaths in the city.

*At about the same time **Ella Parsons**, the optimistic wife of an*
Alberta doctor, described the ravages of the disease just one day after
fighting had finally ended for Canadian troops overseas.

Red Deer Nov 12/18

My dear Mother: –
It has been nothing but "flu" here for two weeks past. Dick has
just been going night and day until 12 every night making
visits; we all are pretty well played out, but I think it is abating. So
many Doctors have died, I was afraid Dick would contact it but he
is fine considering.

Tell Flo I rec'd the parcel to-night. Dick is so pleased with my
hat. It fits much better than the one I got myself. The sweater is also
lovely and I needed it so badly. The veil goes so nicely with my hat
and the underskirt is just the servicable kind I wanted. I expect the
waist will come along later.

The peace celebration yesterday was terribly hard for me. I had
Dick take me away to the country for the day. This is the hard time.

I cannot believe Xmas is so near. I am pretty tired out helping
make it easy for Dick through the epidemic. For two weeks the phone
has rung night and day every few minutes. Fortunately we have a
good office girl.

I shall write you later after I wear my things and see them in daylight.

Love to you all

Your loving daughter
Ella.

Within a few days of writing this letter, Ella, not her husband,
contracted the flu and died.

FLAGS, FLOWERS, AND COFFEE

The fighting ended for Canadians at Mons, Belgium, at 11 a.m. on November 11, 1918. **Major John L.W. Harris** *was with the Canadian division that liberated the town and marched triumphantly past grateful Belgian civilians. Sixteen when he left Moncton, New Brunswick, to go to war in 1914, Jack Harris served first with the Royal Canadian Artillery Fredericton 36 Battery, then was transferred to the 9th Brigade CFA from 1915 to 1918.*

Mons, Belgium, Nov.14th 1918

My dear Father;

At last we have realized our fondest hopes of the last four years. Germany and Austria are beaten and beaten so badly as to never be able to recover, or at least never to repeat the crimes that they have committed since this war started. Our last week of the war has been a busy one and at the same time a glorious one. The Hun had stopped evacuating the civilians and everywhere we were greeted with crowds of people. Flags that were hidden during the German occupation in all sorts of weird corners were brought forth and bunting and flowers were to be seen wherever one looked. As we went through towns crowds of civilians lined the roadsides and passed out flowers and small French and Belgian flags to the troops. Whenever we halted the women dashed out with hot coffee for us. At each new town we entered we had to go through a regular barrage of coffee and flowers. Everywhere we were welcomed as liberators from the cruel oppression of the Hun and everywhere we heard the same stories of the vileness and bestiality of his deeds. I don't think it possible for one who has not actually spoken to some of those who have suffered to understand the way the Boche is universally despised and hated.

But I could write pages of stories I have been told of the Boche without stopping to think about it.

Where we are just now is the place where the English first met the Huns in any strength and I could go on all night and tell stories (told me by eye-witnesses) of how two or three Englishmen with their rifles have held up whole battalions of Huns; how every English bullet found its mark and how the Huns, in their anger at not being able to find any English in towns, when they had captured them brought out civilians and shot them in cold blood. I have talked to civilians who had been pushed forward in front of the Germans and had German rifles fired over their shoulders.

But there is no need to go on. All these things will be accounted for very soon . . .

The last day, (the 10th) was a very exciting one for us and although to look back on it seems rather amusing at the time it was "no picnic". The whole battery was taken on by the Boche in the open with machine-guns, "whizz-bangs" and 5.9's with direct observation. Needless to say we had an exciting few minutes, but it would take too long to write it all and would be very difficult to explain on paper. I am hoping that it will not be long before I am able to tell about it personally. Suffice it to say we came out of a very nasty hole without a scratch except one horse slightly wounded. It was really nothing short of a miracle . . .

Now that it has appeared in the papers there is no harm in telling you that it was our division that took Mons. And the welcome we received was a thing we shall always remember. The whole population turned out to greet us with flags and banners. It was truly a wonderful sight. Our first patrols entered the town at five o'clock in the morning. At this time, of course, all the people were hiding in their cellars, but after our main body passed through they were soon out and by the time the first guns started through it was better than a circus.

Then we had a triumphal procession. Infantry, artillery, some cavalry, motor ambulances, machine gunners etc. all literally groaning under the flowers and flags heaped on them. Of course this was not till 11 o'clock, the hour at which the armistace began.

Must close for this time. Love to all.

Your loving son,
Jack.

P.S. We start in a few days for Germany. Censorship is relaxed and cameras may be carried. Am having my camera sent out from England.

MISSING PERSONS

*Following the carnage of the Great War, Canada enjoyed a decade of relative calm. Prohibition ended in Canada in 1920 (while still in force in the United States), and Canadians were intoxicated by a buoyant economy and the promise of continual growth. One of the contentious issues of the day was the vociferous campaign of the suf-fragettes pressuring governments to give women the vote. Two married women, both writers, led the fight. Ontario-born **Emily Murphy** was a prolific journalist (whose pen name was Janey Canuck) and a self-educated legal specialist who became a magistrate in Alberta, the first woman in that role in the British Empire. Along with Nellie McClung, a popular author and later a Liberal member of the Alberta legislature, and three other women, Murphy fought to have female Canadians declared persons under British law.*

1101 – 33 Avenue
Edmonton, August 5, 1927

<u>PERSONAL</u>

My dear Mrs. McClung:

Enclosed you will find a copy of Section 60 of the Supreme Court Act of Canada . . . with also a letter to the Governor-General in Council, which latter I am asking you to be good enough to sign and return to me by registered mail as soon as possible.

You will recall the National Council of Women, the Women's Institutes, the Women's Church Temperance Union, University clubs and other of our organisations, in convention, submitted resolutions to the Honorable, the Prime Minister at Ottawa [Mackenzie King] requesting of him that women be admitted to the Senate of Canada, thus permitting us to secure our full enfranchisement . . .

It may here be pointed out that while, in 1923, women generally were gratified in having [Ontario] Senator McCoig's motion placed before the Senate of Canada, with a possible prospect of its being later submitted to the House of Commons for added appeal to His Majesty, we have now come to realize that the matter is one which cannot with any degree of fairness be submitted for decision to a body of male persons, many of whom have expressed themselves towards it in a manner that is distinctly hostile . . .

. . . I have not thought it necessary to submit the matter to Canadian women generally, they having already endorsed the principle, but only to the few "interested persons" as specifically required by the [Supreme Court] Act, these being all from the Province of Alberta and women reasonably capable of giving an account of the principles that actuate them should they be required so to do.

The following are the names in alphabetical order, your own among them: –

Henrietta Edwards,·
Irene Parlby
Nellie L. McClung
Louise McKinney
Emily F. Murphy . . .

Yours very sincerely,
Emily F. Murphy

Edmonton. Dec 2/27

My dear Mrs. McClung,
. . . I had a letter from Mrs John Scott to-day. She says that the Montreal Women's Club would not send a resolution [supporting women in the Senate] to the Conservative Convention at Wpg because it was a Conservative Convention, and the majority of the Montreal Club were Liberals.

Vice-Versa, the women at Wpg gave two reasons for not asking the Conservative Convention to go on record (1) The men didn't want it; (2) They were not going to work for anything that might end in Mary Ellen Smith being appointed.

God help us! What small-hearted, stupid, selfish, graceless women we have among us.

I could cry for disappointment were it not for the fact that the Executive of the Ontario Liberal Women's Association passed a resolution in Toronto last week asking for the appointment of women to the Senate. Loud cheers from the gallery!

I hear, though, that it has been a terrible shock to the Eastern women that 5 coal-heavers and plough-pushers from Alberta "(Can anything good come out of Nazareth?") went over their heads to the Supreme Court without even saying, "Please Ma'am can we do it?" We know now how to stir up interest in the East – just start it going ourselves.

Most affectionately
E.F.M.

In 1929 the British Privy Council ruled that women were in fact persons under the British North America Act (now the Constitution Act) of 1867.

RIDING THE RAILS

After the Crash of 1929, when stock markets plummeted and half of Canada's workers went on relief, the world spun into the Great Depression. During the Dirty Thirties **John Patterson**, *out of work and restless, left Hamilton to take to the road for six weeks. Hitching rides and hopping boxcars, as seventy thousand other Canadian men would, the twenty-two-year-old Patterson headed west through the northern United States to Vancouver and back through Jasper, Alberta – where he was among the many jobless people the railway police caught and jailed – to keep them out of Calgary during the annual Stampede. Through it all, Jack wrote to Kay Hamilton, the girl he'd left behind on Nightingale Street.*

Vancouver BC
Sunday, July 9 [1933]

Dear Pal –:

I hope that it hasn't been too long since you got the last letter, but we have been travelling ever since and it is hard to write in a box car. We arrived in Vancouver Sat. night at 9.30 – exactly four days from Winnipeg – and 17 days from "You". This was much faster than I had figured on – too fast from you.

On Tuesday morning we went to the Winnipeg Grain Exchange and it certainly is a busy place. Then we took a street car and went to the outskirts (before this we went to the Post Office – but no luck.) We tried to get a ride for 3 hrs. and then decided we would go on the freight train. I am glad that we did because the traffic is very light through the west. We went back to the C.P.R. yards and waited in what they call the "Jungle", until the train left, which was at 11.30 P.M. . . . About 200 of us got on the train at Winnipeg, but we only stayed on until we got to Portage la Prairie and then we changed to the C.N.R. We arrived there at 2.00 A.M. and had a cup of coffee and then caught the train again at 4.00 oclock. Portage looks like a nice place. We rode on a flat car and it was too cold so at the first stop we got on the tender where it was warmer but very dirty . . .

We arrived in Saskatoon at 2.00 oclock, and had to hide in the grass while the Mounties searched the train. After they left we got back in and then the yard cop chased us out; but we got in again before the train left . . .

When your riding like this you change cars often because at every division point they change engines and some cars are dropped and others put on. Friday we were in a refrigerator car and we had been warned that the police were bad at "Jasper". So we had a fellow lock us in and we didnt have any trouble . . .

. . . In the afternoon four of us played euchre going through the mountains and we would have to stop every few minutes while we went through a tunnel. We rode right into the yards at Vancouver arriving at 9.30 . . .

. . . You sleep when you can and for your meals you buy a loaf of bread and a can of something and eat it on the way.

The scenery was nice all the way, but in the Rockies it was wonderful. I hope that "we" can make the trip together sometime. Vancouver looks like a very interesting place and we are staying here for a week.

Jasper Park Alb.
July 17 – 33
Letter Nº 10

Dear Kay –

Caught at last. We were not so lucky coming back and now we have to spend 10 days [in prison] in Fort Saskatchewan.

On Sunday morning at 9.30, twelve of us were pulled off the train and held over until this morning – we had the option of 10 days or paying a fine – $9.70 – and we couldnt pay the fine. We are on a passenger train now going to Edmonton – 236 miles. We are having a lot of fun and we have been well fed – more than we could eat. We stay in Edmonton overnight and then go to the Fort in the morning . . .

Love

Jack (Convict No. XXXXXX)

Winnipeg Man.
July 29, 1933

Dear Pal – :

It must be nearly two weeks since you got a letter from me so I can imagine how anxious you are . . .

We got out of Fort Saskatchewan on Wednesday at noon – it is supposed to be the hardest jail in Canada <u>and is it</u> <u>tough</u>. They brought us to Edmonton in a bus – 16 of us – and we stayed in Edmonton until 1.10 next morning when we caught the train out . . .

We arrived in Winnipeg Friday night at 10.30 and are leaving tonight – we have to find out what time the train leaves. Don't worry about the trains – they are getting me back to you in a hurry and we are very careful . . .

A farmer was at one of the railway stations and offered us work at $12. a <u>month</u> – but we think that we are worth a <u>little</u> bit more than that. I think that you would be disappointed if you came out to "Portage" for your holidays . . .

I am really awfully home-sick and can't get back fast enough. There isn't any real pleasure to me in seeing all these things without you – they are nice but if you could see them with me they would be wonderful. I knew before I left home that you meant a whole lot to me but now I realize that <u>you</u> mean <u>everything</u> . . .

With <u>all</u> <u>my</u> <u>love</u>

Jack

The finances are very low.

Jack and Kay were married three years later; their romance lasted for another thirty-seven years.

RIDING OUT THE THIRTIES

Jack Patterson's riding of the rails was a youthful lark compared with the travails that most Canadians endured in the 1930s. Thousands of men, women, and even children wrote to the prime minister, R.B. Bennett, pouring out their troubles. The wealthy Bennett, whose annual income never fell below $150,000 during those years, answered many of these letters, sometimes enclosing a few dollars for correspondents like **Christina Arnold**.

Raymore Sask

Oct 11th/32

Dear Sir, – I am a girl thirteen years old and I have to go to school every day its very cold now already and I haven't got a coat to put on. My parents can't afford to buy me anything for this winter. I have to walk to school four and a half mile every morning and night and I'm awfully cold every day. Would you be so kind to sent me enough money to so that I would get one.

My name is

Christina Arnold

Raymore Sask.

Bennett's private secretary sent her five dollars, "which may be of some service to you in securing yourself a coat." Another letter to

Bennett was written by the daughter of a struggling Manitoba farmer,
Jean E. McLean.

127 Jackson Avenue
Hamilton, Ontario
April 6, 1934

To His Excellency The Rt. Hon. R.B. Bennett,
Parliament Buildings,
Ottawa, Ontario.
Att: Mr. Bennett.
Dear Sir:

I am writing you as a last resource to see if I cannot, through your aid, obtain a position and at last, after a period of more than two years, support myself and enjoy again a little independence.

The fact is: this day I am faced with starvation and I see no possible means of counteracting or even averting it temporarily! . . .

I have received a high-school and Business-college education and I have had experience as a Librarian. My business career has been limited to Insurance, Hosiery, and Public Stenography, each time in the capacity of Bookkeeper and Stenographer – briefly, General Office work . . .

When the Stevenson-Harris Co., Ltd., went out of business I had saved a little money and there being no work for me there I came to Hamilton. Since then I have applied for every position that I heard about but there were always so many girls who applied that it was impossible to get work. So time went on and my clothing became very shabby . . .

In the past fortnight I have lost 20 pounds and the result of this deprivation is that I am so very nervous that I could never stand a test along with one, two and three hundred girls. Through this very nervousness I was ruled out of a class yesterday. Today I went to an office for an examination and the examiner just looked me over and said; "I am afraid Miss, you are so awfully shabby I could never have you in my office."

I was so worried and disappointed and frightened that I replied somewhat angrily:

"Do you think clothes can be picked up in the streets?"

"Well," he replied with aggravating insolence, "lots of girls find them there these days."

Mr. Bennett, that almost broke my heart. Above everything else I have been very particular about my friends and since moving here I have never gone out in the evening . . .

Oh please sir, can you do something for me? Can you get me a job anywhere in the Dominion of Canada. I have not had to go on relief during this depression but I cannot get relief even here. Moreover it is a job I want and as long as I get enough to live I shall be happy again . . .

Your humble servant,
(Miss) Jean E. McLean

There is no record of a reply from Bennett, though his private secretary did send five dollars in response to the following letter from **J.H.E. Blackball.**

1211 Bleury St.
Montréal P.Q.
Feby. 13th/35

Rgt. Hon. R.B. Bennett K.C.
Ottawa Ont.
My Dear Sir
Having read what you said, "As long as I am Prime Minister of Canada no one will starve." Well this is my last appeal to you as I owe my landlady both for room rent and milk bill so that by Tuesday the 19th it will be either Starvation or Suicide. I have been trying since last Friday to get on relief here and after being passed from one office to another – all over the city – I at last found a man by the name of Lake in the Sun Life Bdg who gave me a blank to fill out. While I was doing so he came over and said "I'm going out, you wait

here I'll soon be back." I waited and when he returned I took the paper to his desk and he said "Sit down over there. Ill attend to you in a minute." I waited 2 hrs 20 mins then asked him if he had forgotten me. Ans. "Why you have come to the wrong place we have nothing whatever to do with relief go to this address" (handing me a slip) I said these are the people who sent me to you. "Oh, they're simply passing the buck"

What am I going to do? My brother who was helping me died Jan^ry 23rd leaving what <u>little</u> he had to his wife

Yrs Sincerely
J.H.E. Blackball

A BOGUS PEACE

In 1938 British Prime Minister Neville Chamberlain went to Munich to negotiate with German Chancellor Adolf Hitler over the fate of Czechoslovakia. Chamberlain's tactic was to allow Germany to have Czechoslovakia's Sudetenland in exchange for a promise of peace. On September 29 the two leaders signed an agreement "symbolic of the desire of our two peoples never to go to war with one another again," a document soon shown to be worthless. Canadian Prime Minister Mackenzie King supported Chamberlain's policy of appeasement. Like many Canadians, **Muriel Wetmore Teed** *of Saint John, New Brunswick, was relieved that there would, apparently, not be another war with Germany. She rejoiced in this letter to her sixteen-year-old daughter, Mary.*

Sept 29, 1938

My dear Mare,

Isnt it wonderful about the Peace settlement – if it is for the best – Gee, I have been about ill all the week – unable to do a thing – and I hardly went out – and now it is like someone brought back from the dead – and to think our British Premier did it all – he must be a very happy man – and if ever there was a man of God he is one – or he could not have wrought such a miracle. I have just been listening to his arrival in London and at his home – and it even beat the Coronation – Even if Peace is only for a short time – there is that much longer to be happy. I am here all alone but I had to shout and cry – worse than a moving picture – It is beyond belief that one man could have such calm and courage – How could we ever be any thing but a <u>Britisher</u> – forever –

   Now I hope I can settle down to normal – . . .

Heaps of love –

Mother

The dog is getting on well – but we keep him tied up – or he goes away – We call him "Happy"

German troops marched into the Sudetenland on October 1, 1938, the timetable Hitler had intended all along. Britain declared war on Germany on September 3, 1939, two days after Germany invaded Poland.

CAROUSING CANUCKS

Surgeon Lieutenant Commander W.D. Gunn studied medicine at McGill University. Unable to find work as a doctor in Canada during the Depression, he joined the Royal Navy in England. As war began, he was stationed in Hong Kong, where the British had a garrison of twenty thousand men. Gunn's mention of the arrival of the Canadians in this letter to his wife referred to the Royal Rifles of Canada (a Quebec unit), the Winnipeg Grenadiers, and the Canadian Signal Corps, who arrived on November 16, 1941, to reinforce the defence of the crown colony.

28.11.41

My Dearest Joanna: I wish you a very Happy Christmas and I hope it will be the last that we ever have to spend apart. Please don't think I'm [?] for not sending you a package but I had so hoped to bring it myself that it is now too late. But don't let that restrain you, go out and get yourself a big something you want & isn't rationed or couponed – and a nice big bottle of whiskey or something to really celebrate the day. It is going to be hell again but time seems to be going very quickly so maybe it won't be so long before I get a relief now. You will wonder why I'm writing so small & only one sheet, its a free air mail, we are told it will reach you for Christmas and we are only allowed one sheet. So I am trying to get in as much as I can on my ration. It should be a pretty big mail & hope it does arrive on time. Things here will be very quiet – little fuss or decorating in the hospital. We are going to have another combined Xmas dinner . . . The big news about this place is the arrival of the Canadians. They came about two weeks ago, as you probably heard. We were the only people on the island that didn't know what was happening, it had been in the Chinese papers 2 weeks before! They are a grand bunch of chaps & I have all ready met quite a number of them. One of their doctors was in my class at McGill & the other knows a number of folk I do. They have added a new zest to this place and all ready 21 are in Detention! It is grand to hear your own language being spoken – you will have to start in on me all over again when I get back. They brought 2 nursing sisters with them who aren't candidates for any beauty contest – & are living at the military hospital where there is great jealousy as these women get more pay than even the Army Matron – £35/mos! We have had an increase in Colonial Allowance which is back dated to 3.9.39. My share less Income Tax is £19 which I have remitted to the Bank. It may help to cover the Income Tax deficiency, though I've already paid £120 this year! I'm expecting to have a destroyer or corvette or something named after me soon . . .

. . . No one can ever talk to me about active serve M.O.'s [medical officers] being lazy or ignorant any more after some of the reserve people we have met here. One man sent in a case as tonsillitis when even the patient knew he had malaria! And that's a common case. And then they wonder why our diagnoses are always different from theirs. Please give my best to your Mother & Susie & to Phyllis if she comes down to spend the holiday with you. All my love to you,

Joanna Darling, and please give yourself a good Christmas – I mean you in the singular & really will be very unhappy if you don't. Give the small piece some of my love – but the most of it is yours and always will be more than I can possibly give to anyone else ever. It is you I married and you I want most of all things in the world. Good night, Honeybear, Happy Times & it can't be so very long now – always your very own. Bill.

On December 7, 1941, Japanese aircraft bombed the U.S. naval base at Pearl Harbor in Hawaii, bringing the United States into the war. The next day Japan attacked Hong Kong, and on Christmas Day the British colony surrendered. Gunn became a prisoner of war and was eventually transferred to Japan, where he died while working in a coal mine.

YEARS OF SHAME

*After Japan bombed Pearl Harbor, Ottawa ordered 21,000 people of Japanese ancestry – 17,000 of them Canadian citizens – to leave their homes in British Columbia. They were forced into makeshift camps and ghost towns in the B.C. interior and onto farms in Alberta and Manitoba. More than four thousand internees succumbed to government pressure to move to Ontario and Quebec. Their homes, farms, and fishing boats were either sold cheaply or confiscated outright. Second-generation Canadian **Muriel Kitagawa**, a mother of two who was expecting twins, wrote to her brother, Wes.*

March 2, 1942.

Dear Wes:

What a heavenly relief to get your letter. I was just about getting frantic with worry over you. That's why I hope you'll forgive me for writing to Jim Carson. Eddie [Muriel's husband] and I thought that was the only way to find out what really was happening to you. Oh Wes, the things that have been happening out here are beyond words, and though at times I thank goodness you're out of it, at other times I think we really need people like you around to keep us from getting too wrought up for our own good.

Eiko and Fumi [Muriel's friends] were here yesterday, crying, nearly hysterical with hurt and outrage and impotence. All student nurses have been fired from the General [Hospital].

They took our beautiful radio . . . what does it matter that someone bought it off us for a song . . . it's the same thing because we had to do that or suffer the ignominy of having it taken forcibly from us by the RCMP. Not a single being of Japanese race in the protected area will escape. Our cameras, even [younger brother] Nobi's toy one, all are confiscated. They can search our homes without warrant.

As if all this trouble wasn't enough, prepare yourself for a shock. We are forced to move out from our homes, Wes, to where we don't know. Eddie was going to join the Civilian Corps but now will not go near it, as it smells of a daemonic, roundabout way of getting rid of us. There is the very suspicious clause 'within and without' Canada that has all the fellows leery.

The Bank is awfully worried about me and the twins, and the manager has said he will do what he can for us, but as he has to refer to the main office which in turn has to refer to the Head Office, he can't promise a thing, except a hope that surely the Bank won't let us down after all these years of faithful service. Who knows where we will be now tomorrow next week. It isn't as if we Nisei [second-generation Japanese Canadians] were aliens, technical or not. It breaks my heart to think of leaving this house and the little things around it that we have gathered through the years, all those numerous gadgets that have no material value but are irreplaceable. My papers, letters, books . . . the azalea plants, my white iris, the lilac that is just beginning to flower . . . so many things.

Oh Wes, the Nisei are bitter, too bitter for their own good or for Canada. How can cool heads like Tom's prevail when the general feeling is to stand up and fight.

Do you know what curfew means in actual practice? B.C. is falling all over itself in the scramble to be the first to kick us out from jobs and homes. So many night-workers have been fired out of hand. Now they sit at home, which is usually just a bed, or some cramped quarters, since they can't go out at night for even a consoling cup of coffee. Mr. Shimizu is working like mad with the Welfare society to look after the women and children that were left when their men were forced to volunteer to go to the work camps. Now those men are only in unheated bunk-cars, no latrines, no water, snow 15' deep, no work to keep warm with, little food if any. They had been shunted off with such inhuman speed that they got there before any facilities were prepared for them. Now men are afraid to go because they think they will be going to certain disaster . . . anyway, too much uncertainty. After all, they have to think of their families. If snow is 15' deep there is no work, and if there is no work there is no pay, and if there is no pay no one eats. The Province [newspaper] reports that work on frames with tent-coverings is progressing to house the 2,000 expected. Tent coverings where the snow is so deep! And this is Democracy! You should see the faces here, all pinched, grey, uncertain. If the Bank fails Eddie, do you know what the kids and I have to live on? $39. For everything? . . . food, clothing, rent, taxes, upkeep, insurance premiums, emergencies. They will allow for only two kids for the Nisei. $6 per., monthly. It has just boiled down to race persecution, and signs have been posted on all highway . . . JAPS . . . KEEP OUT. Mind you, you can't compare this sort of thing to anything that happens in Germany. That country is an avowed Jew-baiter, totalitarian. Canada is supposed to be a Democracy out to fight against just the sort of things she's boosting at home.

And also, I'll get that $39 only if Eddie joins the Chain Gang, you know, forced to volunteer to let the authorities wash their hands of any responsibilities. All Nisei are liable to imprisonment I suppose if they refuse to volunteer . . . that is the likeliest interpretation of Ian MacKenzie's "volunteer or else." Prisoners in wartime get short shrift . . . and to hell with the wife and kids. Can you wonder there is a deep bitterness among the Nisei who believe so gullibly in the democratic blah-blah that's been dished out . . .

There are a lot of decent people who feel for us, but they can't do a thing.

And the horrors that some young girls have already faced . . . outraged by men in uniform . . . in the hospital . . . hysterical. Oh we are fair prey for the Wolves in democratic clothing. Can you wonder the men are afraid to leave us behind and won't go unless their women go with them? I won't blame you if you can't believe this. It is incredible. Wes, you have to be here right in the middle of it to really know.

How can the hakujin [white people] face us without a sense of shame for their treachery to the principles they fight for? One man was so damned sorry, he came up to me, hat off, squirming like mad, stuttering how sorry he was. My butcher said he knew he could trust me with a side of meat even if I had no money. These kind people too are betrayed by the Wilsonites [an alderman's supporters] . . . God damn his soul! Yet there are other people who, while they wouldn't go so far as to persecute us, are so ignorant, so indifferent they believe we are being very well treated for what we are. The irony of it all is enough to choke me. And we are tightening our belts for the starvation to come. The diseases . . . the crippling . . . the twisting of our souls . . . death would be the easiest to bear.

The Chinese are forced to wear huge buttons and plates and even placards to tell the hakujin the difference between one yellow peril and another. Or else they would be beaten up. It's really ridiculous.

And Wes, we are among the fortunate ones, for above that $39 we may be able to fill it out by renting this house. Now I wish I hadn't given my clothes to Kath. We will need them badly. Uncle has been notified to get ready to move. Dad will be soon too.

There's too much to say and not enough time or words.

Can't send you pictures now unless some hakujin takes the snap . . . STRENG VERBOTEN [German for "strictly forbidden"] to use even little cameras to snap the twins . . . STRENG VERBOTEN is the order of the day.

My apologies to Jim Carson.

Love,

Mur.

March 3, 1942

Dear Wes:

This is just to warn you: Don't you dare come back to B.C., no matter what happens, what reports you read in the papers, whatever details I tell you in letters. You stay out of this province. B.C. is hell.

Rather than have you come back here, we'll come to Toronto if we can.

I'll keep you posted by letters, but I repeat, there is nothing for you here. Even if you quit school, stay in Toronto – anywhere East of the Rockies.

Yoshi Higashi went to Camp last night with 7 hours notice.

Eddie will be about the last to go anywhere, whether to another branch bank or elsewhere. If I really need you I'll come to Toronto. Remember!

For the love of God, don't you come here. Not you, a single male. You'll be more help to me and to others if you stay where you are – free – even if starving.

Love,

Mur.

Muriel Kitagawa moved with her family to Toronto, where she continued to protest Canada's treatment of its Japanese citizens. She began writing an autobiography, which was incomplete when she died in 1974, at the age of sixty-two.

THE DISASTER OF DIEPPE

By 1942 the Allies were reeling. The Japanese were winning in the Far East and the Germans were advancing on the ground in the Middle East, bombing vital convoys in the Mediterranean and sinking merchant ships in the Atlantic. From Britain, where Canadian troops awaited deployment, a series of escalating raids was planned. The largest raid was an attack in August across the English Channel on the German-held port of Dieppe, in northern France. The disastrous

four-hour raid, which was intended to land tanks and men on the
beaches, was supported by aircraft, some of them Canadian. Canadian
Captain G.B. Buchanan *wrote this letter of gratitude to the crew of*
the ship that transported his regiment.

CANADA

SOUTH SASKATCHEWAN REGIMENT

2 Sep 1942

Officers and Men of H.M.S. Princess Beatrix
G.P.O. London
Owing to rush of work, courts of enquiry and demands of other
returns to be made out, I must apologize for not writing sooner.

The Officers and men of the S.Sask.R., one and all, have agreed
that the crews of your Assault Craft are the bravest lads they have
ever seen.

I know that you have been wanting to hear what happened to
us, so I will try to tell you something about that wild battle.

Your craft put us down on the beach at exactly the right time, our
landing was a complete surprise, but thirty seconds later, "Jerry" was
opening up with everything he had. Our right Co^y went through the
town and inland two miles, secured their objective very readily with
some casualties. The left flank gave us all the trouble, as you no doubt
could see from the sea. We were subjected to extremely heavy M.G.
[machine gun] mortar and Art^y fire, and the town fairly rocked with
their explosions all morning. From the cliffs on both sides of the
beach, all hell seemed to break loose at us and it was there that your
lads in the A.I.C.s [assault craft] gained our everlasting admiration
and thanks; repeatedly they made trips from the ship to shore under
a withering cross-fire from M.G. and cannon. If it had not been for
their coolness and bravery very few of our men would have survived.
We lost some of our best friends, and some of whom you knew also.

Our C.O. did not return. He had performed such deeds of daring
that morning that his name will always be a legend in our Regiment.
Other friends of yours who did not return were: Major J.C. MacTavish,

Capt. T.M. Osten, Capt A.J. Edmondson, and Lieuts Wollard, Dawson and Conn, and many of the men. Major J.E. McRae and myself, thanks to the Royal Navy, managed to get back in one piece. Capt N.A. Adams was wounded but is now recovering very speedily. Lieut Mullholland also returned.

Tell "Hank" Saunders that we do not think he was much of a sailor, having to be towed back across the Channel. The sight of Hank sitting on the bow of his craft like some "Norse Viking" and being towed behind a crippled gun-boat was the crowning climax of the day.

Give my regards to Paddy, Alex, and all the other gallant lads of your ship. We thank you one and all for your grand co-operation and friendship, and we are looking forward to the day when we can go for another ride on the H.M.S. Beatrix.

G.B. Buchanan Capt.

S.Sask.R. C.A. (O)

The Dieppe raid was an unmitigated disaster; the causes ranged from untrained troops to poor intelligence to the misguided planning of a full-frontal, daylight assault on the Germans' most formidable fortress on that coast. The German High Command called it "an amateur undertaking in opposition to all good military sense." The Beatrix *actually offloaded the regiment almost two kilometres east of their target, which left the soldiers scrabbling up cliffs in a futile effort to reach a radar station. The commanding officer who did not return was Lieutenant Colonel C.C. Merritt, one of two Canadians who won a Victoria Cross for their roles in the raid. They were among the nine hundred of their countrymen killed and the 1,874 imprisoned. Thirteen of the 106 aircraft and ten of the eighty-one airmen lost were from the Royal Canadian Air Force. Captain Buchanan earned France's Croix de Guerre for gallant and distinguished service.*

THE FINAL GAMBLE

*In 1943 Canadian infantrymen began fighting alongside the British in Sicily and on the Italian mainland, where they played a pivotal role and lost nearly 5,800 men. They were also a key component of the greatest amphibious operation in history: an ambitious scheme in June 1944 to open a second front in France through a surprise assault on the beaches of Normandy – Operation Overlord. Joining the American and British troops were the 3rd Canadian Infantry Division and the 2nd Canadian Armoured Brigade, which landed at Juno and Sword beaches on June 6 – D-Day. Among the Canadians was **Gunner Ross Baker**, who two months later described his role to his brother, RCAF Sergeant Alvin K. Baker.*

ON ACTIVE SERVICE
B44351 Gnr Baker R.E.
14 Fld Reg't 66 Bty R.C.A.
Cdn A.D. 13 W.E.F.
13 Aug 44

Dear Alvin: –

Well I'm back in a hole in the ground again. I received your letter a few days ago but not here. We have just finished having some cocoa for a mid night snack. I'm on duty to-night, so it gives me time to write, which I never had before. We have a very good light that runs off a battery (car) But we are a little crowded. The hole is rather small for three but the reason is that the ground is very rocky . . .

. . . I came over on a barge (L.C.T.) [Landing Craft Tank] We had water proof vehicles which were all tanks, S.P. half tracks [wheel-and-track vehicles bearing men and armaments] & carriers. So it was supposed to be a dry landing for the personnel, but my tank hit a mine and go[t] drowned, so before it filled with water we got out & I had presents enough of mind to take time to get my pack [rifle?] and a few maps and after awhile jumped into water up to my neck. things were blowing up all around us & some fellows were getting nervous & left everything behind. But things happened so fast I didn't have time to get scared. the water wasn't so terrible cold, but the waves were big and I had to let them take me in so I could walk. I nearly jumped in when I remember I had better blow up my Mae West [inflatable life-jacket] it should have been done long before that. The beach was jammed & I waited around there for nearly an hour. Then the major told us to get on some other vehicle & go up to our troop. So I finally got through the town [Bernières-sur-Mer] & found them, at their second position. The first position they went to their place but they got ahead of the infantry and in the first feild outside the town an 88 mm knocked out three SP., so they pulled out of there to a barn yard behind a stone wall where I found them. My other pack was in another vehicle that got in safely so except for my bed roll that was on the out side of the tank I was o.k. My bed roll had my overcoat, a battle dress/gas cape, rain coat, ground sheet, a bag with personnel stuff such a flash-light batteries soap etc. So I don't need a flashlight or batteries now. I could take alot of pictures, but if I had had a camera It would have been lo[s]t or at least ruined in the saltwater likely anyway. As I passed though Caen I seen soldiers with a few pine boxes that had bodies inside, that they were digging out of the ruins and they have been there a month. But I guess there is alot of them to be found yet. The city is ruined & it was a lovely place too. They were some lovely houses and grand stores etc., very fancy. But there were a few fine specimens of gash [women] there. It isn't such a small place either about 85,000. But there are villages that are worse off than that city. I haven't really been able to get any souvenirs. I haven't time to go looking around. If I ever get up with the infantry though, I may. I had the picture taken a few weeks before I left I mailed it from France as I was here when I got it. If you think I have a good tan you should see me now. We can't carry extra stuff around and not as much with this vehicle establishment so all we are particular about is something to eat & I suppose that is something thats hard to get with rationing. But hot chocolate drinks, or fruit drinks honey cheese canned meat is always something that we can carry and that will go with hard tack . . .

Cheerio Best of Luck & Love to you both

Ross

The Allies had learned some hard lessons from the catastrophe of Dieppe. As Lord Louis Mountbatten, director of British combined operations, later wrote: "For every soldier who died at Dieppe, ten were saved on D-Day." The Normandy invasion triggered the final campaign in northwest Europe.

SPOILS OF BATTLE

Captain Joseph Greenblatt *of Ottawa, a medical officer with the Royal Canadian Army Medical Corps, sailed with the invasion armies on D-Day and advanced with them into Germany. He wrote scores of numbered letters to Frances, his sweetheart back home.*

> 24 Sept 44
> Letter #54
> ON ACTIVE SERVICE
> Capt J. Greenblatt
> RCAMC
> 13 Fed Rgt RCA
> C.A.O. B.W.E.F.

Fran Darling –

This letter is being written from a deluxe Jerry dugout built presumably not for our occupation . . .

I must tell you of a funny incident that happened a while ago. We were proceeding along a road in convoy beside a field marked in German "Achtung Minen". You could see the mines all over the place & in one of the innumerable convoy stops we were right alongside it. On the other side of the field another convoy was stopped also. All of the sudden a cow appeared in the field & started to walk around & of course the expected happened. "Wham"! & the cows head was blown off leaving the rest of the body fairly intact. Immediately there was a good deal of hustling & bustling about & out came the mine detectors & from each side of the field you could see a little procession start off. The procession was headed by the chap with the Polish minesweeper followed at a discreet distance by the butcher of each unit brandishing a long carving knife. It was a race from each side of the field. Everyone gathered around to cheer their respective heroes. Our butcher got there first & he had already carved a couple of good quarters when the fellow from the other side reached his objective & skilfully started to cleave away. Our butcher noticing the skilful handiwork of the other chap looked up & recognized the other chap as a man whom he had worked beside in a meat-packing plant in Western Canada & hadn't seen each other for about three years. So while everyone cheered lustily from the sidelines they had a quiet chat & a smoke & reminisced. Then each divided the booty & departed carrying their quarters of beef. What a war – but a bloody good dinner . . .

Yours
Joseph

After the war Joseph returned home and married Frances.

A SOBERING END

In the last days of the war twenty-five-year-old **Erle Shakespeare** *of Winnipeg was servicing aircraft – the "kites" of this letter – as a ground-crew mechanic with the Royal Canadian Air Force in Leeming, England. Just after Germany surrendered, he wrote to his sister, Eileen Porteous.*

London. –
ON ACTIVE SERVICE
[May 15, 1945]

Dear Leen. –

Seems like quite a while since last I wrote so here's a line or so to let you know I'm still in England. This is the first letter to flow from the

79¢ pen since VE day so a word or two about the way we celebrated the occasion should be a good idea.

Well on monday the 7th we knew it was all over. We did nothing that day but get dressed in our best & wait for the official announcement that we were sure would come before supper. However by 6.30 the word still hadn't come so Marc, Floyd & myself with a few other rogues hiked into the little town of Exelby anyhow for a few pints.

A word about the pub before I continue – it's one of the homiest I've seen. Just like an ordinary house with a chesterfield, easy chairs, couches, piano & a radio in it. Also the inevitable fireplace.

There was quite a few of us there – men & women – and there seemed a certain tenseness in the room. Then over the radio came the chimes of Big Ben pealing out the hour of nine, and the announcer's voice – very dramatic & very English – saying: "This is the news from London – Germany surrendered unconditionally to the Allies today –" that's all we heard. The place became a bedlam with everybody hysterical with joy. Some of the women, due to either joy or alcohol, wept & wailed, but everyone else just yelled & laughed & threw glasses into the fireplace (damn near put the fire out, they did).

We stayed on there till almost midnite singing patriotic songs etc. & then staggered, still singing, across the fields back to camp, where we rolled into our sacks to recuperate for the doings on Tuesday VE day.

We got a rude shock tho' when they rustled us up at 7 to get the kites all serviced & ready for take-off at 10 A.M., to pick up P.O.W.'s from Brussels.

They got back about 5 & by 6 we were all set to celebrate. We pitched into the ale at Jack's with a vengeance. Left there at eight & came back to the station because there was 32 thirty-six gallon barrels of beer there, that was for free. By eleven o'clock I don't think there was a single sober person on the camp. There was a dance going in one of the hangars & that's where we all went – jumping & kicking & bouncing around till 3:30 A.M.

Back at the barracks somebody had dragged a 10 gallon milk can full of beer & we wasted no time getting into that. By 6.30 we'd cleaned that up & then came the voice over the P.A. to get the kites ready for another load of P.O.W.'s.

Well the idea didn't appeal to us much, but we went out & I'm damned if there wasn't another 20 gals. of suds out at the drome. Somehow or other (between glasses of ale) we got them in the air at 11.30 & then just lay down on the drome & slept till they came back.

That was all the celebrating we did at Leeming, cause the next day (Thursday) Marc, Floyd & myself went on leave to London, which is where I'm writing from.

We pulled into King's Cross station at 6.30 & after getting rooms & supper took a tube to Trafalgar Square. Everything out there was lit up with floodlites – such places as the Art Gallery, Nelson's monument, Admiralty arch, Buckingham Palace, Houses of Parliament, Big Ben etc. The place was jammed with thousands of fanatical Londoners – mad with joy at seeing bright lites again. All the way from the Admiralty arch, clear up to the gates of the Palace was a solid mass of humanity. We made our way to the gates, however, & just as we did the King & Queen stepped out on the balcony. I thought I knew what noise was, but the roar that went up from that crowd beat everything. The ground actually shook from the vibration!

This is my fifth day in London & I've enjoyed myself immensely so far. During the days we've been visiting such places of interest as Westminster Abbey, St Pauls Cathedral, the wax works, Tower of London, Hyde Park etc. & at nite have tried our luck with the London girls. Taken all in all there's not much wrong with the English girls that a few new clothes, a girdle & an American uplift couldn't improve. But maybe I'm just hard to please.

Yesterday we walked thru one of the hardest hit parts of London but I'm not even going to try to describe it. It sure makes a person wonder how in hell they stood up under such hellish pounding.

Kind of a sober note to end this with but it's supper time & I'm pow'ful hungry. Bye for now,

Erle

THE GUSHER

After the war Canada flourished, and in the West geologists sought new sources of energy to fuel the boom. Among the active exploration companies was Imperial Oil, which by 1946 – after drilling 133 consecutive dry holes across the prairies – was intending to rely in future on offshore petroleum supplies. But geologist Dr. Ted Link convinced the company's directors to try tapping a belt of central Alberta plains south of Edmonton, near the sleepy town of Leduc. What happened in early 1947 was recollected a decade later, in a letter that **Vern Hunter***, a supervisor, or toolpush, sent to an Imperial colleague.*

January 7, 1957

Mr. R. J. Johnstone

After drilling a series of dry holes in Saskatchewan and earning the name "dry hole" or, affectionately, "salt water" Hunter, we moved the rig (Wilson #2) to Provost, Alberta . . . When we moved into the sandhills at Provost, they had quite a laugh on us. I remember one day a sheep herder came out of the sand dunes, one of the most disreputable characters I have ever seen, with a slouch hat pulled down over his ears and a suit that would have fit Alan McClatchie before the famine; Jack Grosenick took a look at him and said, and I quote: "typical Albertan".

We drilled two wells in Provost, one of which was a short-lived oil producer, the other a fair gas well and then early in October of 1946 Charlie Visser informed us we were to go to Leduc. We were quite happy to move as we were getting itchy feet from staying too long in one town, but fully realized that no oil could possibly be found within 20 miles of a city like Edmonton.

I made a trip up to Leduc where I met Walt Dingle and together we went out to stake the rig site which Walt had already surveyed in . . . Walt drove the stake, and being of little faith, left immediately for South America. A short time later we moved the rig, shacks and trailers, into Leduc and began to settle down in the town park right next to the Curling Rink.

The rig was located on Mike Turta's farm just outside his barnyard. Mike refused to let us go around his yard, for some reason, and I am afraid that with the constant traffic some of his chickens and ducks came to an untimely end. I was always afraid that it would be one of his kids. Walking through his yard was too dangerous, with the ganders snapping at your heels like the hounddogs after little Eva. However, we had very good relations with the Turtas and were always welcome for a cup of tea or a meal. The whole crew made a point of buying their cream, eggs and chickens and Mike Turta seemed to thoroughly enjoy the company the crew provided.

The weather turned very cold the night we spudded in and "Mousie" McIntyre, who had just been set up as driller, on the graveyard shift, had the misfortune of the stand-pipe and Kelly hose freezing up on his first tour. Mousie was a pretty sorry looking fellow when he brought the reports in that morning. No hole and lots of trouble. I don't imagine he thought it portended a great future for Leduc #1 . . .

. . . I cannot be sure after all these years, but I think it was George McClintock [a geologist] who first noticed some porosity in the samples one cold night and insisted that we take a core. (Note: drilling crews don't like to pull out a fresh bit in the middle of a winter's night and run in with a core barrel just to satisfy the whim of some geologist who can then go to bed knowing that it will be several hours before anyone will wake him up.)

Well, we cut a core and on visual examination it didn't look too hot. The porosity was so good that the washing action of the mud had removed all the oil. However, we ran in with the tester, hooked up to the flare line and dropped the dart. Without any hesitation there was action. Air from the empty pipe started to flow, to be followed by gas and mud and then oil, flowing by heads. We lit the flare and all stood around it, grateful for the heat even though we were frying on one side and freezing on the other. After about an hour we shut it in, let the pressure build up for information purposes and then pulled out of the hole, little realizing that this event was changing the whole economy of Western Canada.

Several cores and drillstem tests later, on instructions from Calgary, we called it deep enough and ran casing.

I have forgotten the exact date, probably about February 10, the two Taylor boys – Walker and Vern – told me that a celebration was to be held on the day the well was to be brought in with invitations being sent to the Government and Industry officials. They wanted me to name the day which I did under protest, as so many things can happen when fooling with temperamental oil wells. Another thing that scared me was that the crew, including myself, were experts at abandoning wells, but didn't know too much about completing oil wells. However, I named February 13 and started praying . . .

Shortly before 4:00 p.m., the well started to show some signs of life, greatly to my relief, as I was having trouble dodging Walker Taylor [the western production manager]. He was at least as concerned as I was and possibly more so as he had to face the invited guests. Then, with a roar, the well came in, flowing into the sump near the rig. We switched it to the flare line, lit the flare and the most beautiful smoke ring you ever saw went floating skywards. Shortly after that, Campbell Aird turned the production through the separator to the tanks and my day was over. I didn't even go to the reception in Edmonton as bed looked more inviting to me.

If I ever learned a lesson that day it was this: never predict when a well will come in.

V.H. (Vern) Hunter

The front page of The Edmonton Bulletin *of May 16, 1947, reported: "A surging, angry voice from the depths of the earth Thursday at 1:30 p.m. announced to the world that the Leduc area may become one of the most prolific producers of petroleum crude in the West." For many years thereafter, Canada was self-sufficient in oil.*

YOUNG JOEY

Joseph (Joey) Smallwood was the crafty, consummate politician who brought the British colony of Newfoundland into Confederation as the tenth province in 1949. In the 1920s he had been an idealistic young journalist; while writing for leftist newspapers in New York he corresponded with George Tucker, who worked for Newfoundland Light and Power, about the never-realized possibility of forming a Newfoundland Labour Party. Reading some of his letters from this period, Smallwood's granddaughter, Dale FitzPatrick, remarked, "Wow! He had some forward-thinking ideas for a twenty-five-year-old!"

123 West 15th Street
New York City
Feb. 17, 1924

Dear Comrade Tucker:

. . . There is nothing that Newfoundland needs so much at the present time as some party of honest, enlightened, capable, sincere men who would bend every effort to the really herculian (and thankless) job of cleaning up the national house. Public affairs have never been so corrupt; graft has never been so nakedly rampant. We have passed thru and, for all we know, may still be passing thru a saturnalia of rottenness unequalled in our public history. Mispractice and looseness have never been so prevalent. Side by side with this there has been a good deal of incapability and floundering. I feel certain the public would be startled if they knew the full facts . . .

. . . The thing to do, it seems to me, is organize sufficiently to be in the position to criticise, expose, heckle and attack existing parties, and drive home to the masses that they will never get good government as long as they have parties that are organized and conducted along the lines of the present parties. That is to say, a propaganda, educational group tha[t] should prepare ground for the establishment of a Labor party. That propaganda, in my opinion, ought to take on four phases: to expose the graft and corruption of the old-line parties; to agitate for good government for Newfoundland; to agitate for progressive social legislation; and to agitate for workers' legislation . . .

. . . The mere desire to gain power would make the party opportunistic and adventuristic, and encourage the very career-mongering that would kill it. A mere cut and dried program or platform would in time be exhausted, and the party should be left high and dry. We must at the beginning set up some high principles which, even with the passing of time, shall prove a fountain of inspiration. From this you will readily see that my ideal of a party is a crusade imbued with love and comradeship – "the dear love of comrades," indeed. Unless there be these high principles to start with, a movement is so apt to degenerate, as we can see when we study the history of many unions and parties . . .

Fraternally,

J.R. Smallwood

By 1948 Smallwood had been a union organizer, radio broadcaster, pig farmer, and failed political candidate. That year he ran a campaign for the Newfoundland Confederate Association to end Newfoundland's colonial link to Britain and encourage a confederation with Canada.

July 14, 1948.

Mr. Frank I. Robinson,
Buchans.
Dear Mr. Robinson,
It was good to hear from you again. Your letter was most encouraging indeed. Such reports from the North and West indicate that our victory this time is beyond all possible doubt. When we started this movement – such a long time ago – we did not imagine things could have turned out so well, so far we have not suffered a single defeat

or set-back, whereas Responsible Government has lost steadily all along the line . . .

With best wishes.

Sincerely yours,

NEWFOUNDLAND CONFEDERATE ASSOCIATION

Per. J.R. Smallwood, Campaign Manager.

Voters narrowly supported the referendum on Confederation, 52 to 48 percent. Smallwood became a formidable Liberal premier and, some critics say, fell prey to the kind of excesses of power he had railed against a quarter century before. He came to be seen as a friend of the industrial magnate, not the worker. His government was defeated by the Conservatives in 1971, and Smallwood finally gave up his seat in the legislature six years later to write the Encyclopedia of Newfoundland and Labrador.

LETTERS FROM UNDERGROUND

Less than a decade after Newfoundland embraced Canada, another Atlantic province made Canadians sit up and take notice. In Springhill, Nova Scotia, on Thursday, November 1, 1956, an explosion ripped through the town's No. 4 mine, trapping 127 coal miners. Fifty-four of the men were at the 5,200-foot level, among them underground supervisor **Con Embree**. *As hope faded on their third day of entomb-ment without food and water, Embree tore a page from his logbook to write to his family, referring to his wife as "Mother."*

[November 4, 1956]

Sunday 3 p.m.

Mother you will have to sell
the place and the best thing to do
is get the vet to give Rocky

a needle. Florrie be good to Mum
and Donald and Freddie see that she
is looked after.

God bless you all
Dad

Some miners, including **Charles (Sonny) Michelson,** *used brown
lunch bags as writing paper.*

[November 4, 1956]

dear Marilyn make sure
you look after the kids
I guess this is the way it
has to be. tell Nan
and the rest of the family
it couldnt be helped

love Sonny

Make sure this note
gets to my wife

Sonny

Deborah xxxx
Wayne xxoo
Wife ooxx
Nan xxoo

*Miraculously both Embree and Michelson were among the eighty-
eight miners rescued after four days underground. The mine was
sealed on November 7; the following January the bodies of twenty-
six of the thirty-nine victims were recovered. Two years later, at the
same mine, a tunnel collapsed and buried 101 men. A quarter of
them were saved in a rescue attempt that galvanized Canada as the
CBC television network did its first continuous remote reporting of a
major disaster.*

BOOKMAN JACK

Jack McClelland turned the stodgy domestic publishing industry upside down. Joining the family business in 1946, he made McClelland & Stewart the premier Canadian publisher by aggressively promoting the likes of Farley Mowat, Pierre Berton, Leonard Cohen, Peter C. Newman, Margaret Laurence, Irving Layton, Mordecai Richler, and Margaret Atwood. He was a shameless promoter – dressing up as Santa Claus in July to hand out free books in Saskatoon, costuming author Sylvia Fraser as a Roman empress and himself as a toga-draped emperor in Toronto to promote one of her books – but also a lover of Canadian writing who, despite horrendous financial difficulties, helped his authors get international exposure and supported them stalwartly. In 1965 he wrote to Leonard Cohen about the manuscript that would become Beautiful Losers, *mentioning at the start their mutual friend Irving Layton.*

June 15, 1965

Mr. Leonard Cohen
Hydra, Greece
Dear Leonard:
When I talked to Irving, I had only had a chance to read the first thirty-odd pages. I've now finished it. Migod, it's a fantastic book. It astounds me and baffles me and I don't really know what to say about it. It's wild and incredible and marvellously well written, and at the same time appalling, shocking, revolting, disgusting, sick and just maybe it's a great novel. I'm damned if I know. I have no way of knowing. It's the majority view at Viking [in New York] that it's a superior piece of work. All I can say is that I think it is an amazing book. I'm not going to pretend that I dig it, because I don't. So leave us not pretend. I enjoyed reading it, I would like to reread it and will when I have a chance.

Are we going to publish? At the moment I don't know. My guess would be yes, but I'd better wait and see what sort of reaction I get from some of my associates. They could scream, although I really don't anticipate that they will. I'm a little apprehensive about the reaction of the Catholic Church. It's either pretty damn sacriligeous or it isn't. Certainly it is in extract, but whether it is in total is for the author to say. You could fool me. The odds are, though, that we will make a publishing offer and I'll let you know as quickly as possible. Let me be truthful about this. If it were being published in the U.S.A. by Grove, I'd be very apprehensive. When it is published by Viking, I think we have a fighting chance. I'm sure it will end up in the courts here, but that might be worth trying.

You are a nice chap, Leonard, and it's lovely knowing you. All I have to decide now is whether I love you enough to want to spend the rest of my days in jail because of you, and even though I can't pretend to understand the goddamn book, I do congratulate you. It's a wild and incredible effort.

Cheers!

J.G. McClelland

As McClelland feared, Beautiful Losers *proved controversial, though it was never banned. One of its critics wrote the publisher to say: "I don't know who Mr. Cohen is, I wish him no harm, but he must be a sick man to write such garbage."*

August 26, 1966

Mr. John Fisher
271 Truman Road
Willowdale, Ontario
Dear Mr. Fisher:

. . . You say you don't know who he is. Cohen is a poet. I think it is no exaggeration to say that in the opinion of the majority of responsible critics, he is one of Canada's most gifted and accomplished poets. Many would say he is our best . . .

. . . *Beautiful Losers* is a serious work. Undoubtedly it may offend some people, but I cannot feel that this is sufficient justification for suppressing such a work . . .

I do not believe in censorship. I think there is abundant evidence available to thoughtful people that the evils of censorship are far greater than whatever evils the censors might attempt to correct. However, I do respect the right of any citizen to care, and I do respect the right of any citizen to endeavour to do something about any matter on which they feel strongly. However, Mr. Fisher, if you do feel that you must make a stand, if you do care, and if you do feel that you must do something about it, I suggest that you might find it a far more worthwhile starting point by looking at the "pulps" on the local newsstand instead of attacking the work of a serious writer.

Yours sincerely,

J.G. McClelland

WE ARE THE WORLD

*As their nation marked its one-hundredth birthday in 1967, Canadians were feeling a newfound cockiness. Centennial celebrations across the country reminded them of their heritage, and in Montreal Expo 67 was dazzling the world. **Nathalie** (whose last name is unknown) communicated her excitement (in French) to a distant friend.*

30 April, 1967

Dear Françoise,

Expo has finally begun – you must have been thinking about it on April 28, opening day – If you could just see how proud we are to be Montrealers. It's Huge, Splendid, Astounding, Marvellous, Unique. All with capital letters. There isn't a word strong enough to do it justice. Dad and I spent all day Sunday the 30th on the grounds – we knew the crowds would be insane but we rushed down there anyway. There must have been 400,000 of us. Unbelievable! Around 3 p.m., they had to stop the subway at Berri-Demontigny station to prevent anyone else going down, so the crowd could thin out a bit and people who wanted to leave Expo could get through. It's not only the States that can claim the biggest – here too, let me tell you. The weather is great, and that just makes things even better. So far we've visited the Russian pavilion, which is very popular, and Thailand and the Union of Burma, they're as sculptured and delicate as a piece of lace, they're absolutely fascinating. Also went to Place d'Afrique, that's a whole group of republics – Ivory Coast, Cameroon, Uganda, Togo, and Congo will be there too but it's not open yet. Those guys are slow. But the most beautiful of all, as far as I'm concerned, of all the ones we've seen, is the Czech pavilion. It's so lovely, it's like a dream. So anyway, I can't wait for you to arrive so I can show you everything. In fact, you should come straight here, don't stop for anything along the way, because you don't have enough vacation time to take everything in. The whole world is right here on our doorstep.

With love,
Nathalie

WE ARE CANADA

A year later the magnetic Pierre Elliott Trudeau, elected on a tide of Trudeaumania, became Canada's fifteenth prime minister. Meanwhile, the charismatic René Lévesque had deserted the Quebec Liberal government of Jean Lesage to found the separatist Parti Québécois in 1968. Writing in French, a perceptive young Québécois, **Julien Martin,** *set the stage for the political drama that would consume Canadians for decades to come.*

15 May '68
Bromptonville, Qué.

"We are Québécois, and what that means first and foremost and of necessity exclusively, is that we are deeply attached to this one corner of the world where we can fully be ourselves, this Quebec which, we know in our bones, is the one place where we can truly feel at home."

– René Lévesque

Good evening Gilberte,
This evening, I think I'm finally going to write something about Quebec. I'll begin by sending you the quotation above to add to your collection. Even though I'm pretty tired, since I went riding this afternoon.

Sorry – I lay down for a bit after that last sentence and I'm still tired! But I'll try to have some second thoughts about this second century . . . (Oh, I'm falling asleep!)

16 May '68

Good evening once again: I meant to finish this letter yesterday evening, but that didn't work out, and today I had gardening to do and then I gave blood . . . so, finally, here I am!

The 100th anniversary celebrations for Confederation made a lot of Canadians feel very nationalistic (full of national pride). There was a spirit of confidence in the air and friendship reigned. Then one month after St-Jean-Baptiste [the annual holiday in June], along came General de Gaulle to burst the balloon [by shouting "Vive le Québec libre!"] . . . That was enough to convince any Canadian with a head on his shoulders that the future won't be built through a continuing pursuit of vague abstractions and "vainglorious" dreams of destiny, poorly defined and bluntly expressed. However, the experience has turned out to be a blessing. Since then, we've seen the articulation of the alternatives facing Canada – and before Canada, Québec.

René Lévesque presented the first last October, when he proposed political independence for Québec. If the break takes place, this is the path that Quebec will follow . . .

Pierre Elliot[t] Trudeau presented the second, known as "Option-Canada," in January of this year. It calls for a pragmatic political arrangement, based on hard realities, not dreams . . .

All levels of government share responsibility for the lives of Canadian citizens, no capital has the right to decide the destiny of any group. No single administration exclusively represents the interests of a unique and distinct group, for example French-Canadians. At the

Ottawa conference, other governments addressed this issue just as seriously as Québec. The separatists forget that fact. Lévesque can try to shrug off all French-Canadians who live outside the province, on the grounds that "they're already anglicized," but it's a thoughtless attitude and unfortunately representative of much of the nationalist thinking in Québec today.

My brother has already put this question to Lévesque: If, tomorrow, you could take power in an independent Québec, what would you do? What would happen? etc.? . . . Well, Lévesque replied that he couldn't answer because he didn't know what he'd do or have to do. You asked me my opinion of separatism. (Okay, here I go.) I'd be against it, because Québec isn't ready to be independent; a lot of people say that Québec isn't ready financially speaking, etc., but as far as I'm concerned, we're not ready politically speaking. I'm also opposed to it because of the injustice it would mean for our minority groups (linguistic, religious, whatever). So if that's your opinion too, then we don't have to debate it . . .

Julien

MEDICARE AND MATERIALISM

*The 1960s overturned some of Canada's most conservative conventions. In Saskatchewan **T.C. (Tommy) Douglas**, a bespectacled Baptist minister turned socialist premier, fought the province's medical establishment to introduce the nation's first medicare program, which was implemented in 1962. He then pressed the matter as a member of Parliament, urging Ottawa to pass a Medical Care Act, which the Liberal government finally introduced in 1966 (but did not make truly national in scope until 1972). Canada's other domestic upheaval was the hippie revolution; young Canadians joined their American counterparts in challenging "straight" society, using drugs, rock music, and protests – particularly against the Vietnam war. Tommy Douglas responded to both movements in these letters to voters.*

January 25, 1968

Mr. R. L. Foster,
6498 Buchanan Street
Burnaby 2, B.C.

Dear Mr. Foster:

Thank you very much for your recent letter and for your comments concerning Medicare.

I agree with you when you say that Medicare is too often thought of as mere "sickness insurance", and that our thinking should be directed towards "health insurance". Quite frankly, it was with this in mind that we first introduced Medicare in Saskatchewan.

Since 1962, when Medicare became a reality in Saskatchewan, there has been a tremendous increase in interest and activity in preventative medicine. Once the financial barrier between the doctor and a patient was removed, more emphasis could be placed on keeping people healthy rather than merely treating them after they became sick.

For example, in many Saskatchewan centres we had the development of what are called community clinics which are operated as a co-operative venture involving both the people of the community and the medical personnel serving those clinics. An over-riding principle of these clinics is that people should be kept healthy, not merely treated after they become sick.

With best wishes to you for 1968.

Sincerely yours,
T.C. Douglas

March 19, 1968

Miss F. Menzies
Box 2396
Vancouver, B.C.

Dear Miss Menzies:

I suppose there is some truth to your statement that all politicians are cut from the same cloth. We all have our lapses; we all have our periods of disorganization. I hope you will accept my apology for the treatment your recent letters have received. My personal secretary and my executive assistant were both lost to me recently, my secretary through a serious illness and my executive assistant died suddenly. The result has been that my operation has not been as efficient for a month or so, as it normally is.

The article enclosed with your letter of 28th February dealing with the Mental Hospital in Edmonton was extremely interesting. I am at a loss to know why in this day and age such institutions continue to exist. As a long-time C.C.F.'er you will recall that the C.C.F. Government of Saskatchewan, as one of its first moves, began to improve the facilities and methods of treatment of mental patients. One of my proudest moments was when Doctor Karl Menninger of the Menninger Clinic visited the province and its mental institutions and found it proper to state that they were the finest on the continent . . .

I can understand your anguish about the sort of social phenomena that you see around you. This country, as is the rest of the world, is going through a revolutionary phase. Young people have found the crass materialistic ethos of the 1950's and early 1960's to be empty and have become alienated from society as a result in their struggle to find a new touchstone. Their reactions demonstrate that they know what they are against, and have not yet discovered what they are for. I know it is difficult, but try to summon up the interest to take another look at these people. Despite their extravagances and excesses, despite their weird garb, despite their aversion to soap and water, I find some cause for hope in them. My hope is based on the sole factor that these young people have rejected materialism. They have not yet found the moral course to commit themselves to some other philosophy, but I have sufficient faith in man to think that a purely negative approach to life, will not long satisfy most of these young people, and that they will turn their energies to more productive endeavours . . .

Sincerely yours,

T.C. Douglas

THE TROUBLE WITH HIPPIES

One of the enduring offshoots of the hippie movement is The Georgia Straight, *a weekly newspaper launched in 1967 in Vancouver as an outraged, outrageous voice of youth. It survives today under founding publisher Dan McLeod as a serious alternative publication. In its early years it attracted such writers as Marxist/existentialist poet Milton Acorn; music editor Bob Geldolf, who became a member of the Boomtown Rats and was knighted for his charitable work; and* **George Bowering**, *now an esteemed poet and author, who was not above trashing fellow contributors in a letter to the editor.*

[August 5–12, 1970]

The trouble with hippies is they take on such a pretentious air when they are writing reviews of books & things, an air that wouldn't be so bad if they weren't so ignorant. The combination of the two is something that pisses me off.

George Bowering

I'M PETER GZOWSKI

Peter Gzowski, rumpled host of CBC Radio's "Morningside" from 1982 to 1997, was a genius at inspiring people to open up. He was also a champion of literacy and an unabashed lover of Canada. Before his broadcasting career, he was the editor of Maclean's *and* The Star Weekly *and a gifted magazine writer with a passion for hockey – which prompted this infuriated fan's letter to the editor on a subject that resonates to this day.*

[December 13, 1968]

The Editor
The Globe and Mail
As your sports pages have already indicated, the Montreal-Toronto hockey game played Wednesday night at Maple Leaf Gardens was a

stirring one. It must have made exciting television fare. I wonder, though, if the people who saw it on television realized how much of the game's edge was taken off by the catering of the men who presumably run hockey to the commercial sponsors of the telecast.

I'm talking about the pauses in the flow of play imposed for the sake of commercials. There were several occasions on Wednesday when a faceoff was delayed for no reason at all, other than to permit the ramming in of 60 full seconds of advertising. These pauses may be tolerable if you're watching the game at home, free, and want to go to the john or something. But at the Gardens they're a pain in what [*Globe and Mail* sportswriter] Scott Young would probably call one's a-dash-s.

The worst case, on Wednesday, occurred late in the third period. Until then, many of the highlights of the evening had been provided by the Leaf line of Keon, Ellis and Oliver, whose forechecking and artistic passing (artistic by Leaf standards, anyway) had gone a long way toward making up for the defence's habit of getting out of position. Now, with the score tied 4-4 and time running out, the line skated out for what appeared to be one last chance to beat the best hockey team in the world.

And what happened? We got a *pause*. The players skated around; the referees scratched their heads and the balloon of excitement that had been expanding all evening began to shrink in a chorus of impatient boos. Commercial . . .

. . . Instead of booing, let's hit those sponsors and the collaborative owners where they live: in the wallet. Were the offending sponsors Molson's? (There are ways – tiny portable TVs or even FM radios – of finding this out.) Then let's have the fans set up a chant during the pause of "We love Carling's Red Cap." Or any other beer. And keep it going. Meteor? Then how about something like "Wide track, Eddie Shack, we love Pontiac"? Anything at all. Just yell. Knock the product. Or sing the praises of a competitor. Are you listening, university students? For the fun alone it would be worth it. But there could be practical effects, too . . .

. . . the advertisers will learn that they have no right to interrupt – and help to spoil – a game that 16,000 people have paid to see. Or, for that matter, to dampen the climax of an event they are sponsoring, presumably entertaining the fans at home.

In any case, I think even The Globe and Mail would agree that this is an unparalleled opportunity for free enterprise.

Peter Gzowski
Toronto

Gzowski's enthusiasm for Canada and his support of literacy came together when he encouraged listeners to send him letters to be read on air. One of his correspondents was **Vic Daradick,** *a dyslexic Alberta farmer whose error-ridden letters delighted the broadcaster with their folksy wit and wise observations. This one was broadcast on Gzowski's first daily CBC show, "This Country in the Morning," which ran from 1971 to 1974. (Daradick used a variant of his own surname.)*

Vic Dardick
Box 321, High Level, Alta
Oct. 11, 1972

Dear Peter Zotskii? hope I spelled that right I know how you feel you should see the fun they hav with my name I am also a lousy speler.

I listen to your program when ever I can mostly becaus CBC is about all we get hear. HE! HE! But seriusly I do like your program some times you get a little beyond me but its different and I like it.

I herd your program today and you ried a powem about a [fellow?] leaving his citifid ant hill typ job and taking off for a cotage in the woods I wonder how meny men have don that. I have don it I lived in Welland Ont for 15 years and worked in just about all the factoryes there I married a girl there had 4 children but after pining for my prairie hom for 15 yr I finnaly took off for 2 years found this place in High Level it is the most northerly farming cuntry in Canada I believe and I have found my sele here (finally) but It cost me dearly my wife took one look at this cold God forsacken Cuntry and took off as fast as that old bus would taek her I somtimes whis I had forst her to stay but I love my freedom to mutch to fors my will on eny one elles freedom   I miss them verry mutch so I worck like hell clearing the bush off the land burnying roots bracking new land with a 24 in bracking plow. and work it is. only 4 out of 10 peopl stay in this cuntry. But I have promised my silf I would stay I have quit so meny good jobs that I would be emberest to tell how many. I figer a fellas got to make a stand sooner or latter you cant run for ever. but I shure wish my family was hear with me. but if I went back there I would only be thincking about this place.

All the time I was in them smocky factories I used to think of the open praries, the free blowing wind with not a house in sight. When I came back I drove out in an old 51 ford 1/2 ton and I drove night and day. The second moring I was in Saskatchewan it was in the spring the wind was flowing the ducks were mateing, and the antelop were troting aross the prairie I stoped the truck and I took a deep breeth of freedom I never fellt so close to God in all my life and that was when I said to my self there aint enuf money in Ontario to mack me stay there.

I have a new famely her. I have a famely of bares living on the south west quarter. She dug her den right under my corner post and it's a real good one too. I get a wild stalion that comes to visit every now and then and a wesel lives uner my shack. the littl devil stole my duck the other morning. there is also a pure white timber wolf comes throw here every week or so to chick on me. Walks right threw the yard but I hardly ever see him but I shure see his tracks they are larger than the palm of my hand. I don't have T.V. here but I would'nt have tim to watch it with all these wild criters around here to watch. Like how many people have seen the mating dance of the sand hill crain or watched a wild stalion macking love to a spirited little filly or seen the wheet fields in spring with so many ducks and geese you could'nt count them all or wathch all the beatfull colers off the sunsett at mide nite

I have read the paper at 11.ocok at nite hear meny times. I have driven the tractor all night with out turning on the lights. this is a very exciteing cuntry for those how are yong at hart. It is the last fronter. I don't know why I am telling you all this exept to say that a man only lives onec and if he is brave enofe he lives it the way he likes and likes it all the time he lives.

Yours Truly,

V.L. Dardick

PS. shure hope you can read this mess.

When Peter Gzowski died in early 2002, Canadians poured out their emotions in a way they hadn't since the death of Pierre Trudeau. "Peter was a plain ordinary down-to-earth guy," Vic Daradick reminisced from High Level. "He brought people together. He wasn't afraid of talking to prime ministers or farmers like myself. He was Canadian."

THE END OF INNOCENCE

While other young Canadians were smoking weed and staging "be-ins" throughout the late 1960s, a small band of radicals in Quebec was plotting violent revolution. On October 5, 1970, four gunmen from a cell of the Front de Libération du Québec – the FLQ – kidnapped British Trade Commissioner James Cross in Montreal. Five days later four members of another cell grabbed **Pierre Laporte**, *Quebec's labour minister and deputy premier, from the front of his house in a city suburb. The next day police found an anguished letter (here translated from French) addressed to Laporte's friend, the Quebec premier.*

Sunday, October 11, 3 p.m.

Mr. Robert Bourassa

My dear Robert:

1. I feel I am writing the most important letter of my life.

2. At the moment I am in perfect health. I am well treated, even with courtesy.

3. I insist that police stop all their searches to find me. If they succeeded this would result in a murderous shoot-out from which I shall certainly not come out alive. This is absolutely urgent.

4. In short, you have the power to dispose of my life. If this were the only question and if this sacrifice were to produce good results, one could entertain it, but we are facing a well-organized uprising, which will only end with the release of the "political prisoners." After me, there will be a third one, then a fourth, and a twentieth. If all politicians are protected, they will strike elsewhere, in other classes of society. Act now and avoid a bloodbath and an altogether unnecessary panic.

5. You know my own case, which should be borne in mind. I had two brothers. They are dead, both of them. I remain alone as head of a large family which includes my mother, my sisters, my own wife, and my children as well as Roland's children, whose guardian I am. My death would mean an irreparable loss, for you know the ties that bind the members of my family. I am no longer the only one whose fate is at stake, but a dozen people are involved – all women and young children. I think that you understand!

6. If the departure of the "political prisoners" is organized and completed satisfactorily, I am certain that my personal security will be assured. Mine, and that of the others who could follow.

This could be done rapidly, as by taking more time, I should continue to die little by little in captivity. Decide . . . on my life or death. I rely on you and thank you.

Friendly greetings,
Pierre Laporte

P.S. I repeat: have the searches stopped and don't let the police carry them on without your knowledge. The success of such a search would mean a death warrant for me.

Laporte wrote Bourassa again, at midnight on October 11, remarking: "While eating very frugally this evening, I sometimes had the impression of having my last meal" – but ending with "I hope to be free . . . and at work within twenty-four hours." Four days later, Ottawa called out federal troops; the day after that, the Bourassa government asked Prime Minister Pierre Trudeau for sweeping powers to crush the FLQ.

GOVERNMENT OF QUEBEC

THE PRIME MINISTER

Quebec City, October 16, 1970

Mr. Prime Minister,

. . . After consultation with authorities directly responsible for the administration of justice in Quebec, the Quebec Government is convinced that the law, as it stands now, is inadequate to meet this situation satisfactorily.

Under the circumstances, on behalf of the Government of Quebec, I request that emergency powers be provided as soon as possible so that more effective steps may be taken. I request particularly that such powers encompass the authority to apprehend and keep in custody individuals who, the Attorney General of Quebec has valid reasons to believe, are determined to overthrow the government through violence and illegal means. According to the information we have and which is available to you, we are facing a concerted effort to intimidate and overthrow the government and the democratic institutions of this province through planned and systematic illegal action, including insurrection. It is obvious that those participating in this concerted effort completely reject the principle of freedom under the rule of law . . .

Please accept, Mr. Prime Minister, my very best regards.

Robert Bourassa

Ottawa proclaimed the War Measures Act, which suspended civil liberties, banned the FLQ, and led to the detention of nearly five hundred people without charges being laid. On October 17, 1970, Laporte was found strangled to death in the trunk of a car; two FLQ

members received life sentences for his murder. James Cross's kid-
nappers released him on December 3 in exchange for passage to
Cuba. Fewer than twenty of the detainees were ever convicted.
Bourassa acknowledged later that the War Measures Act had been
imposed for public show rather than for quelling what politicians
had labelled "an apprehended insurrection." His admission further
incensed civil libertarians across the country.

PERMISSION TO COME ABOARD

The environmental organization Greenpeace, born in Canada, chose
as its first target nuclear-weapons testing around Amchitka in Alaska's
Aleutian Islands. Jim Bohlen and Irving Stowe, Americans with Sierra
Club experience, and Canadian law student Paul Cote launched it in
1970 as the Don't Make a Wave Committee in Vancouver. One of the
*prominent early Greenpeacers was **Bob Hunter**, an author and a*
columnist who espoused radical ideas in the conservative Vancouver
Sun. *In a letter that defined the media-attracting tactics he honed so*
brilliantly, Hunter applied for a position on a twenty-four-metre fishing
vessel renamed Greenpeace, *which was heading to the testing range.*

The Vancouver Sun
March 15 [1971]
Bob Hunter

Jim Bohlen,
Don't Make A Wave Committee,
Dear Jim:
I have been meaning to write this for ages . . . I guess you'd call it a
formal application for passage on the Greenpeace. And I guess you've
had quite a few such applications.

Presumably you want on-the-spot coverage. The idea is to focus
as much attention on the effort as possible. Yet at the same time I
gather the problem comes down to getting as much useful coverage
as possible without loading the ship down with journalists.

I'd like to submit my reasons for believing that I might be able to make a fair contribution.

First of all, I have two books out and a third will be out by the time the Greenpeace sails. The last two of these books deal with environmental collapse, with special reference to the problems of nuclear radiation. (See The Enemies of Anarchy, McClelland & Stewart Ltd.) So I feel that I am qualified to write on these subjects. Further, as a writer on the subject I have some credibility with the other non-newspaper media which I would not have if my role was limited to strictly that of a journalist. I have in the past functioned as an "articulator" of the environmental point of view both on television and radio and at rallies. I was one of the first journalists in this part of the country to scream about the original Amchitka blast and played some part in making the public more generally aware of the dangers by speaking out on CBC across Canada as well as within the confines of my own column at The Vancouver Sun.

Through these activities, I have come to be identified with the struggle to preserve the environment, to reverse the insane priorities which now dominate the thinking of governments.

Pardon the tub-thumping, but my feeling is very strongly that I would be your best bet so far as exposure in the mass media is concerned. Even if I were not engaged in this type of work, I would want to go along, to put my genes where my mouth is, as it were. However, I would not have much to contribute otherwise. This way, I feel I do have something to contribute. Moreover, my knowledge of the ways in which media function is sufficient to guarantee that mere hysteria would not dominate what I write – I can make it cool enough to reach a lot of people who might otherwise not be paying attention. I could also, in effect, offer my services as a public relations man, if you like . . .

Sincerely,

Bob Hunter

P.S. Further to our telephone conversation, I will, while in Toronto, ask Peter Newman of MacLean's [sic] Magazine, what he would be willing to pay for exclusive rights to the Greenpeace story. Also I will press Jack McClelland to agree to a paperback on short order. I'll contact you immediately upon getting back.

Hunter signed up for the voyage and helped generate worldwide publicity for the group that became Greenpeace. He was its president for two years, until 1977, and later became an ecology specialist for Toronto's CITY TV, *ran unsuccessfully as an Ontario Liberal, and co-authored a book about native concerns that won a Governor General's Award for non-fiction. The establishment magazine* Time *named him one of the "Heroes of the Century" for his work in the environmental movement.*

Rex Weyler *was one of the early environmental activists aboard the* Phyllis Cormack (Greenpeace V) *in 1975, when it confronted whalers in the Pacific Ocean off San Francisco. In a letter to his Dutch-Indonesian wife in Vancouver, he reported on the first bloody encounter with the Russian whaling fleet – which helped alert the world to the ongoing slaughter on the seas. (Lieve means "dear" in Dutch,* kusjes *"kisses,"* ik hou van jou *"I love you," and* tot gauw *"see you soon.")*

June 30, 1975

Lieve Glenn,

We're just a day out of San Francisco. For the last three days I have barely had the chance to think. I don't know if I can explain what has happened . . .

The first sight of the factory ship was something I'll never forget. Fred and Pat went in one Zodiac, and I went in another, just to get close and figure out what was going on. The harpoon boats come up behind the factory ship and off-load dead whales which are dragged up through a slip in the stern. The factory ship is like a floating city. There could easily have been 500 or more people on board. There was blood everywhere. There were huge cranes on the deck, peeling slabs of pink flesh and blubber from the whales and a pipe on the side of the ship where blood just poured into the water. A steady red stream of blood. There were sharks all over the place. The stench made me sick. It's just a floating slaughterhouse. I wanted to scream it was all so insane . . .

. . . A pod of sperm whales were fleeing the harpoon boat and George managed to manoeuvre the Zodiac between them. I was off to the side in a Zodiac with Pat. I have some decent shots, but I won't know exactly until I see them. When the whale was hit by the harpoon, I could see the blood spraying out with [its] breath.

Everyone is very emotional. Most everyone is feeling angry, but I just feel sad. Will anything ever change? . . .

We played music to the Russians. That was the one moment when the mood was happy. Mel wrote a song that was supposed to sound like Russian music. I don't know if it did, but they loved it. The crew on the factory ship seemed like they wanted to communicate. They waved and clapped.

I don't know when we're coming home. Some people want to get more fuel and go back out after the whalers, but I think we've done it. We might go back out after them, but we may just come home. I'll call from San Francisco. There's so much more to tell you. It's 4:00 in the morning. I'm on watch, but time to wake up Fred. Kusjes. Ik hou van jou.

Tot gauw,
Rex

THE NEW PLAGUE

If any single disaster marked the 1980s, it was AIDS. Acquired immune deficiency syndrome decimated a generation of homosexuals around the world and spread through the heterosexual population as a result of drug use and tainted blood supplies. The first known case of AIDS in Canada was reported in 1979. By the mid-1980s fewer than three hundred victims were recorded, but a decade later that figure swelled to more than ten thousand. Among those infected was **Jack Pollock,** *the self-styled "gentleman of excess" who owned*

Toronto's prestigious Pollock Gallery. Addicted to drugs, he survived
open heart surgery and bankruptcy to live in southern France, where
he wrote revealing letters back home to his psychiatrist and friend,
identified only as M.

March 21/86
Lou Paradou
Gordes

Dear M,

Well, it's really the 22nd (1:30 AM!) and I have just arrived home from
a long, exhausting and exhilarating day . . . Good news. my valve is
fine. not so good news, my heart is racing far beyond its capacity . . .

Living here gives one a perspective on daily news. The elections
here were, to me, frightening as Le Pen and the fachist right won
over 35 seats. Then, yesterday in the Herald Tribune, that asshole
Buckley wrote an article (enclosed) demanding all AIDS persons be
tattooed on the arm, and the ass!

Aids is a problem we (you, me, and the world of alternate choice)
cannot ignore. It is ugly – murderous, and spreading. I feel you and
your brothers in the proffession have a truly special role to play, as
the tragedy unfolds.

Can you imagine, dear M, "coming out" now – not only with
society against you, but with the ever present fear of death & despair?

Ignoring its horrific presence will not make it go away. The
promiscuity of much of the "gay" world is being challenged and,
probably rightly so. A society such as ours, that on one hand, has
condemned, and on the other permitted places such as baths, blackened rooms of bars, etc, for purely sexual purposes, is in deep
trouble. No such places for sexual relief exist in the so-called heterosexual world. We cannot have our cake, and eat it too – so to speak.

I say all this, being a product, a result, of the two faced social
dilemma, and the world of twilight lust and passion. I probably have
never felt the singular love and caring of another to any great depth
because of my continued appetite for the fantasy of the physical. I

fear for the young – realizing their desires, and the terrible burden of disease – death, added to the acceptance of a life style not accepted. The Church (read right wing Moral Majority) have a wonderful caché of ammunition for the on-going battle of prejudice.

Maybe, out of it all, will come a sense of committment for many, and an empathy, which as we are well aware, has been lacking. My past was doubly dangerous, as intervenus drug use, and sexual promiscuity are both major factors in the plague. It is also strange that the "passive" partner is more prone. "The meek shall inherit the earth"? – well, so much for that . . .

But I continue to survive, and paint again each day. I have decided – who needs another Pollock?

Pollock does –!!!

Je T.M. Jack

Jack Pollock died in 1992 of an AIDS-related illness.

FREE-TRADE FOLLIES

After the Progressive Conservative government of Brian Mulroney signed a free-trade agreement with the United States in 1987, opponents of the pact counted on the Liberals to repeal it when they came to power. Among free trade's most vocal opponents was Edmonton publisher and passionate economic nationalist **Mel Hurtig.** *By 1992 he had sold his publishing house, which created the landmark* Canadian Encyclopedia, *and founded the Council of Canadians. In a provocative and prophetic letter to Jean Chrétien, he pointed out the Opposition leader's contradictory stances on the issue.*

15th May, 1992

Dear Mr. Chretien:

In the past you have referred to the Free Trade Agreement as "an omelette that cannot be unscrambled." . . .

On the other hand, you have said that you will renegotiate the trade agreement and that you wish to keep "the good parts" and scrap the "bad parts" . . .

I have yet to meet an informed observer who believes that the FTA can be successfully renegotiated on terms that would be favourable to Canada. Since you would be dealing with the U.S. Congress and since the U.S. has already in place an agreement very favourable to American corporations, and since U.S. corporate interests would lobby very hard and very effectively against any deterioration in their position, I cannot understand your rationale for "renegotiation". As [American trade negotiator] Peter Murphy has said "What happens if they ask you for more?"

Since you will not be renegotiating from a position of strength but rather from a position of weakness, why do you not simply come out and make it clear that the FTA has to be abrogated? If you are not being totally honest with the people of Canada, how are you then any better than the Mulroney government? If you already know in advance that the FTA cannot be successfully renegotiated, why adopt that as your position and the position of your party?

Perhaps there's something you know that the rest of us don't know . . .

What troubles me, personally, most of all, is that I believe that you fully understand that renegotiation will <u>not</u> be successful and so do most of your caucus (many of them have told me that already). If this is the case, I cannot, for the life of me, understand why you and your party would adopt this strategy . . .

Sincerely,

Mel Hurtig

That same month Hurtig turned down an invitation to run for the Liberals in the 1993 federal election, in which the Conservatives were reduced to two seats in all of Canada. Instead, Hurtig became the catalyst behind the brief-lived National Party of Canada. His prediction about Canadians' inability to renegotiate a free-trade agreement in any substantive way proved well founded. And the obstacles the United States raised to the prime Canadian exports of lumber and grain, which The Globe *had complained about in 1851, still existed 150 years later.*

THE ICE STORM

"Unconsciously, Canadians feel that any people can live where the climate is gentle," wrote Canadian-bred novelist and broadcaster Robert MacNeil. "It takes a special people to prosper where nature makes it so hard." Nature made it even more difficult than usual in eastern Canada in January 1998, when the Great Ice Storm affected more Canadians – four million of them – than any one weather phenomenon ever had. As the freezing rain toppled millions of trees and 130 key hydro towers, about 900,000 households in Quebec and 100,000 in Ontario lost their power. Three weeks later, 700,000 of them were still without electricity. At least twenty-five people died, many from hypothermia, as a direct result of the storm. Fourteen thousand troops were called out to clean up, maintain order, and assist people in distress. But it was the individual acts of kindness, such as those related by **Suzanne and Wayne Martel** *in this letter to the editor of* The Ottawa Citizen, *that helped warm the hearts as well as the homes of those whom nature walloped.*

January 15, 1998

It has been a full week since my family has had power. We live in St. Pascal [near Ottawa] and my husband and I have physical disabilities. Our three children, 9, 12 and 15, have helped this past week in bailing water from the sump pump to avoid a basement flood.

On day five, we were so exhausted and cold despite having a wood furnace (which heated very little) that we decided to seek help at our local fire station in Clarence Creek. We were told that Barry Flood and his wife, Brenda, have generously donated their generator and their services to help individuals in the community empty their sump wells.

Barry works from early morning until very late at night. We know because he comes by around 11:30 p.m. and is back around 9 a.m. He goes from house to house helping others in need, on his own time and in his own vehicle.

On day six his car lost its muffler, but he kept going. He also brought us some lamp oil and a heater which he plugs in to his generator. He has invited the whole family to take a shower or do our washing and has kindly invited us to dinner.

A big special thanks to the Flood family for all their help in this community's time of need. A special thank you also to the officials at Clarence Creek Arena, all volunteers and the companies that have donated food and time to help shelter and feed so many families.

We once asked Barry what his last name was. He said, "Guess." Here he is trying to help others avoid exactly what his last name is . . . Flood. We all had a good laugh. His kindness and generosity will be remembered always.

The Martel Family, St. Pascal

THANKS BUT NO THANKS

*As the 20th century drew to a close Canada welcomed its newest and largest territory, Nunavut – "Our Land" in Inuktitut. Created in 1999, Nunavut spreads north and northeast of the tree line across 1.6 million square kilometres east of the Northwest Territories. Nunavut has a legislature, a supreme court, and a feisty population of 27,000, more than 80 percent of them Inuit. One of them, **Jack Anawak** of Nunavut's capital, Iqaluit, wrote to the magazine* Up Here *about a southerner's objection to the policy of replacing English names with Inuit ones.*

[September/October 2000]

How magnanimous of C.E. Sheppard to at least suggest that names of communities should have Inuktitut in brackets so as not to confuse the Inuit up here (Speaking Up, May/June). Most of the Inuit names of those same communities that he/she is suggesting should be bracketed in Inuktitut can record the history of their names in thousands of years whereas the English names can be recorded not much more than 200 years, if that at all.

So based on this, whose history are we trying to preserve here? I was not asked whether I approved of the Anglicization of all the communities' names when those same communities always had names. Thanks but no thanks, Mr. or Miss or Mrs. C. E. Sheppard.

Jack Anawak

Iqaluit, Nunavut

A MAN LIKE NO OTHER

When eighty-year-old Pierre Elliott Trudeau died on September 28, 2000, the nation responded with a flood of emotion. Day after day, newspapers devoted entire sections to his life, career, and legacy. Television offered continuous coverage of his final rail trip to Montreal and his state funeral there. The former prime minister (1968–79, 1980–84) was not universally loved: many westerners never forgave him for his National Energy Program, and civil libertarians objected vehemently to his imposition of the War Measures Act during the FLQ crisis. But even his critics respected his dazzling intellect and commitment to principle. Canadians especially empathized with him during his marriage to Margaret Sinclair and sympathized with him when one of their three sons, Michel, died in a B.C. avalanche in 1998. Ivan Head, a friend and a colleague, wrote to Trudeau's remaining sons after their father's death.

8 November 2000

Dear Justin and Sacha,

In the Spring of 1967, while teaching at the University of Alberta, I received a totally unexpected telephone call from your father asking me to fly down to Ottawa to talk about constitutional issues. Once there, and following a conversation that lasted the better part of a day, I realized that this was a man unlike any other I had ever encountered; a person whom I could follow for the rest of my life. For 33 years I did – and I have never doubted how fortunate I have been. Your father raised my sights and demanded of me higher standards of performance than I had previously thought possible. I shall be forever grateful to him. Over the years my admiration became joined with genuine affection.

Much more important, however, I have been witness over the years to the warm regard that your father earned among the billions of people in the developing countries around the world. Not in the past, nor since, has any leader from the industrialized North championed so consistently the interests – the basic rights – of the world's poorest as did he. His quest for a global ethic was a plea to respect the dignity of humans everywhere. In the United Nations, in the Commonwealth, and in the G-7 he argued for fairer deals, for hope, and for opportunity for the peoples of the South.

You both know how extensively your father traveled in the developing countries, of his friendships there with persons within government and without. Following his death the tributes from these places and the people who live there have been numerous and deeply touching. As one example of many, an elderly, retired Chinese diplomat, once Ambassador to Canada, telephoned me from Beijing at his own expense to ask that his grief and his sorrow be communicated to you. His name is Zhang Wenpu; the telephone call likely cost him the equivalent of a month's pension.

Perhaps the most articulate comment to reach me took the form of an editorial in the Kingston, Jamaica "Daily Observer". It concluded:

"People like Pierre Trudeau understood clearly the power they had was not an end in itself, but a means to an end – of improving the quality of life of the people they served, and that ultimately we all shared a single world.

"All the ideas and visions did not come to fruition. Some were flawed. What made the difference is that Pierre Trudeau dared to try. Our world is better because he did."

He was an extraordinary guy, your father, and his sons reflect in their own characters just how special he was. To each of you I extend heartfelt condolences. Be assured that in countries around the world countless persons are now burnishing their memories of a man who understood their plight and who carried their cause with him constantly. In those places he represented Canada, but he represented as well the best of the human spirit. Because of that he will be remembered fondly forever.

Sincerely,

Ivan L. Head

Head, a law professor, first advised Trudeau on the constitution and continued as his special assistant, focusing on external affairs, when Trudeau became prime minister in 1968. Head is a professor emeritus of law and political science at the University of British Columbia.

GLOBAL WARNING

*The debate about global warming has been raging for more than a decade. At the dawn of the new millennium some journalists and bureaucrats continued to absolve politicians – and humankind generally – from responsibility for planetary stewardship. In protest, a University of Alberta professor, **Alexander P. Wolfe**, fired off this letter.*

December 12, 2001

The Editor
The Montreal Gazette
It was with a certain degree of disbelief and disappointment that I read that the "warmest autumn on record" has arisen for "no obvious reason" in the eyes of Environment Canada meteorologists (*Gazette*, Dec. 6). In actual fact, there is mounting evidence that a globally registered warming trend is causally related to the enhanced efficiency of our planet's greenhouse effect. This effect is in turn the result of

the acceleration of human emissions of gases such as carbon dioxide, which are very good at absorbing Earth's radiation before it can escape to space.

At present, carbon dioxide concentrations are more than 30 per cent above levels in the pre-industrial atmosphere. It therefore seems perfectly reasonable – if not entirely predictable – to interpret the unseasonable warmth being witnessed coast to coast as but one component of global warming. Indeed, we witnessed record monthly warmth for November here in central Alberta, with similar trends elsewhere in North America. The nine hottest years in the climate record have all occurred since 1987.

Readers of the popular press surely deserve this factual context when assessing reports of unusual weather trends, given the unlikelihood that they are purely random events.

It is my view that the precocious swelling of lilac buds, the wearing of shorts in the streets of Montreal in December and the disappearance of outdoor hockey in southern Canada are merely harbingers of what is yet to come. Therefore, it is time to decide collectively, whether to do nothing and wait to see what happens next or to engage ourselves proactively in modifying our behaviours and policies in the face of potentially more severe consequences of climate change.

It is worth recalling that Alberta's environment minister has recently deemed Canada's participation in the Kyoto Protocol, which aims to reduce greenhouse gas emissions to 1990 levels by the second decade of this century, as "suicidal" and "disastrous." Should this manner of political nearsightedness, which emphasizes the short-term economic gains of domestic hydrocarbon exploitation, preclude both the urgency of planetary stewardship as well as the excitement of building an innovative long-term federal energy strategy?

Climate change is real in terms of impacting our daily lives, as the *Gazette* article clearly demonstrates. Moreover, its intimate association with national and international policies should be presented in such a way as to challenge readers into thinking critically about the complexities of the issues involved.

ALEXANDER P. WOLFE
Associate Professor, Department of Earth and Atmospheric Sciences,
University of Alberta
Edmonton

LOVE AND FRIENDSHIP

"I shall write a little of my love to you"

L ove impels the pen. The words may be the boisterous effusions of
a truck driver or the precise phrases of a literate physician, but
the emotion the writers feel leads to a near-compulsion to communicate. Separation, of course, inspires love letters. It also imbues them
with sadness, even if the lovers are confident they will soon be reunited.
Separations chosen out of patriotism are perhaps the saddest of all.
Canadian soldiers in the two world wars wrote more sombre letters.
They expressed their love by protecting their wives or girlfriends from
the reality of war, by assuring them of their invincibility, or by com-
posing a message to be delivered after their deaths.

In the nineteenth century, separated lovers wrote about the minu-
tiae of their lives – social conditions, modes of travel, sermons heard
in church, songs sung at concerts. Suitors wrote prospective parents-
in-law asking permission to marry, and the elders, knowing the realities, replied with ardour-dashing advice and stipulations. The
contemporary letters in this section deal with the commitment of long-
married couples, the farewell of a partner facing death, grief over the
loss of a child, the undying love of a rejected woman.

If these more recent letters reveal less about how we live – we now
dispose of practicalities by telephone or e-mail – they nonetheless

reflect the timeless need to mark extraordinary feeling with written declarations. A prominent Canadian novelist wrote to the woman he would marry, "I no longer belong to myself, but to you." A woman told her paramour, "I have used my letter writing to make a spiritual map of myself for you." And a soldier in wartime France wrote to his darling, explaining why he discussed politics in a love letter: "I would not like you to have me & not know me." As these letters demonstrate, there are few better ways to make oneself known than by committing one's thoughts and feelings to the page.

BUT A FEW MILES

Catharine Parr Traill, pioneer, author, and botanist, was befriended by Frances Stewart in 1832 when Traill and her husband, Thomas, emigrated from England to settle in Upper Canada. The Stewart family home, Auburn, was just north of Peterborough. In 1851 the Traills lived south of the city on Rice Lake. By 1870, the date of the last excerpt, both women were widows and Catharine was living at her cottage, Westove, a short distance north of Auburn – but still too far away for the two friends to get together.

17 January 1851

My Dearest Friend,

. . . My dear husband is sadly depressed again. This is a season of the year when ones creditors are sure to remember us if no one else does – and though he did get relief from Nicholls [Robert Nicholls, a friend and partner in a general store in Peterborough] it was not adequate to the calls for it. I for my own part am more cheerful than I was when his spirits were more hopeful for I am looking to the future not as I think unreasonably for help to pay all that we owe. I do not forget that I am in your debt my kindest of friends but I do not feel uneasy on that account. Your loan of love sits light and is treasured in my heart to be repaid as soon as I can, but how can I repay your kindness to me and mine my most generous and faithful friend! Your

goodness to my [daughter] Anne is another proof of your affection –
I hope she may never be ungrateful for it . . .
Wednesday night –
Though it is very late I will finish my letter in case a good opportu-
nity occurs of sending it – . . .

Tell William [the eldest Stewart son] that I hope he will not forget
his parting promise to drive a <u>good sleigh</u> load over. We will find
beds for the ladies and a shake down for the gentlemen. I need not
say how much pleasure it would give us dear Mrs Stewart if you would
come with William. Could you not spare us a few days this Winter?
The next fall of snow I shall begin to look out for our friends. I used
to reckon in old times on a friendly sociable visit from dear Auburn
in the sleighing time. When dear dear Mr. Stewart used to come up
with Anna and Ellen and Bessie. It was one of our bright days when
a family party came up either to Stricklands or to our place – I wish
we could revive those cheerful meetings – To see you all again under
our roof would be delightful – When we look back to the years that
are past how changed does every thing appear the past like a dream.
A new race springing up around us, nothing remains as it was; even
we ourselves are not what we were – All – all is changed. It is strange
but true that we always seem to value our former happiness more
than the present enjoyment – Time seems to lay a hallowing finger
on the past, smooth all the rough points and gild the dark shades of
the picture. Goethe says 'The past – the past, seems only true to me.'
I think that I have a happy faculty of forgetting past sorrows and
only remembering the pleasures –

[1851]

My Dearest Friend,
. . . Our propects become each day more gloomy – there is a cloud
gathering over us that I see no means of averting – I am trying to
brace my mind to bear it when it does burst with fortitude and resignation – I would wish indeed if possible to have done something better
than passively enduring the evil – I have the impression upon my mind

that something ought to be done, but I know not what that something is – Our dear childs sick state and the overwhelming difficulties of our situation seems to have paralized my dear husband – he cannot think – unfortunately – he can only feel – We have no friend – with whom we can advise – The fresh delay that seems to arise respecting this vexatious legacy has thrown us all aback and unless something occurs shortly – I fear we shall be involved in great trouble –

I am full of perplexing thoughts – It is not for myself that I care, but I cannot endure to see my poor husband so utterly cast down – It is for me and for the children that he feels so keenly – I wish that he could look beyond the present and remember that the brightest of earthly prospects endure but for a season – and it is the same with the trials and sorrows of life – they too come to an end – and those who now sow in tears may reap in joy – I wish I were able to come over for a day or two to Peterboro[.] I want to see my brother but at present I cannot leave home. I have no one to fill my place and then this poor child is not fit to be left – I must bide my time – . . .

Sunday night – I think I have almost made up my mind my dear friend to get my son James to drive me up to Peterboro on Tuesday God willing – I believe I must see Nicholls and I will consult you about some things that your advice may be serviceable to me on – I am writing nevertheless for if I see a chance of sending this by post I will for I may be prevented from going to P. If [I] do it will shew that I had been thinking of you – My poor girl has been ill all the last week with ague her cough distresses her greatly – she looks very ill – and is so weak she can hardly move from room to room – she has had the fits every day till yesterday – I hope it is gone.

Sunday
4 September 1853

My Dearest Friend,
I had been anxiously looking for a letter from you and was glad indeed when my husband gave me your welcome packet though I do not feel quite satisfied at the account you give of your health. This

month has I know always had a bad effect on your complaint [asthma] and now a fresh series of very hot weather seems to have set in which I fear you will feel very oppressive. How greatly I wish you were near me or I nearer to you my beloved friend, though I fear I might be too often breaking in upon your solitary hours. Yet much comfort and solace it would doubtless be to us both in our old age to be nearer to each other. I fancy at times you must feel lonely for the society of young people is often too lively at times to be enjoyed when we are not in the humour for it – . . .

14 November 1870

My Dear Friend –

I ought not to have been so long without writing to you and I reproach myself day after day with not sending off a letter to one whom I ought not to neglect and whom I dearly value – but I have had many letters to write of late and these not short ones – The family being so scattered calls for longer letters . . .

How many things we should find to talk of could we meet for a few hours but that I see no hope of – It does seem hard that so few miles of distance should prove such a barrier to the meeting of old and tried friends, not even once in twelve months – Nay it is far more since we saw each other. Well we must submit to this as well as to other privations – Of one thing I feel certain that absence does not lessen our faithful affection for each other. I must now close this long epistle with the assurance that I ever am my dear Mrs Stewart Your very faithful affectionate old friend

Cath. Parr Traill

Frances, who was eight years older than Catharine, died in 1872 at the age of seventy-eight. Catharine was ninety-seven when she died in 1899.

JOY AND PASSION

Raymond Renault's declaration of his love for Mademoiselle Nicole is a perfect expression of infatuation. Intoxicated with love, Raymond poured out his feelings in a way that seems typically French, quite unlike the studied locutions of English writers of the time. (This letter has been translated.)

Pointe aux Esquimaux
10 June 1861

Mademoiselle,

I have finally received from your very own hand a pledge of hope and of joy. Oh, happiness! in adoring you with more ardour than ever before, I may, ignoring the rest of the world, allow you alone to fill my heart and my spirit. There was a moment, I acknowledge, when I feared your indifference, and I envied the languid ease of those who feel no love; but today, intoxicated with my love, I disdain all those hearts that know nothing of love . . . It is for you, for you alone Mademoiselle, that I am resolved to live. A sweet idea accompanies me in my every action, and everything traces yet again before my eyes the future that is promised me. I feel that I am with my Nicole in every moment, I see her, I hear her, I speak to her, charming illusions, which soon will be reality. I have as guarantor this letter written by a beloved hand, which I kiss with such tender emotion. Oh, delicious image that is my constant companion, you no longer bring me the torment of anxious uncertainty, on the contrary you pour into my heart a tranquil joy and serene hope. Soon it shall be vouchsafed to me to see my Nicole, to have reappear before my eyes a sight of such loveliness, and to hear from her own mouth the confession that she has made to me of her sentiments! May our souls, animated by the same ardour, be filled with the same joy and blend forever in the voluptuousness of a pure love.

I am, Mademoiselle,
The most passionate and the most sincere
of your admirers
Raymond Renault

SEEKING GOLD

James Thompson, a baker's apprentice, emigrated from Scotland in 1844 to farm near the present-day town of Cardinal, in eastern Ontario. Two decades later a gold rush lured him west, at age forty, to the rugged Cariboo country of British Columbia, still part of the Hudson's Bay Company's vast territory. Thompson's heart remained with Mary, the daughter of a United Empire Loyalist, and their five children, as expressed in this postscript to one of many letters chronicling his travels.

Williams Lake, British Columbia.
July 27ᵗʰ 1862.

Mary my Beloved Companion, I have written you quite a long letter. It may be that you will have to read some of it to enquiring friends. I would now wish to have a little talk between ourselves. Oh Mary were you by my side I have much that I would like to say. Mary I have thought of you more, prayed for you more, and if possible loved you more this summer than ever before. Volumes would not contain all the thoughts I have of Home and the loved ones there. Mary I often wish that I had more of your courage and energy and resignation to battle with the disappointments of life. I sometimes wonder how I ever came to leave a kind and affectionate wife and all that the heart of man could desire of a family to sojourn in this land. But then the thought comes up that we were poor, that you had to deny yourself many of the comforts of life that a little money would have secured, and then I think of my poor old Father toiling and labouring when he ought to be enjoying the evening of his days in ease and comfort. Then I pray God to strengthen my arm and encourage my heart and bless my exertions to procure the means to make you comfortable. Our prospects at present are rather poor for making much, yet I cannot say that I regret [coming] to this country for God has softened my heart and enabled me to see myself in the gospel glass as I never did before, and I never yet have been able to get over the conviction that God in His providence pointed it out as my duty to come. If so, good must come although it may not come just as we would wish. Mary continue praying for me, keep up your spirits, be cheerful and happy. We have much to be thankful for. May God enable us to be truly grateful.

Mary, I really hardly know what to think about this country I cannot make up my mind to remain long away from home and then to think of returning without making something, to be as poor as when I left and in debt besides, and it might be to be laughed at into the bargain is hard to think of. To think of bringing you to this country unless it were to Victoria, is out of the question, I cannot say much about Victoria, but for this upper country if it were nothing else than mosquitos and bad water I would never think of settling here to say nothing of bad roads and poor society. I sometimes think that I would like to go home, sell half my farm, build a little cottage for you to live in and stay with you and Minnie and the boys and let the world laugh and talk as they please. Then again I think if by staying here a little longer I would make enough to pay my debts and build the cottage it would be so much better. But I will not decide till I hear from you. I expect to go to Victoria in the Fall, when we can correspond regularly and I will be able to get your views on the subject.

What troubles me most is how you are to put in the long cold winter in that old house. Could you do anything by papering it to make it warmer? Could <u>Aunty</u> paper her house to keep out the wind some? I hope to be able to send you some money perhaps by Christmas to help you to rig up for winter. Try to get warm clothing for all.

I suppose the children have forgotten all about Pa. Tell them I have not forgotten them. I have got a Bible lesson for them to learn, I hope to hear them repeat it yet. Oh if God would enable one to return and hear Minnie repeat that verse I would be a happy man. It is the 2nd verse of the 4th chapter of Micah, ommitting the first and the last clause, get down to paths. May God bless all, and bring us to that land, where <u>farewells</u> are unknown.

J.T.

Although Thompson returned home to Mary just as poor after nine months in the goldfields, he became a bookkeeper to supplement his farm income and served as a popular reeve of Cardinal.

A DARK AND STORMY NIGHT

Dr. Richmond Sands, *returning home to Ontario in 1862 after visiting his intended, Margaret Stuart Fisher, in Michigan, compared himself to Robert Burns's Tam o' Shanter.*

Thursday, 13th Nov./62

My ever Dear Maggie

I arrived here to-day & am sorry that I was too late to send you a few lines by to-day's mail. I got to Detroit Monday evening & stopped there all night. Next morning took the train to Pt. Huron, crossed to Sarnia, & thence to Forrest where I arrived about 11. O clock P.M., found my Pony all right & immediately started for James', like Tam O Shanter "I skelpit on through dub an' mire Despising wind and rain and-" Well there was no fire but there was mud, wind & rain enough to make up for it so much so that I rather regretted the absence of fire as it would have given me an occasional glimpse of the road which I earnestly desired. I got to the Dr's a little after "That hour o' night's black arch the keystane" & to my surprise found the house lighted. On entering I found the Dr & Joe Fenner who had just returned from Michigan. The Dr being pretty long winded 'twas Wednesday evening before I got away & when I got to Mother's there were some messages for me to visit some patients in the neighbourhood, so I stopped to morning, visited the sick & got here this afternoon. And now my Dear Maggie my only trouble is concerning yourself. I would God that thou wert with me. I hope that by this time you are entirely recovered from your sickness & are again in the enjoyment of your wonted health. Oh my own Dear Maggie since my return I feel doubly anxious for our union & chafe with impatience at my own inability to hasten it & various plans have I thought of to forward it but there are only two which seem at all feasible one is I think of borrowing money enough to furnish a House etc the other is for us to board out till such times as we could save enough to have a house to ourselves. Both have their objections: to the first is that I am already in debt & do not wish to draw you into any more trouble than I can help; the second I dislike as I wish to see you Mistress of your own house & besides it would be more expensive than even the former. What do you think? I believe I shall try the former as soon as I make up my mind finally to settle here & my own Darling I do anticipate being happy with you for is not the foundation of domestic happiness; faith. Faith in the virtue of woman & is not my faith in thee unbounded & is not the foundation of all happiness, reliance on the goodness of God & do we not both rely upon & trust in Him

Please write immediately on receipt of this & let me know how you are, & if there be anything you would wish to tell write it down do not be backward about it. ever thine own

Richmond

I hope you have got the Quinine. It will not only remove the remains of the fever but also improve your health <u>generally</u>

RX	Quinine	grains XX
	Acid Sulphur	drops XX (oil of vitriol)
	Aqua (water)	VIII (ounces)

Dose A tablespoonful three times a day or if you prefer it you can take about a grain of the quinine in a little jelly (preserves) three or four times a day.

Richmond and Margaret married the following year. Richmond Sands set up practice in Nairn, Ontario, where he was revered as the poor man's physician, willing to ride out in any weather and at any hour to tend the sick. He died at forty-five, his health perhaps compromised by his arduous work; the local paper reported his funeral was the

"largest ever witnessed in this county." Maggie raised their three
children and eventually moved to Manitoba.

CIPHERED LOVE

As Canada's fourth prime minister (1892–1894), **Sir John Sparrow**
David Thompson *is noted chiefly for his role in developing the*
Criminal Code of Canada. As a young man he exploited a quite dif-
ferent code in his courtship of Annie Affleck, whose Catholic family
in Halifax disapproved of this Methodist suitor. Thompson taught
Annie a form of shorthand, which they used in smuggled notes and
on the inside pages of letters written in longhand. The innocuous
letter below from twenty-four-year-old Thompson was followed by
two pages in which he spoke more frankly.

Barrington [Nova Scotia]
Dec 3rd 1869

Dear Annie

I suppose it is very bold of me to write again and your ma & Joey
[Annie's sister] will be cross but I will be there soon I hope to apolo-
gise in person. Barrington is like a perpetual Sunday – the people are
very nice and all very good. It seems strange though how they all live
for you see no one going about and even those that keep shop only
seem to be there for about an hour a day. Two or three vessels have
run ashore in honor of my arrival to their own great personal incon-
venience and the embarrassment of their owners. See what it is to
make a Sensation. With love to all.

I Remain Yrs
JSDT

This is a portion of the ciphered message:

My own baby dear yesterday morning the first thing after breakfast I
went up to the Way Office to see if the mail had come for I had been

thinking the time is long [?] Annie's letters could come. The mail had not come in but presently a wagon stopped at the house and a [?] and valise were left but no letters and I felt just as if I had not a friend in the world but soon afterwards Dan'l came in with my darling's letters in his hand. My heart jumped up to the ceiling but I put them into my pocket until I could kiss them all four before reading them. My own pet pet there never were such darling notes written before. They made me so happy and I laughed over them and kissed them and prayed for Annie when I went to bed . . . Darling it seems so long since I got a petting from Annie . . . I have just kissed that little round spot that Annie made in her letter and I send to baby 100,000 kisses in this little spot O . . . Darling I wish I could give you a kiss now and get a box on my ears and then a hug and a kiss and be called your darling [?] and won't you give me a lot when I come home. My pet I pray God to bless pet whatever becomes of me and to make her happy all her life. Good bye darling your boy sees you just as plain as if you were here and he remembers pet last thing every night.

Good bye good bye my own baby
Your own own boy.

After marrying in 1870, John and Annie Thompson corresponded frequently while he was away as a member of the Nova Scotia legislative assembly, premier of the province, a judge of the Supreme Court of Nova Scotia, a member of Sir John A. Macdonald's cabinet, and finally a Conservative prime minister. The historian P.B. Waite writes that Annie was "bold and spirited" while John was "quiet and controlled." Since he referred to himself as "your ugly coward boy that nobody likes but Annie," it's not surprising that she assumed the role of cheerleader.

Halifax
Monday Oct 31, 1881

Baby dear
Your letter dated 27th came this morning. My poor child I almost think that you have the blues the way you write. Now pet don't get

dull and you are just as stiff as they are [but?] who cares for those grand judges or for any one else in Ottawa for that matter. I posted a letter to you last night and I am only sending you these few lines just to bully you back in to not losing heart . . .

Goodby my own pet
Annie

Thompson died at forty-nine – two years after becoming prime minister – just after Queen Victoria appointed him to the Privy Council in a ceremony at Windsor Castle.

NO OTHER FORTUNE

In the 1860s Samuel Medlen left England to work at the Halifax Citadel as clerk of the works, the highest civilian position at the British-built fort. He rented a home for his family next door to **Edward Lordly** *and his wife. The children in these families – Montagu Medlen and Florence Lordly, both born in 1861 – were childhood friends and wrote to one another after the Medlen family was transferred to Belfast. Montagu studied engineering in England before working for a mining firm in Calcutta. This letter was Edward Lordly's response to Montagu's proposal of marriage to Florence.*

Halifax 5 July 1883

Dear Mont

Mrs Lordly has written You in reply to Yours and I fully Endorse all she has written You in regard to Your engagement to Florence – Having lived long enough to see that it is not wise to be in too great a hurry in so important a Matter as taken a Partner for Life – And this is no doubt the most important step any man can take, as his whole future happiness depends on the Wisdom he displays in his choice. I think it will be well to let Your present arrangement with Your Firm run out the three Years – Then make Your arrangements for future Business, take your Hollidays and come on, and if we are spared You will receive a hearty Welcome get Married and enter on Your New Role.

In taken Florence for Your wife You have selected an affectionate Conscientious and Religious Girl but You will receive no other Fortune. My Business only gives me a living. I did Promise Louisa & Florence when ever they got married (and I can still carry out my promise) $20,000 <u>each</u> in <u>bad debts</u> with a supplement of five or ten thousand of the same value if necessary. This will give You some idea of how I have been Victimized I do not imagine however You are thinking of what she is to have so long as You get herself and I am quite Satisfied to trust her in Your Keeping and so long as You Stick to the Principles You have upheld from Your Boyhood I have no fear of You and her leading any other than a happy life

Sincerely wishing You every Prosperity and Happiness – Believe Me Yours

Effectionately

Edw J Lordly

Montagu and Florence were married in St. Paul's Church, Halifax, in 1887. They lived in London, England, until the late 1890s. The last of their four children was born in Rockingham, Nova Scotia, in 1903.

LAST LETTER

Louis Riel, head of the Metis provisional government and leader of the Northwest Rebellion in 1884–85, was taken prisoner on May 15, 1885. He was tried for high treason and convicted. From prison he wrote to his twenty-four-year-old wife, Marguerite, who was ill after giving birth to a third child; the baby lived only briefly.

[November 16, 1885]

My dear beloved Marguerite:

I am writing you in the early hours of the morning. It is around one o'clock. Today is the 16th: a very significant day.

I wish you well. I offer you advice today out of the love that I have always felt for you. Take good care of your little children. The children belong more to God than to you. Do your utmost to raise them according to the dictates of religion; have them pray for me.

Write your Good Father often; tell him that I never forget him, not for a single day. He must take heart. Life seems sad sometimes, but when it seems saddest, sometimes that is when it provides God with the greatest glory.

Louis "David" Riel, your husband who loves you in Our Lord's name.

I have some words of encouragement, in the Good Lord's name, for my little, little Jean; words of encouragement, of tenderness as well for my little, little Marie-Angélique.

Take heart. You have my blessings.

Your Father,

Louis "David" Riel

Riel was hanged later that day, in Regina. Marguerite died the following year.

A WEDDING BET

Although **Tom Hunt** *and* **Mary Stinson** *lived not far apart in small towns near Portage la Prairie, Manitoba, the "miserable weather" of January 1888 separated them for many weeks and prevented Mary from proceeding with their wedding arrangements. Meanwhile Tom contrived to get news of Mary without letting the neighbours know of their engagement.*

Wellington

Jan 15th–88

Dear Tom

I received your kind letter last night & was very glad to hear from you, but I would have been better pleased to have seen you today which of course is impossible for it is anything but a nice day. You spoke of not coming up till next month but oh you must try to get up before that. I am lonely & want to see you so much, if the roads are at all fit, do come up next Sunday. You ask me how I am getting along with my wedding arraingements – well, I am about as far ahead as when I saw you last. I cant get a chance to get down to Portage & even if I could the weather is not fit for me to go. I am afraid I wont be ready by next month but a few weeks wont make any difference, will it, dear. Some of our people were saying it would be better to put if off till nearer Spring but I suppose that would not suit you & your will will have to be my law . . .

Well now I will give an account of myself & how I behaved at the Oyster supper. We all went with Crighton's team & I was a very good girl, did'nt flirt any. I went home with McElrevys & spent New Year there. Annie came home with me & stayed over a week, & I may tell you that I asked her to be my bridesmaid. She was somewhat surprised to hear that I was going to be married, as she had money bet on it that I would'nt. I suppose you have heard that Dougall is married you wont get a chance to laugh at him any more.

I have'nt much more to say this time. I hope to see you very soon so please my dear old boy, dont disappoint me. I may tell you W.J. is working in the new store at McGregor.

Well I think it is about time I finished. Hoping this may find you in good health as I am happy to say it leaves us all at present.

I am & always will be

your loving

Mary

I shall expect to see you next Sunday or at the very latest the Sunday after. do come dear

Good bye my darling

soon to be my <u>darling husband</u>

Burnside Jan 22nd 1888

Dear Mary

I received your kind and welcome letter last night and was glad to
hear that you were well as I was afraid that if you had ventured to
go to the Portage that you might be laid up after the trip there has
been such horrible weather ever since Christmass I am very well
pleased that you were sensible enough to stop at home dear. Any
time that I was out past Elliotts for hay I always asked how many
teams had been down from the west – knowing that if you had been
down I would find it out that way. They never tumbled to the racket
as I always put it off on wanting to find out how the roads were up to
our hay. Well dear by what you said in your letter you were expecting
me up to-day but it is impossible for me to get away just now our
horses are on the road every day that it is fit to be out and lots of
days that is not and they need what little rest that they can get on
sunday as they are tired right out every week. I never saw such a miserable winter as what it has been this last month back. I have been
frost-bitten about fifty different times so I will be a nice looking
pickle to look at next time you see me. Maybe I had better not go up
to see you dear untill I get a new face on me if I get frozen much
more I think I will get the hens to pick a face on me or at least to
take the colored parts off. However I will try and get up next sunday
if possible if not I will take the train up to McGregor a week from
next saturday if the roads are not good enough to drive. I may be able
to get a ride out near your place from there if not I am very well able to
walk out. Let me know when you write again darling if Wm James
goes home from McG – r saturday evening as I would like to have
company if I go that way. There has been two parties down here
since I was up to your place last. I did not go to either of them there
is to be a social held at Ferriss'es next thursday by the Methodists
they are expecting a good time and a big turn out all the way from
Portage. So you broke the ice at last and asked Annie to be your
Bridesmaid did you ask her who she had made the bet with I think
likely it would be Tom I wonder if there is any one got money up on

her & Tom for my part I do not know whether I would risk any or not. Dear Mary if this cold weather continues do not risk going to Portage. hoping that I may see you soon again as I am longing to see your dear face once more.

Good bye dear old Girl

From Your intended Old Man. Tom

A FRIENDSHIP MANIFESTO

Pauline Johnson, daughter of a Mohawk chief and a wealthy white woman, grew up in a mansion on the Six Nations Indian Reserve near Brantford, Ontario. In her youth she wrote poetry; in her thirties she recited it in a hugely popular stage show for which she dressed as a Mohawk princess. Her first book of poems was published in 1895; five books followed, the last after her death in 1913, of breast cancer, just before her fifty-second birthday. Authors Veronica Strong-Boag and Carole Gerson (in their book Paddling Her Own Canoe) *speculate about an absent lover, "unrelenting leagues" away, to whom Johnson might have addressed some of her poems of the late 1880s and early 1890s. The authors had not seen Johnson's eighteen letters to Archibald Kains, recently given to the National Archives of Canada. An American banker who had been born in London, Ontario, Kains escorted Johnson when she was visiting New York in 1889.*

Brantford Sept 25th 1889

My dear Mr. Kains:

. . . You will find me a moody fitful correspondent I fear, and you must take me just as I feel without restraint or disguise. I never dissemble with those I write to and you will have to put up with an expression of my ideas more than a list of town items – with my impressions of thought observation and feeling more than bits of social news, either you must let me sing to you when I am mournful, complain when I am discouraged, write gloomily when I feel gloomy, or you must not hear from me at all, will you choose? . . .

      Your friend

      E. Pauline Johnson

              Brantford

              Nov 7th '90

My dear Archie

It is just a month ago I find since you wrote me last, and such a delightful letter too old boy, and tonight as I re-read it everything is just as new and interesting to me as if it had for the first time been opened for to tell you the truth I have not kept in this instance to my usual practice – that of reading a letter many times for I have been so busy while at home that even you have come in for a share of neglect, and that has not happened before. My letters I always keep on my desk until replied to – that is, those that I do not immediately burn, and often when very late at night . . . I am retiring after a whole evening of study at composition, I pick up my favorite letters and read them before I sleep. They always put me into touch and feeling with my friends and with humanity again, and I know by them that <u>all</u> is not fancy – <u>all</u> imagination such as I perhaps have been struggling to create or devise in some of my work.

 The usual rush in Christmas work this last month has compelled me to write on business only and oh Archie I have "made" my first story – sent it on a venturesome voyage in which I am sure you wish me success, I'm proud of that story, and at the request of my dear old editor have entered it in the lists for the prize competition for "Saturday Night" – it does not stand the ghost of a chance you know for it is my first attempt, but it will be published finally, tho' it may fail just in the present venture, and you shall have the very first copy for you like Indians, and it is of course an Indian story. Then I've had my holiday orders to fill – poems "made to order", to be completed by such a date etc, and with making myself a new gown, and my other home duties I have not been idle . . .

. . . Mr. Bell and Courtney Thorp did some criticising for me that will be of great advantage to me in future. They both recite magnificently, and have asked me to write them a semi-dramatic poem. In this purpose, are they not kind? Well – every one is kind to me, I meet with nothing but good-will and seeming approval from strangers – after all the world treats me very well, and I must not growl, because I have every thing – everything but ease, and romance. Well I suppose servants and dressmakers could not make up the sum total of ones happiness – neither could love if ones health was gone or if one were steeped in ignorance and had an ambitionless life. I wonder how people without ambition live. I do not mean the chase for fame – but the desire to better one's self morally and materially – the ambition that cries for advancement in all things. The excelling of perhaps one pet idea, scheme, or talent – the attainment of some height – in fact the ambition that means purpose, and despises to stand still. Some people say there is no such state as standing still, that one either steps forward or falls backwards, and it must surely be so, for in all the created world, nothing ceases for an hour, but to live the purposeless humdrum life of some I know would be nothing but a misery to me . . .

Do you know I have a great inclination to scold you? I believe you have been down by the sea all this summer flirting like all fury hence the depth of feeling conveyed in your remarks about the golden summer hours which are now at best but a sweet memory. You make these dreamy observations in connection with a dissertation on flirtations. I hate too the "calculating" individual, the human clod that never loses his head, never forgets his self-possession. but – Ah Archie my dear old boy you must think of at least <u>one</u> thing in these little amusements – dont forget that you may leave your seaside girl just a bit heart sore – a little lonely – a scrap desolate, and alas – women dont get rid of these things by putting on their hats, and lounging off to the theatre or smoking a consoling cigar. Girls must grin and bear it in silence and the fun you enjoy may be so serious to her. You may perhaps tell me this state of things will reverse easily – but not so. If it is the man who loves he may & does speak, if he has any "sand" about him he wins – If the woman loves what is there for her but silence, assumed indifference, and – desolation?

What am I scribbling of? I who believe so little in this love people tell me of – I who have never seen it but have often been forced to look upon base imitations thereof – Ah well – dont mind my scolding. I know as well as I know my Creed that you would not give a dog pain – consciously that is, and I don't think Archie that either you or I will ever get ourselves madly disliked for assaulting hearts at summer resorts with intent to kill, or for thoughtlessly decorating our belts with the scalps of victimized sentiment . . .

Dont forget me, it is always such a pleasure to hear from you.

With affectionate

regard

Your friend

Pauline.

A ROSE-FILLED BOWER

Born in Llannefydd, North Wales, in 1857, tailor **William Herbert Griffiths** *came to Canada around 1881 and settled in Ontario. His lady of the bower was Elizabeth Ann Barrett, daughter of Augustus Barrett, a photographer with studios in Oshawa, Whitby, Cannington, and Toronto. She met Griffiths in Cannington; they were married in 1891 and moved to Toronto, where they raised three daughters.*

Simcoe House

Orillia, Ont.

[1891]

I really must write to tell you of something that happened to me last night. I had a most delightful dream, with you in it. [Though?] that is not remarkable for I am thinking of you all the time. I thought that you and I were walking in a most beautiful garden, full of the loveliest flowers, and trees and fruits, and you the loveliest of them all. Your arm was on mine and we talked just like lovers. I thought that we came to a bower all covered with roses and sat there forgetting all the world but our two selves and that I told you how I loved you and you did not frown and asked if you loved me and [you?] did not say no. The birds were singing over us. The breeze was wafting a thousand odors round us and all was like paradise itself. I cannot tell you half what we talked about, but we were happy as the day is long. Then I asked you if you would be mine and you turned away your face for a while but left your hand in mine and then I stole my arm round your waist and you looked at me and our face[s] drew near each other and I awoke: never was such disappointement the grey dawn was stealing in at the window. There was no garden no bower no dear one, all was changed. But the question is what does the dream mean one thing is true about it I love you dearly and would give all the world if the vision was true. Supposing that we were walking in a such garden or anywhere else, and I was to ask you what I ask you in my dream. Would [you?] answer as you answered then to the question of

[signed with a personal mark]

A PM'S PASSION

*In the last decade of the 19th century, Liberal Party leader – and later prime minister – **Wilfrid Laurier** wrote a series of letters to Émilie Lavergne, a married woman in Arthabaska, the town in rural Quebec where he had begun his law career. Sir Wilfrid, also married but childless, insisted his friendship with Émilie was purely platonic, although some historians suspect otherwise. Certainly his words, written in English, betray his passion for the mother of two, whom he compares to Madame de Staël (Anne Louise Germaine Necker), the French-Swiss novelist and intellectual who pursued an unconventional love life.*

[Ottawa, Sunday, August] 23rd [1891]
. . . I also, my dearest friend, I would like to be near you, not however to hear your explanations. I knew very well, I always knew

that you never intended to wound me, but wounded I was because your words revealed to me that since on a certain subject I felt a certain way, you thought me cross & unkind. How else could I construe those words of yours: "Don't be cross, don't be unkind, but let me talk with etc." Confess, dear friend, that in those words no half-jesting, no humorous play; there was on the contrary great earnestness. I know your heart too well, not to be aware that you would have erased those words, torn them to pieces, if the thought had then occurred to you that they might sting & grieve, but dear friend, would not the feeling have been there all the same in your heart, though not conveyed by your pen. This is really what still torments me. Am I unkind, am I unjust, & whether you express it or not, have I really given you cause to believe me unkind, ungenerous, unjust. My friends & even my foes have generally given me credit for generosity of conduct, & that I should [be] ungenerous to you, of all beings on earth, to you my friend so dear, & every day dearer, I cannot bear the thought. The expression is only secondary, but if the feeling is there in your heart, do you think it makes much difference to me whether it is expressed, or whether out of kindness, you keep it unexpressed.

I would like to see you, my friend, not to have your explanations, but simply to see you, to hear you, to look in your eyes, to listen to your voice, to feel that it is you, to be sure of it, to enjoy the consciousness of it; & next I would like to see you, to convince you that it is you who are unjust to me. <u>Chère injuste</u>, this is an expression which you once applied to me, & which I would like to utter to you in so many words . . .

It is true, my dear friend, you never sang for me; that is one of the sacrifices of life. How often have I pictured to myself, when I was sitting by your piano, listening to your voice. I heard you once, last summer. From the open window of my room, I heard your voice, faint it is true from the distance, still audible. My heart was big that night, & the words went deep into my heart, though I could hardly then respond to the sentiment which they gave expression to (it was the barcarolle song by Coquelin). All the emotions which that voice evoked, are still as rich in my soul as they were these thirteen months ago.

You protest, my dear friend, that you have not made the conquest of the great man. Oh! but I am sure you have! I was sure you would! And I have no fault whatever to find with that. What would you say, if I were to tell you & to insist on it, that I am not moody, not ungenerous, not unkind, not unjust? What would you say, my dear, so dear friend? Would you insist that I can be all that, & without cause too? Answer in the affirmative, if you can, if you dare . . . be so dishonest to your conscience . . .

I will send you another book, but I will not return the one which contains the too short notice on Madame de S[taël]. I will take it to you myself, & will make you read under my eyes, certain passages which have singularly impressed me. I quite agree with you, my dear friend, that that woman is altogether admirable. If you are not insensible to vanity, there is cause of vanity for you, for you are closely akin to that woman, with a touch in addition of Madame Necker. Yes, I do not doubt, I am quite sure, absolutely certain that all she did, you could be capable of, all the generosity, devotion, sacrifices which she so gladly showered, you would also have showered, & therein found the happiness of your life . . .

The last words of your letter are very good, very kind; good, kind, loving like yourself, & yet good, kind, loving as they are, they make me sad & lonely – sad & lonely because I crave all the more to see you. Do you not believe this my dear, ever dearer friend.

Again goodbye. May the love of your little ones, convey [to] you a part – a part I say, it cannot be more – of what there is in this heart for you.

W.L.

Émilie Lavergne's son, Armand, looked strikingly like Laurier, which helped prompt politically inspired rumours that the prime minister had sired him. Armand, who had a good relationship with his mother's friend, once said that whether it was Lavergne or Laurier, he had a good father. In 1917 young Lavergne was a prominent

Quebec nationalist who defied the federal government of Robert Borden, which was attempting to conscript soldiers for the First World War; he insisted he'd rather be hanged or shot.

THE BARREN GROUNDS

In fifteen expeditions in the Canadian west and north, **Joseph Burr Tyrrell,** *a geologist and historian, explored and mapped for the Geological Survey of Canada. He is famous for having discovered dinosaur remains in southern Alberta. In 1893 he and his brother, James, and six Iroquois and Metis canoeists set out from Fond du Lac in northern Saskatchewan and, following rivers in the Northwest Territories, reached Hudson Bay. Along the way, he wrote his fiancée, Edith Carey, about the native and mixed-blood people vital in guiding and even feeding his expedition. (The precise and respectful Tyrrell, in using the word "promiscuous" in this letter, likely means it in the dictionary definition "of mixed or disorderly composition.")*

Fond du Lac
June 29 1893

My dearest Edith

We arrived here about noon today and I am now surrounded by a promiscuous rabble of Indian men and boys. Last year this was quite a little village, but during the winter old Jose Mercredi died and now it has been abandoned as a summer Trading Post, and a man will be stationed here in winter to trade with the few Indians in the vicinity. On this account it is quite uncertain when this letter will go out to you, perhaps not till after my return in the Autumn, but whenever it goes it will take out my best love.

We are passing right along, hurrying to the Barren Grounds, where we hope to arrive in a couple of weeks, and if we have any sort of good fortune we shall be on the shore of Hudson's Bay about the tenth of August. Our course back must then be guided by circumstances.

I have just had an interesting parley with a lot of the Indians; one has to be used to looking pleasant with about a dozen men and women talking around you as fast as they can; in about a quarter of an hour you ask the interpreter what they have said and he answers you in a couple of words. The talk is very much one-sided, and very few ideas are interchanged, the result of about an hour hard work being the gift of a few ounces of tea.

Now darling I must be off for the summer here is very short and we have a long way to go. Wherever you may be I hope that you are having a pleasant time. The leaves are not much more than out on the trees here while you in the east are in the midst of summer. Eleven months ago today I wrote you from here and we have had many a happy day since then, and the future has many more happy ones in store for us.

Give my kind regards to all at home, and with fondest love to yourself.

I remain

Your own true lover

J. B. Tyrrell

The expedition returned overland to Winnipeg by January 1894. A month later Joseph Tyrrell and Edith Carey were married. He died in 1957, at the age of ninety-eight; she had predeceased him by twelve years.

AND SO TO WED

William Wight Robson, born in Galt, Ontario, in 1865, worked as a machinist apprentice but quit because the foreman swore. He then studied photography and opened studios in two locations in Nova Scotia. Harriet May Currie, a descendant of Dr. Samuel Fuller, the physician on the Mayflower, was born in Windsor, Nova Scotia, in 1864. In 1883–84 she travelled the world on the sailing ship Tuskar with her half-brother, Charlie, who was the ship's master. William

wrote to Harriet while she was visiting Charlie in the United States.
Harriet wrote her letter while returning home by rail.

Wolfville, N.S. Apr. 8, 1894

My beloved:

You see that I didn't manage to withstand the fascinations of the 'Old Homestead Quartet' – They sang here last night and I am glad, very glad that I stayed for the blending of those four male voices was about as near to perfection as I expect to hear for many and many a day. The first tenor was perhaps a little overstrong in his solo work but we would be 'finicky' indeed to criticize such renditions as they gave us last night. But, I think you have heard them, have you not? So you will know for yourself just how fine they are. The elocution-ist Miss Girardian is a dainty little fairhaired sprite who charmed the house before she opened her lips . . .

This morning I have been to Methodist Church with Miss Randall (the milliner) and Charley Weeks, a student from P.E.I. Heard a fairly good sermon from a young man named Henneson (?) and some awful singing – tenor bad and soprano worse, alto fairly good.

This afternoon I go to Presbyterian and tonight to Baptist Church. The Presbyterians have a very brainy young man, Mr. Fraser, and awful singing – the Baptists have not such awful singing but they have Mr. Higgins so I guess church service in Wolfville is about an even thing all round – Can't get time to go down and hear Ken Hind (Rev. K.C. he is now) at the English church but I am thinking things are not an awful lot better there than any place else. Tomorrow a.m. I go home, Tuesday night we shriek the cantata 'Belshazzar' – and Thursday night Miss Harrison of Sackville sings in the old hall. You remember her, do you not? She sings 'The ivory gates and golden' and she sang the 'Inflammatus' once with the choral society . . .

Have just finished 'L'homme qui rit' (The man who laughs) by Victor Hugo and in it he was raking over the muck heap of English court society in the time of Queen Anne and her predecessors. It was bad I acknowledge even in the time of the Virgin Queen Bess, but can anyone show us any country under the canopy that was not wicked in those times? There are some beautiful love passages, though, in the book between Dea, the blind girl, and Grymplaine, the boy whom the wickedness of James II had mutilated into a frightfully mirth-provoking monstrosity – but to Dea's sightless love, the soul of his – pure and true and strong was worthy of all the wealth of her love. Church time, dearie, good-bye a little.

Church is over and "I'm come back home where my beau lives at", at least when I am talking to her via the pen and ink long-distance telephone – Am glad you so much enjoyed Faust, have read lots of and about it, heard bits of the opera and often wanted to see, but as yet never seen either opera or drama . . .

More snow fell last week. Friday, strangely enough, the 6th April, saw several inches of the beautiful come down and exactly eight years ago that day there was a fall of two feet – I have cause to remember it for that day I left Galt to go to Petrolia and commence the study of the art and science of photography. But for my taking up that delight-ful and also aggravatingly bothersome business, my chance of seeing H.M.C. [Harriet May Currie] would have been pretty slim I guess . . .

. . . When Maude was in the studio yesterday I told her your letter was due to come in on the evening mail and that, as Seminary strictness forbade my speaking to her or seeing her home from the concert, that she was to look at my handkerchief pocket and if the flag were flying high she would know that I had good news but if she could manage to find me and she would fail to see even the smallest tip of my handkerchief protruding then the news was the same old story and when the letter came my 'wipe' was put away down along with my expectations.

Wordsworth and Marion Crawford both appear to have much the same ideas as to the soul's former life, only Crawford widens it more and seems to see that the soul had existed countless times before it comes to sojourn here upon earth. These men must have some foundation away deep in their inner consciousness for their belief, so when a man honestly believes anything we <u>must</u> listen to him. Carlyle I think it is says it is a much easier thing to refuse to listen to an argument from one who holds a different view but such a course blocks at once development of truth, and our refusal to hear the truth does not make it any the less true. Surely the world is not growing worse, Hat, as it grows broader – today in church the minister held that the inspiration of God's Holy Word was not at all in the old sense of absolute verbatim dictation. If such were true, why should the differences in the writing of St. Paul and John be so marked. The men were servants of God delivering His message and tell of His work and surely it is a grander thing to believe that God inspired these men with the love of His infinite goodness so that they were constrained to write of Him rather than to think they became temporarily mere automata holding the pen and their brains doing no work at all. I have little patience with the men who see no good at all in any other religion under the heavens than our own Christian, it looks too much like the spirit of the Inquisition to suit me . . .

Oh my sweetheart, come home soon. I get tired of work, tired of friends, tired yes sometimes of my good friends and all because there is a place in my heart that none of them can fill and she who can is so long kept away from me – but, forgive me dear for talking so and making your stay harder, but the complaint slipped out of me . . .

Now, my love, good-night, and may the next mail bring me word of your speedy home-coming.

Your own Will

May 19, 1894

Dearest Will: " 'O'er the desert I come to thee' and though my steam horse I expect is making better time even than the Bedouin's 'Arab shod with fire', yet I find that still 'My heart outruns my steed On the wings of my desire'. I wonder, by the way, if the fellow in the song looked as disreputable and dirty as I do. You can't imagine what it is travelling through these plains. The porter comes along and brushes me occasionally but five minutes afterward, you would never know it. And my face and hair and hands! O my, will they ever get clean again? I am glad, Billy, that you are not going to be in Boston to meet me for I know that the longest course of brushing and washing is not going to make me look half decent for a week at least.

There is a lady who had the berth above me last night going to take the G.T. [Grand Trunk] train in Chicago and is going to stop at Nappalene (is that spelt right?), Ont. She is worrying about the quarantine regulations but the conductor told her that he thinks that as her trunks are checked from California, they will only examine her smaller luggage. I wish so much that I were going that way so I could see your mother. Do you think she will be disappointed?

Charlie felt dreadfully when I left last night and I assure you I felt badly. It did not seem possible that I could feel as I did but somehow his loneliness struck me more forcibly than ever before and it seemed to me I was doing a dreadful selfish thing in leaving him. Do you think I am selfish or is this wish of mine to have someone of my very own to love and be loved by, a natural womanly one? I have been so mixed up since I left that I can't think straight myself any more. But I am going to try not to think about it. The big step from the old to the new life has been taken and the gladness in my heart from the thought of seeing you soon over-balances the pain of parting with all others. Yet you will not blame me will you for having some sad and a little remorseful thoughts of Charlie.

Chicago – Nickle Plate Station. Here we are transferred bag and baggage and I feel much better for a cup of coffee and something substantial to eat. It is so cold here this morning, those who came through from California in light wraps are feeling the cold so much and I started with a travelling acquaintance to see the wrecks on the lake from the storm last night but we were glad to turn back. I wondered whether I ought to have started with him after we were fairly on our way but in my impetuous fashion I thought too late. Charlie would scold me I know and I am thinking maybe you will but he was kind to me all day yesterday and there is nothing of the 'fresh' order about him and I did want to see the wrecks, so I went. There were twenty-two people drowned they say. And after all I could not get to shore for my hat blew off and I guess my hair would have followed suit if it had not been fastened on by natur'! So we had to come back. And now my acquaintance has gone to get shaved and I am once more with the ladies of the party so you see he was a safe cavalier . . .

I am feeling so much better since I started. The day I left I was so miserable that I was really almost afraid to venture but kept it to myself for fear Charlie would make me wait another week. And now I am almost well, I think, though you would be surprised to see how much flesh I have lost. I shall have to take Cod Liver Oil or something in Lynn and hurry up if I want to get back all the pounds of flesh my imperious lord and master demands. How many weeks are you going to give me to get ready, Billy? This is the 20th, 11 more days in May only. If I am to get home in time for the commencement exercises at Wolfville, I will have to hurry not a little for it will not be <u>three</u> weeks. Fancy seeing each other in three weeks time! But then you know maybe I can't make it – I have such a lot of things to do. It is so lovely though to be where I can hear from you in less than a week and to know I am only a day's journey away from you or not much more . . .

. . . One night this week we went to hear The Bohemian Girl, W.G. Carleton's opera troupe. I enjoyed it so much for old as it is I never heard the whole opera before. Then the tenor who sings that lovely 'When other lips, etc.' was glorious. And Carleton's 'Hearts bowed down' also; and the soprano, a pretty little actor, simpatica to the core, sang that old 'I dreamt that I dwelt in, etc.' most beautifully. I <u>do</u> like opera it is not wicked do you think to love beautiful music even if it is sung on the stage.

Now goodbye my own boy. I am going to drop this here. Won't it be funny to know I am going as fast as my letter towards you? Do you love me as much as when I was so far away?

Your own Hattie.

Will and Hattie were married in 1894 and eventually moved to Winnipeg, where Will became an eminent photographer. His signature, W.W. Robson, appears on many photographic portraits of the politicians of the time.

A MIXED MARRIAGE

Charles Spalding, a no-nonsense Scot, wrote his love letters to Mary Dyck on the letterhead of his business – Reuter & Spalding, Dealers in Hardware and Harness – from Lowe Farm, a community seventy kilometres south of Winnipeg. Mary, a Mennonite, lived in Plum Coulee, twenty kilometres farther south. The idea of marrying outside her faith clearly troubled her.

April 6, 1909

My dearest Mary,

I received your letter this morning and it makes me think all the more of you for writing thus. I admit it is sudden but in all my life I have done things that I made up my mind to in a hurry. In buying our business here in 1 hour I had it settled. I have been considering our union for longer than you imagine & please do not compare it to those trifle dances and gatherings we had here. I did not like to set the people talking as they sure would over an affair like this, as I am aware of your church being very objectionable to mixed marriages with English people, but I am scotch & so it will not matter. But Mary I will write your mother but if she is not willing what will happen then. I want you or I would not have asked you and we will have to wait till the answer comes. I would not for the world cause her any more trouble. But really Mary we will get along. I could have made things more pleasent for you while here but I wanted to keep those big mouths shut around here, and if your ministers get wind of it they will try & change your mind, so lighten up your heart for I think you like me a little and I am sure I care for you, although I have never made any spread about it, and we will let things stand just the way they are till we get your mothers consent and we will pospone matters for 1 week & if the roads are passible Sunday I will be over to Plum Coulee. I hate to pospone it but if you think better to wait till we hear from your mother we will wait, we are young as yet. I was at the phone last night but we could not get the wire. The mud is about 4 ft deep around here. Hoping you will brighten up and not worry about things that you shouldn't, I will close as ever

answer soon

Your Charles xxxx

Charles did write to Mary's mother, who had remarried and moved to Aberdeen, Saskatchewan. She immediately replied to Charles.

[April 10, 1909]

Dear Sir,

I received your letter asking me for the hand of my daughter Mary. It is a hard question to answer. But in hopes that it is the happiness of my daughter, I may say yes. The Lord may be with you.

Yours truly,

Mrs. Wm Vogt

Charles soon wrote to his "Marie."

April 14, 1909

My Dearest Marie,

At last I rec'd your letter. I thought you were never going to write, and say I am enclosing your mother's letter which I rec'd yesterday and now you are sure mine, and I am writing to her to-night thanking her for it & for you as now we have nothing else to do but get married, nicely & quietly, and it will be done with. I think my Marie, you take this occasion too seriously, surely I am not such a bad fellow, that, I was going to get you only to be cruel to you and mean. On the other hand, I am hoping to get you to be good to you and for us to love each other as long as it is Gods will to live on this earth, and the first unhappy hour I cause you may God punish me for it. I want you to keep this letter for future references and see if I am not as good as my word, and for my sake cut out this different nationality business. I know what I am doing, and you are a sensible girl that knows right from wrong, and my experience with people here is I have more friends, that I appreciate, and am used better among the German people than any of those white-washed english people. I am a poor devil and am working for a living as every body else is and if I am spared another year with prosperity to our country I will be out of debt & with you will be the happiest fellow in the country, so please Marie get all those foolish notions out of your head and begin to think you have a fellow in Lowe Farm that really loves you, and that your right place is with him . . . I better close or I will have to start another page and say there is not much use of me going to Plum Coulee. I hate the darn place anyway and it would take about 5 hours to drive there as the roads are so muddy so if you stop your foolishness and get to business you might state in your answer how soon you will be ready . . . Good night just 10:30.

Your Charles xxxxx

We will give Old Heppner & Butcher Penner enough to talk about all summer.

Mary and Charles were wed and had two children. Charles owned a hotel for a time, farmed, and practised as a chiropractor. His gambling problem ultimately strained the marriage. Old Heppner, who apparently liked to gossip, was the reeve of the municipality of Morris when Charles served on the municipal council.

MOTHER-IN-LAW

*When William Sutherland, who owned a silver mine in Cobalt, Ontario, visited an injured friend in hospital, he met a nurse named Mary Jackson – whom he swept off her feet and into marriage. A few weeks before the wedding William's mother, **Elizabeth Sutherland**, wrote a gracious letter, which her daughter-in-law would keep throughout the years.*

Toronto, Dec. 12, 1910

Dear Miss Jackson,

I was indeed pleased to get your letter. I am sure that you will be so busy for the next two weeks getting your things ready that you will have very little time for correspondence.

I had a letter from that (<u>good</u> <u>son</u>) William today. He is coming to Toronto this week. He may spend most of his time here during the holidays. We are always pleased to have him. He has always been so kind and good to us. If he makes as good a husband as he has a son you will not have to regret your choice. I do hope that you will both be very happy and be long spared to be a blessing to each other.

We are in hope that you will decide to live in Toronto so we can enjoy your company.

I have my Christmas cake baked. We are trying to get some sewing done this week. We shall be kept busy preparing for our family gathering at Christmas. If we are all spared to meet on that occasion, we must have our pictures taken again.

The children are all very busy with Xmas exams, they will be glad of a holiday.

Maud and Alma are at the church tonight. They are both taking part in a concert the Sunday school is getting up for Xmas.

Mr. Sutherland joins me in sending best wishes & love.

Yours Sincerely,

Mrs. J. Sutherland

A successful businessman, William hired a private rail car when the couple travelled to Atlantic City. He succumbed to influenza ten years later, leaving Mary with three small children and no insurance benefits. She managed to support her family and lived to the age of ninety-one.

LOVE EVERYTHING

*The painter **Frederick Horsman Varley** moved to Canada from England in 1913 and worked as a commercial artist while his wife, Maud, remained in England. Already a friend of the British artist Arthur Lismer, who had preceded him to Canada, Varley soon met other Canadian artists and later participated with them in the first Group of Seven exhibition, at the Art Gallery of Toronto in 1920.*

22 Henry Street [Toronto]
Friday March 28th [1913]

My darling little girl,

Shall I have another chat with you just for a few minutes? I find now, that the mails have gone dotty. And you will get quite a budget all by one post. There's been no overtime work today – I've put in a full day though and may work over tomorrow. I've got quite a bit of humorous work to do and do you know I revel in it – I can make others laugh over it. It is not at all serious. I dont care a button about drawing – It's the spirit of the work that they consider over here – Winter has come again all in a day – We have snow about 8" deep – and freezing hard; out in the sunlight it is altogether conquered – The sun is quite hot. I've come to the conclusion that it's a good thing to have a day or two off occasionally – Robson 'grouched' to others while I was away – saying that it always happens, as soon as it's a bit slack, a man stays away and then work comes that only he can do etc etc – He's specially nice now I've returned and as he says "damned glad to see me". Well, dear I didn't pick up my pen to talk shop – but just to let you feel that I'm always thinking of you. And holding you to me. The good people of the house are always slightly changing my arrangement of photographs – I must say I like it. There is a freshness and sweetness about it. But photos are just a stepping-stone for the memory. Poor little Dorothy – I hope she sleeps better now. It's pitiful to think of the little soul getting up 5 times in one night – Oh that she could walk to me!

Do you know dear, it might have been wrong – I dont think it was, but coming home tonight I would have given much for a talk with a girl – I longed ever so. To talk quietly in a cosy room. To make a life of 2 hours: to live in reality a little of life nearer to you and I – I felt it would be nearer – I could not be with any girl without having you there. It would be no pleasure . . . simply a sense of wrong through all. Well, I didnt see that girl who could have been a chum so I came home – and passed on my way a house from which came the cry of a little babe – and I said – "Everywoman in the world is not equal to a little babe. Oh! for a little bairn to hold and kiss – to love – to bury my face in its soft flesh – the warm milky scent of a little child" – I longed until I ached. At home, I said I would make myself so sweet that I in myself will be complete. So stripped for a bath. I found the boiler had burst and there was no hot water for bathing – so I shaved smoothly – scrubbed my face and neck and arms – brushed my teeth and . . . sat down to speak to you and live with my children. Bless you all – make yourselves as pure and sweet as flowers specked with crystal dew – Love with all your hearts, everything and everyone. What a game it is! All of us, individually going our way – a different outlook in nearly all things and yet so similar. How grand it is for them who have companions near to them – I'm awful sorry for the lonely ones. They have not half the chance, but then they are given often more spirit to fight and their vision is very vivid. Well, my sweet little wife (I've cultivated a sense of smell, and think of you as an odour. The same with my children.) the clocks have just struck midnight. I'm going to bed – to lie quietly with my own thoughts. To be content – to make the most of time between work. It's all very beautiful to feel so happy. This chat has done me good – I shall smile as I lay me down, perfectly content and calmly happy – Goodnight my darlings

Your loving one –
Fred

TO BE YOURS

William Seath Brown came to Canada from Scotland in 1905. He was a sergeant with the Canadian forces in France during the First World War when he wrote many letters to his fiancée, Lila M. Scott, of Dominion City, Manitoba.

Febr. 18th 1916
France

My Dearest Lila

. . . well dearie this letter is to be uncensored as you will notice my signature on the envelope giving my word of honour as to the style of letter. Well darling I can write you what I want to say without eyes prying through but your own dear. I miss you darling as much as you do me & hope & pray that I may safely return to you, as my love for you darling is as great as ever and have only one wish & that is to be yours all my life until we are Called above . . . How is Dad & Mother getting along I do hope they may find a nice place to go to in their declining years, perhaps we yet be able to give them some comfort after this horrible war is over. I may be of the other side of politics & I am yet but God forbid if the milk of human kindness has or will die in my breast, when there is someone to help, I do hope that Dad & Mother bear me no ill-will seeing I'm opposed to them in certain things. It is not because of pretty speeches by politicians which has given me my Liberal principles & I mean not Liberal as in politics, but in the true meaning of the word, that is to help as far as the people's wishes are in regards to social betterment & taking evils out of the path of youth which are a menace to them & also helping to legislate along lines which will give a better living to the working-men also a better understanding between the Capitalist & labour parties. I do not hate neither rich or poor, but fully believe a way is possible where rich & poor may be as brothers to one another & each have respect for one another instead of this trying to cut one another's throats. Well Lila this is dilating too much but those are some of my thoughts & you whom I claim as mine are entitled to them as I would not like you to have me & not know me. I do not know why my thoughts are to help those who are the toilers, as our people I mean my people altho' hard working, would in the way the classes range be considered in comfortable circumstances, still they do not hate the working man & have always shown kindness towards them & it is, as it should be. Well darling I at anyrate love you so very much that perhaps I may also become selfish & wish all for our own selves, but dearest I think you also love those who work hard & would like to make their path less arduous. Now darling I only get one of those envelopes once a week where I can safely put my sincere thoughts in them which I have to you. I will have to close dearest as lights have been ordered out in 10 minutes, Im so sorry as I wanted to write more but we are in the Military zone now where they have certain rules. I am in good health darling altho' bothered with a chilblain on my foot which is nasty if you can find a remedy send it & I will be grateful for it. With the best of love to you my darling & all, the best I wish you, Kind regards to all

I am

Ever Yours

Bill

Bill and Lila were married after the war and had one daughter. In 1958 Bill died of cancer in the Winnipeg General Hospital. Lila died two minutes later – of grief.

AN APOSTROPHE TO CANADA

Charles William Howatt, *a truck driver with D Company, 184th Battalion of the Canadian contingent of the British Expeditionary Force, was stationed in France from November 1916 until the end of the First World War.*

France 14/4/18

Dear Jennie: –

A little talk tonight before I turn in. it is almost two weeks since I last wrote and since then have had two lovely long letter's from you was sure glad to hear that my little girl was in good health as this leave's me fine and dandy getting along o.k. my cold is all better so don't nead a nurse now

But to tell the truth sweetheart if I dont soon get back to see you I will die of heart trouble for I sure get lonely to see you at times but suppose there is no use feeling like that as it wont make the day's any shorter.

It sure is an aful war and from what I can see it is just starting and a lot of hard fighting ahead off us yet . . .

This is Sunday night sweetheart and a cold old night it is the wind is blowing it seem's about 40 below. Makes a fellow feel like getting in by a good old fire makes me think of the good old day's gone by and the day's that is yet to come when I land back in dear old Canada and take you with me to that little home that I plan and dream about day in and day out then I will tell you the thing's dear that I cant put on paper.

Your little ring sure does stand for comradeship as well as love Jennie but I cant tell you the thing's that I would like too . . .

Now Jennie dear – it is getting late and I have very little new's you will have to excuse short letter's for a few week's till we get settled down

So good night sweetheart with all my love
Charlie

Charlie was repatriated in April 1919 and married Jennie Rebecca Silcox in Morden, Manitoba, three months later. They bought a farm near Kaleida, Manitoba, where they raised five daughters and a son. The farm is still operated by Charlie and Jennie's descendants.

FAIR WARNING

In 1920 Lorne Ratz asked **Amasa Winger** *for the hand of his daughter in marriage. Winger replied on the letterhead of the store he owned
in Elmira, Ontario, which sold dress goods, silks, ribbons, house fur-
nishings, carpets, groceries, ladies' and misses' ready-to-wear suits,
coats, underwear, and hosiery. Winger spelled his daughter's name as
Adell, and she herself used that spelling when she filled in a certificate for a drawing competition in 1909. However, on her marriage
certificate of June 1922 she gave her name as Effie Adele.*

Elmira, Ontario
April 2nd, 1920

Mr. Lorne Ratz
Dear Sir
We received your letter asking for our consent to your marriage to
our daughter Adell.

I suppose you have seriously considered this important step,
which you intend to take, and with a view to the future comfort and
welfare of Adell and yourself have decided that it is necessary to stick
closely to your work, save your money, and not let any inclination to
loaf, or play poker get the better of you, like it did last summer.

You know Adell is our only child is not very strong, and will
require a husband who will look after her comfort, and save her from
hard, heavy work wherever possible, and this can be done in many
things which are ordinar[i]ly not looked upon as a man's work.

Further, if the marriage takes place, as Adells parents, (and you
not having any living) we would like to be consulted on any important
change you intended to make, and our advice carefully considered
therewith, and also expect to receive the consideration and respect,
which as Adells father and mother, we feel we would be entitled to.

Our minister just mentioned last Sunday at the Confirmation
Services, that parents should feel free to advise their children, in important matters, even up to 40 years of age, and that one of these was

which Church they should join: – but this is a subject which can be taken up later.

If you feel that it will be a pleasure to you to carry out the above suggestions, Mrs Winger and myself will be glad to give our consent to your engagement with Adell, provided she is willing, and hope and trust that the Lord will bless the undertaking.

Will be glad to see you any time you can arrange to come up.

Yours Truly,

A. Winger

After their marriage Lorne and Adell moved to Oshawa, where Lorne worked for the McLaughlin Motor Car Co. The couple had two sons. Unfortunately Amasa Winger's assessment of his daughter's health was accurate: she died of tuberculosis six years into the marriage.

A BITTERSWEET FAREWELL

*Frederick Banting and a team of researchers discovered insulin in Toronto during 1921–22, a time when Banting was romantically involved with **Edith Roach**, a willowy, clever, minister's daughter. When he later fell in love with an X-ray technician named Marion, Banting was forced to sign a "non-interference" agreement with Edith, giving her two thousand dollars and custody of an engagement ring. A day after their deal was drafted, Edith wrote to Frederick.*

Toronto, May 12, 1924

. . . The bitterness has gone out of my heart and as time goes by I know that only the good old memories of our love will remain for these I will cherish and the unpleasant ones must die from neglect. A little more than a week ago I buried my mother; yesterday I felt that I buried you and my love too, but no, the love for the old Fred has conquered to-night and I think will always be with me, the love of our youth. When I come through Alliston, coming down from home,

I always gaze with longing and pleasure at the banks of the old river and at the old house. These are the memories I want to live and I pray that they may soften and not harden us both.

The time may come when like yourself I may turn to another. It is and will be hard to be sure but if it is to come I pray that it won't be too late. I believe that things happen in this world for a purpose. The way is hard but there is a reason for it all, and this thought gives me strength. Won't you try to see it this way too and it will help.

You may have thought me hard yesterday Fred. I don't think deep in your heart that you did. You will never know what it cost me to go through with it. I had to do it and I don't think you understand, but then none of us understand each other perfectly. My mind heart and soul is at peace. I believe peace to be the secret of happiness and I wish you would believe it too and obtain peace. I think we are both stronger in character than we were two years ago and if that is true we have not failed for life is character building. I have regained my self-control and my self-respect and I am confident I can smile and go forward and make my life count something, though perhaps little. I have faith in you, trust, respect and admiration, for your good points are many and these will stay with me.

We have had our ups and downs and have hurt each other as it is only possible for people who love deeply to hurt, but I hope the storm is over. We have loved each other through it all, even be it only the love of our old selves. That will never quite die. I am your friend, I hope I always will be. I believe that you try to do what you believe to be right. As for our private affairs I trust you to do and to say only that for which you have good cause, and nothing which may lead to any future trouble for either of us, remembering the words of our agreement, and you may trust me to do the same.

It will be 13 years this next summer since we first met. The times that you have made me supremely happy during those years are beyond number and are the times that really count. I am glad I have had them and I do not regret. It is better to have loved and lost than never to have loved at all, but I don't feel that we have really lost.

May God bless you and keep you Fred and make you a greater man.

Yours sincerely

Edith

Years later Edith married another man; she never saw Fred again. Banting would one day be knighted for his co-discovery of the life-saving therapy for diabetes but, according to some friends, came to rue his marriage to Marion and his loss of Edith.

POET TO PIANIST

*When **Sir Charles G.D. Roberts** died in 1943, he was regarded as Canada's foremost man of letters. Born in New Brunswick in 1860, Roberts published his first book of poems at twenty. Part of a group called the Poets of Confederation, he also wrote prose, of which his animal stories were the most successful. He served with the Canadian forces in the First World War in a training capacity. A formal portrait photograph shows him with a beribboned pince-nez and a brush moustache. Later in the war, by then a major, Roberts was one of the authors of the official war history. In 1925 he returned to Canada to live in Toronto and then travelled the country giving lectures. He was knighted in 1935. While in Vancouver on a lecture tour, the sixty-eight-year-old poet met a gorgeous, vivacious twenty-four-year-old pianist named Kathleen Strathearn. Love-stricken, he began an effusive correspondence.*

New Washington Hotel

Seattle

Thursday, Mch 22/28

My Adorable Loveliest –

I have your dear letter this morning, bless you. I am <u>so</u> sorry to learn that you are feeling so wretched & lifeless. You poor Darling! And you are depriving your audiences of so much, when you do not shed your wonderful personality & imagination forth upon them. But perhaps you are recovering by this time, Beloved. And in any case they have the thrill of seeing you as well as hearing you.

I am terribly anxious to learn the Doctor's report. But I will be back to you on Monday morning, & will try to cheer & stimulate you. Please drop me a wee line at once to tell me what time to listen for you on the radio, CKWX, Sunday night. I plan to take the night boat from here, at midnight Sunday, – though I <u>may</u> not get away till the <u>train, Monday morning.</u> In either case, I will phone my Lady at once on arrival.

Everyone is being most attentive to me here, & over-whelming me with <u>entertainments</u> – but only two recitals! I must run.

I <u>love you</u>, Deliciousness. And I kiss your hands & your feet.

Your devoted
C.

Charles chided Kathleen for addressing him as Dr. Roberts but eventually took the hint and offered to "efface" himself from her life. In 1930 she married a wealthy insurance company executive and moved to China, where for ten years she was a soloist with the Shanghai Municipal Orchestra. Roberts found other adorable darlings to woo by mail. His seven letters and two greeting cards to Kathleen were found in 1990 by her son, Arthur Hughes, who remembers his mother telling him: "Arthur, you might have been the son of Canada's leading poet."

OUR AGONY

Roderick Haig-Brown was a crusading conservationist, a sportsman, a judge, and the author of more than two dozen books. He won the Governor General's Award for Juvenile Literature in 1949. The British-born Haig-Brown was introduced to Ann Elmore in 1929 in the Seattle bookstore where she worked. When he returned to England, they corresponded for two years. In 1933, when he was back in Seattle, the pair decided to marry, but first Roddy had to finish writing Panther (Ki-yu), *which he would do while living at a friend's house in Campbell River, British Columbia.*

14th June, [1993] 10.30 a.m.
309 Sylvia Court
Beach Avenue
Vancouver
B.C.

Ann Darling – I wonder how it all seemed to you? I seemed to pass over it on a surge of doing things until now. I walked around the boat, bought a magazine, drank some coffee, looked at Seattle & cursed it for hiding you, blessed it for having owned you for nearly 25 years, then went to bed – &, surprisingly, slept quite quickly. I noticed vaguely that there must have been a westerly swell in the straits, but I wouldn't let myself wake up till 6.30 & then dressed very slowly. Ate a sort of breakfast & came through the customs easily with my two flat fifties [cigarettes]! . . .

. . . and now here I am writing to you. But writing's dross & it's agony too in a way. In doing a host of more or less mechanical things one can almost forget for the time being. But writing to you seems so awful after being with you. And I've found another horribly painful thing too: remember what we said about forgetting one another's faces? I say to myself: "I won't forget Ann's. I can remember it in a hundred different moods, nearly all of them only a few hours ago, in the kitchen, while we were making coffee." And I can remember & see you right in front of me – but I have to stop quickly because it hurts so. So I suppose I'll shrink & shrink from bringing you right in front of me like that until I can't do it any more. And then I'll be miserable.

I'm wondering if I'm going to be able to work. That's so much alone & leaves me so much time to think of you or look at your photograph. But I'll just have to do it & I expect I shall be able to when I keep reminding myself: I'll just finish the first time through. Then I can send it to Ann. And after that I can say: just half-way through the second time & I can send that to Ann.

Oh darling, darling, darling, I love you so much – you know how much, almost. And you know, too, that I'll never care a least small bit about anyone else, even for an hour. Because Ann's precious, ever so precious: & all we have is precious. Sweetest heart, I love you utterly, completely, with every shade & side & kink of me, with all my best things, all my worst things, all my just ordinary things: good bad & indifferent, they're all yours, to use as you wish & keep as you wish. And every bit of you is mine. Sweetest & best, know you're lovely every way, mind & soul, heart & soul's soul, face & body, movements & thoughts & dreams. I adore you, darling heart, & six months will slip away somehow; even if it had to be six months of solid, unbroken agony, it'd be gone in the end. And we understand. We can break our own agony a little, steal away from it in doing things, awaken it & calm it at the same time by writing to one another. I love you, sweet, for always, but don't let's go away from each other when we're married . . .

Ann, my own, I didn't think of you enough last night. I'm horribly selfish when I'm being hurt & can only see my own hurt, don't try & save you enough. Sweetest, I'm sorry . . . I've got to try not to think of you too much. That's the hell of it: I want to think of you all the time, but if I do I'll just go into little pieces & if I don't the world will be vaguely empty, utterly miserable.

But I'm not going to be miserable. Nor are you. And I'll see you in ten days. In a little while I'll write again, Best Beloved. Love me always

Roddy

HARRY HARTMAN, BOOKSELLER
INCORPORATED
SEATTLE, WASHINGTON

Thursday at 5:30
[June 15, 1933]

Darling

I'm a good deal more of a coward than you are about writing . . .

This letter will do you no good, darling heart. I'm being selfish but after the first awful stab of waking up in the morning when all the conscious defenses are down and I only know that you've gone, I'm afraid to feel at all because it would surely hurt. And there are a thousand things to do, so I only do them with the feeling that, as you say, the world is vaguely empty. But I do belong to you, dearest, every second of every day, don't I?

Ann

Roddy and Ann were married in January 1934 and set up house-keeping in Campbell River, where they raised four children. Roddy died in 1976; Ann survived him by fourteen years.

WOMEN IN LOVE

Dr. Edith Bickerton Williams, known as Bud, and Dr. Frieda Fraser, or Lamb, lived near one another as children and fell in love in 1917 as students at Victoria College in Toronto. Edith attended the Ontario Veterinary College in Guelph, Ontario, graduated in 1941 – the second woman in Canada to become a vet – and practised in Toronto. A medical doctor, Frieda was a professor of epidemiology at the University of Toronto. The two women were frequently apart while pursuing their studies and their careers, but in 1939 they began to live together in the Fraser family home outside Burlington, Ontario. During their many separations, they wrote hundreds of letters.

[February 27, 1935]

Dear Lamb.

I'm better but I won't come in to town until Saturday . . .

    I'm getting up to-day for a bit.

    Here are some verses for you.

Something must have happened. Time
          stood still.
Here is our moment, glowing and
          alive.
It looks so sturdy I'm afraid
          it will
Live to be 70 or 75.
It can't be love. Love comes and
          goes so fast.
What do they call it when it seems to last?

    . . . I'll come in on Sat morn. and have lunch with you. The skiing
looks elegant – isn't it a shame to miss it?

               Yours

               B

After enduring a series of strokes, Edith died in 1979. Frieda survived until 1994.

FOR THIS RING

From 1937 to 1940 **Jean Blair Woodburn** *worked as a bookkeeper in a church-sponsored hospital in Hearst, a bar-and-brothel town in northern Ontario. During her first summer there she met Homer Dean, a student minister sent to the mission fields. The couple planned to be married in June 1940. That April, while Homer was finishing his theology degree at Emmanuel College, University of Toronto, he found time to buy Jean an engagement ring.*

St. Paul's Hospital
Hearst, Ontario
April 12, 1940

Dearest –

I should have put the above in Red Letters, because this is a red-letter day. Homer, darling, you perfectly wonderful one, no letter can possibly carry to you the feeling in my heart today.

As I sat and looked at my ring this morning, I kept telling it how sweet you are. The ring is quite perfect, I love its simplicity, I love the four little diamonds in the leaf design, I love the setting of the big center one.

When I got it this morning, after reading your note, I was so excited. But from the note I never suspected a diamond – I thought of a dinner ring, of a man's ring like you had looked at – but nothing as thrilling as a diamond.

I had locked myself in the bathroom, as the really only private place around here, and I'm glad I did, because I'm quite sure my hand shook as I read. I wore it down to dinner, and even though I had to serve the pie, made the wrong remarks several times to questions put to me, was so excited I could not eat much.

But no-one noticed it!!

I never realised I would be so self-conscious wearing it. I kept it under the table most of the time. I also never knew I would be so thrilled. When I came back upstairs, though, one of the girls noticed it – at last! – and in no time the news had spread like wildfire, and they were all around me . . . almost as excited as I was . . . and wanting to know all about it.

[The next day]

. . . I wish you had been here for all the excitement yesterday . . . it was really fun! . . . Before the night staff were up, someone had told them, and they came rushing to see it! Everyone loves it – one girl said it was the nicest one she had ever seen, and it is certainly the nicest one I!! Have ever seen!

But then, of course, I am more partial to the sender than she is . . .

This morning Dr Margaret [Arkinstall] came in the office, wondering, with a sober face, what made the office so bright – "far brighter than outside!" She finally discovered Why . . . my ring, of course!!

I must not rave on for ever – I will be writing again tomorrow, and until then my arms . . . and my lips . . . and my heart . . . are all yours.

Jean.

Homer Dean was ordained as a minister in the United Church in the month that he and Jean married. The couple moved to Parry Sound, where they spent four years before returning to southern Ontario.

A SLUSHY LETTER

Twenty-six-year-old **W.O. Mitchell** *dashed off this letter to Merna Hirtle (misspelling her first name) in bold, upward-slanting longhand.*

STRATHCONA HOTEL
"WHERE YOU FEEL AT HOME"
EDMONTON

Wednesday [August 1940]

Dearest:

Its no use. I told myself before you left that I wouldn't write you a slushy letter – that I'd only write once a week. Here I am writing again after having sent one last night. As to the second rule I'm afraid that feeling as I do tonight any letter I write would have to be shoveled though the mail. Well they can just bloody well shovel because Myrna when I'm in the mood to write a slushy letter – I write a slushy letter.

In the first place dear, I love you. I don't mean that I just 'love you' I mean that you've packed your overnight bag and moved into my heart – or maybe it was a steamer trunk because I have a feeling you'll be there for a long long time.

I hope you remembered to bring your tooth brush and have a room with a nice view of the lungs and liver. I have to add things like that because If I don't I'll be saying extravagant things like "you're part of me" and "I miss you horribly" and things like that. I have to watch myself in it because you are part of me now and I do miss you horribly. When you remember that I love you too you can see I'm in a bad way. I've found a way to help that though. The hotel lobby is a great place for strangers to pass through. I just sit in one of the chairs and when a stranger begins to pass through I stop him –

"Lovely day," I say brightly or "Dull day," dully if it is a dull day. "Been to Banff at all lately," I usually say.

If they say no I tell them you're there and my I miss you. I tell them all about you and then show them your picture. "She's one of the kind with black hair and dark eyes. Vest pocket edition and with the nicest["] – well you know dearest – shocked?

One fellow said, "Yes I know her[.] Daughter of the minister of my church. I agree heartily with you on that last. Noticed it myself numerous Sundays."

"Oh you did, did you," I said. He looked kind of funny walking out of the lobby, wearing a spitoon on his head.

I ran out of strangers to talk to about you, last night. That may explain why I'm so full of love tonight, dear. I love you, Myrna – so damn much it hurts. Good night my dear

Bill

Ahead of Bill Mitchell was the classic Who Has Seen the Wind *and other novels, as well as many radio and TV plays. Ahead of both Merna and Bill was a long marriage, about which Mitchell would write in a letter of sympathy to a widow: "Each of us are in our sixties – and believe me – can understand what it means. Each of us fears the loss of one from the other. The only balm is the sweet memory, which I'm sure you have."*

AUTUMN LOVE STORY

In the 1930s **Margaret Lawrence** *was a Roman Catholic magazine editor in Toronto who lectured to thousands of women across Canada on the embryonic women's rights movement. Benedict Greene, the son of a noted Jewish scholar, was the publisher of* Who's Who in Canada. *Their dissimilar faiths led him to jilt her after a secret love affair – only to come to her for comfort five years later when his wife died. Margaret called him "Baruch."*

July 21, 1942

My Beloved,

As you said today a woman is a complex being and your love is perhaps more complex than even a woman's – as sensitive and shy as a creature out of the deep Celtic forest – as shadowy and elusive as the light that filters through it. And you must help me always. For it is never you that makes me retreat, my own love, but things as they were and things as they are that are faint reminders of the past. For I am inclined to look for the past to repeat its history and am on guard against it with all my carefully reared defences called immediately into action.

I need so much of the open road and the bright strong light and the fine direct command. I do, beloved, I appeal to you for it, always.

It is too soon, perhaps, or at least not long enough, since I convinced myself you did not ever love me at all, nor ever would and that all the signs I thought I read of your love were made out of my own need. You see, my dearest, I used to say to myself it is greater to love than to be loved. It was not that I thought you did not love me but that I did not blame you. I did not struggle with you for your love. I saw you as a man pulled by the emotions of women – the primitive clutching need of women. I always believed, my own love, that you let me go because I needed or seemed to need you, least of all the women around you. I let you go easily, not just because of my code as a lady, but because of a deeper code – I believed it was what soul owed and owes to soul. My dearest, for me to be able to do that, there was a struggle so consuming within me it consumed many things. It consumed what little trust I had, beloved. Is that a hard thing for me to say to you? But we are fair with each other, so it is not hard. One does not quite trust oneself to love. For love, as I considered it afterwards was the least certain of things. It was not, as I have said, that I believed you loved me deeply. I believed that you loved me peculiarly. I was part of life to you, and suddenly I was a part you had no desire for any more, and so even that peculiar bond became in my soul just part of fading, dying mortal things.

And in all those years, not once, did I ever think it would return. I have written those things to you before, but it is a help to me and perhaps to you for me to write them again.

Baruch, my beloved, the suffering was so intense, so prolonged and under iron necessity to be hidden, well – I just cannot ever tell you. I may tell you that even in my close relation to my spiritual director, I mentioned this love, only casually, only generally, as something which finished me as far as mortal love was concerned, forever. It was only at the last of my training with him that it rose to the surface of my mind enough for me to acknowledge it, to myself and in confession, as guilty love and a sin. And it dominated the centre of my being, always. I never knew that, dearest. I thought I was a free soul. Women are complex, beloved and I, most of all women, am made up of complexities.

Now, I believe that I struggle back to you, as I struggled away from you. Now and then some faint thing vividly recalls the anguish of that past struggle. It could not be otherwise, could it? Nor would you have me otherwise, would you, dearest?

All is well, beloved. It was a miracle that we, when all else was over, might return to each other.

So much is strangely over for you, for me. I am still stunned a little by the strangeness of it and I think I may always be a little awed by it. But that will not hurt our love. Really, it will protect it.

I am so happy. These days are beautiful beyond words. It is the first time in years I have known surrender to days of dreaming and enjoyment of life. Life is so good, my beloved man, and in a woman's way, I am so utterly surrendered to its joy. Maybe, day by day, as we stay among these blue Laurentians and their mists, watching the great river's moods, I shall write a little of my love to you. It will only be a little, Baruch. For that is all as yet which can lift itself up to the surface; but this little part will be the sweet beginning of an autumn love story.

Your Margaret

Margaret and Benedict married in 1943; they were still together forty years later when she died at the age of seventy-six.

BE BRAVE, DARLING

On August 19, 1942, troops of the 2nd Canadian Infantry Division crossed the English Channel to attempt an amphibious assault at Dieppe on the coast of France. Among them was **James Walmsley,** *a private in the Essex Scottish Regiment, whose family had emigrated from England when he was an infant and had settled in Acton West, near London, before moving to Windsor, Ontario.*

[August 19, 1942]

Darling Maude
  & Jimmie

This is a note my dearest I hope you never have to receive. We are going into action, we are on the boat now. In a few hours Maude, I will have had my baptismal of fire & only God can know right now what my fate may be. Sweetheart, I want you to be the brave soldier I know you will be. Can only write to you precious, so if anything happens to me, comfort Mum & Dad and always let Jimmie know his Daddy loved him. I am placing my Faith in God dear, to bring me back safely to you. Always know Maude I love you & my last thoughts will ever be of you. Thank you darling for being the finest wife any man could ever wish to have.

Do not be unhappy love, only feel that what has happened was not in vain. May the world be better for what ever sacrifices any of us have to make. We shall win darling, and we are all going in to do our very utmost. God Bless you & Jimmie, Maude dear. I love you probably never more than at this minute

We are not even nervous dear, only tensed with the importance of the job we have to do. We have waited a long time for our chance and I know we will make Canada proud of us all.

Can't tell you precious of all the thoughts in my mind just now. They are filled with happy memories of our married life together.

Give my love to my Mum & Dad, your Mum & Dad, Flo & Ev, Bea & Jim, Grace, Doug & Dot & Anna Mae & Roy & all the kiddies. All my friends too darling.

Carry on & be brave darling. I love you.

Your always loving husband & Jimmie's Daddy.

Jimmie

Kiss Jimmie for me Maude & tell him Daddy wants
him to always be good to his Mummy.
I love you my dearest.

The Dieppe Raid was a disaster (see pages 79–81); Jimmie Walmsley was among the nine hundred inadequately trained Canadian soldiers who did not survive this "baptismal of fire."

NOW AND FOREVER

Sergeant Joseph Tye French Jr. was selected for the First Special Service Force, an amalgamation of Canadian and American soldiers who were to undertake sabotage operations in snow-covered regions of Europe. The Black Devils, as they were known, were assembled initially in Helena, Montana. Joe wrote to his darling Winnifred during his training, which included the handling of explosives, skiing, rock climbing, and parachuting from Douglas C-47 airplanes.

Helena, Montana
Sept. 3rd, 1942

Darling,

This note was left with Corporal Cope, at least in his pack, with the envelope addressed to you. He will send it only if I can't get to it to stop him.

That will mean curtains for me Hon, but when I go out I'll be thinking of you.

You know, all heroics aside, somebody has to do this job and the war must be won. We could never live under the Nazi regime or under Tokyo; it would mean abject slavery, and we're not slaves nor can we ever be, so I'm going out convinced that those behind will carry on.

I was never much on mush, but you know deep down you're the only girl in all the world for me, and I know the sacrifices I could call on for you at any time.

Good-bye darling, don't take it too hard. I wouldn't want it that way, now would I?

Its awfully hard to tell you all the things that are in my heart right now – go out and see Mother and Dad and tell them that you're all to tell each other that it isn't that I haven't had fun and after all anything else is only repetition.

Good-bye and be a soldier. I would do it all over again just the same way if I could.

I love you dearly, now and forever.

Joe

Joe injured his knee on his final test jump and never saw action in Europe. He completed his military service as a drill sergeant in Debert, Nova Scotia.

THE SAILOR'S BRIDE

Douglas Armour, a handsome Ontario boy, and Libby McCurdy Armour, a comely Cape Breton girl, had been married for little more than a year in December 1942 and were living in Halifax, expecting their first child in three months' time. Then Doug was lent to the Royal Navy for convoy duty in the North Atlantic. On the day he left, the couple exchanged sealed letters, to be opened when they were alone.

December 11 [1942]

To My Darling Wife,

There is no use telling you how much I love you in a letter just now because my whole body seems so filled with my love and devotion to you – you once said love was not an adequate word – I agree – but what is the correct word – I don't think there is a word that can describe our love and affection which has become stronger and stronger every minute we are together – so many minutes that we can have a thousand million happy memories to think on.

When you do remember these happy times, Darling, don't think with the regret that we can't be living them now but think of them as they were and how many many more happy times we are going to have when these next few months have whistled by – and whistle by they must my love because we need each other for our very existence. I give you my pledge, Darling, to look after your husband and work hard for a quicker reunion – I won't be foolish, Dear, because I no longer belong to my self but to you alone. I could write on and on but I want to crush you in my arms and kiss you and kiss you. My time is almost up, Darling, and you were a perfect wife these last two weeks and I found myself very very proud of you and your strength – not to "let go."

I love you my Bride and live only for the day when we shall be crushed in one another's arms on our second honeymoon.

Love,

Your husband and lover,

Douglas

XXXXX

I love you so much! how can I tell you better?

My Darling Husband,

I promise to try my best to be a good wife for your sake and the baby's, while you are away. It will be awfully hard, Darling, and it will never be a casual feeling, don't ever think that the longer you are away from me, this awful loneliness will wear off, for it will always be as it is now, only perhaps a little deeper. Darling, no other woman has ever loved her husband as I love you. Remember that sweet and I will always come to you wherever you are, no matter how dangerous the way may be. Our love is strong enough to take us through <u>anything</u>.

Sweetheart, I will live through the winter months, in the hope of your coming back to me and "your baby" in the summer. You have "got to" Doug and I will pray for our reunion next summer, every night. Darling, please try to feel my spirit of love within you all the time, for it will always be there, especially when you feel sad. I am glad and will thank God that I can feel your spirit and love within me so easily. I will take good care of your baby Dear, he will be so lucky to have such a wonderful father. I am so terribly proud of you Dear and you have made me happy and contented. The time is drawing close Doug, and I will try to be strong after you leave. I will write you soon again.

I adore you darling and I will love you for eternity,
Your
Libya.

These were the first of 850 letters Doug and Libya sent one another in the seventeen months Doug was serving as a torpedo officer in Scotland. Their son was born the following March, but Doug wouldn't see him until he came home in March 1944. Doug and Libya met at the Château Laurier in Ottawa – without the baby. "We wasted no time [before] making love," Libby recalled.

LIKE NO OTHER

Percy John Brown was stationed in Rome during the Second World War when his wife, Hilda, gave birth to a baby girl in Toronto on January 23, 1943.

[1943]

To my Darling Daughter Ruth

> Little girl I have not seen,
> I greet you from afar.
> Hair like silky mist of gold,
> Eyes that hold a star –
> And in your rounded baby face
> (Miracle like no other)
> I catch a glimpse of all I love
> In the smile of your Mother.

After the war John returned home to Hilda and Ruth.

PASSIONATE DREAMS

Walter Scragg served in England, France, and Germany as an auxiliary service supervisor with the Canadian War Services of the Salvation Army during the Second World War. Two years after signing up (and winning the Canadian Volunteer Service Medal), he wrote to his wife, Pearl, at home with their daughter in Toronto.

Aurich, Germany
June 45

Dear Heart,
Just finished a fast game of table tennis and I'm still going 60 m.p.h.
I love you, all of time, but especially now.

Dearest I want to fold you deep inside my heart so you can never be away from me again.

The consciousness of your love is with me every day & night. The last thing I see as I turn out the light is your smiling face by my bed.

No wonder then, that after I am blessed with passionate dreams.

I wish there was some definite way in which I could demonstrate my affection for you. I do want you to be sure of my love all the while.

Dearest, how long it is since that dismal day when you kissed me in parting. I think I've told you that when you sent Carol in to sit upon my knee as I sat at the radio I practically broke down.

I was and am amazed at your composure. Perhaps as you say, you could not realize that I was really going away for so long.

I'm sure that since that time you have and I also have experienced the agony of loneliness. I got over it partially when W. Bunton was here but this new fellow Herb Brown while nice enough doesn't seem to be the same. I hope Carol has helped you to overcome the ache of being alone.

Dear One, my own precious jewel, I trust our sacrifice will soon be over, I know I pray so every night & day.

Love & kisses to both of you
Walter

After Walter came home in 1946, he and Pearl had a son, Vernon, who said of his father's letter: "It is filled with the deepest love ever, and continued throughout their lives."

LOVE AND REMEMBRANCE

Donald Arthur Fawthrop and Anna Keays Edey grew up around the corner from one another in Cornwall, Ontario. In 1939, when war was declared, they were both sixteen. Donnie enlisted in the Royal Canadian Air Force in 1941 and received his wings in Yorkton, Saskatchewan. Anna, meanwhile, trained to be a nurse at the Montreal General Hospital. They were married in July 1943 and lived together briefly in Belleville, Ontario, before Donnie was sent overseas as a fighter pilot with the rank of pilot officer and later flying officer in the 421 ("Red Indian") Squadron.

Jan 16/45

My Dearest Anne:

I am packing this a little early but I would rather it would be early than late. Also Toots this is <u>half</u> of the little surprise and secret I mentioned in one of my letters.

Once more to use an over worked term this will be your first birthday that we have been parted, and I hope and am sure it will be the last one. So seeing where I was I figured this gift would sort of be approp[r]iate and would also serve as a memoir of the [occasion]. I don't know much about perfumes Toots other than Lotus but the girl in the perfumerie said it was pretty good and I remember of hearing of Lelong so we bought it. You see Anne, Dorothy, Bill's wife's, birthday is on Apr 4, so he made a purchase too.

I hope you received this ok Anne and that the top stays on ok. I opened it to check the top and also add some extra packing so that explains the torn cel[l]ophane. Also you will notice that the Christmas seals have come in handy after all.

So my Darling my every thought is with you on your twenty-second birthday and may we see many more of them together. I love you Anna and as you once said if it is at all possible I just love you more every day.

Your loving husband
Donnie

When Anna received this letter, she had been a widow for twenty-two days. Donnie had been killed while returning from an operational flight over Germany. Anna eventually remarried and raised two children in Toronto. She has visited Donnie's gravesite in Belgium; the inscription on his headstone reads, "There is a link death cannot sever. Love and remembrance last forever."

ALONE IN THREE HILLS

In 1947, before **Walter Dickie** *and his wife, Evelyn, began their thirty-five-year marriage, Walter was employed by an electrical supply company as a lines inspector in Three Hills, Alberta. He wrote Evelyn many letters, often commenting on his experiences in keeping the power going for the town and a large prairie district. They were married in 1948 and raised five children in Drumheller. In this letter, he indicated the town he was writing from with a little sketch of three hills.*

July 8/47.

Hello my Darling Devil,

I really should be going to bed, sweet, as it's after ten, but I'll be very daring tonight and stay up real late.

It was sure warm around here today, but I didn't mind it too much. I took the truck and went up to Delburne for the day. Had a very nice day all by myself, but didn't have much luck with the gophers. Guess they all hide when they see me coming now.

I was glad to hear that you people got home safely that Sun. night. I was going to suggest that you all spend the night here – only I had no place for Harry & Betty to sleep.

Has your Dad really decided to move to the coast, or is this another false alarm? It must be great to be a member of a wealthy family. You never told me, darling, that your parents had bags of money. How much of a dowry has the old gentleman allowed for his daughters? Not that I'm interested in anything as cold & heartless as a beautiful woman with a lot of money!! However, darling, I may be able to overlook the fact that you have a lot of money – maybe we can give it away to some poor widow with fourteen kids.

It's a good thing I didn't go over to Drum[heller] last Sunday sweet, because we had one hell of a lightning storm here Sunday morning which kept us working all day Sunday & most of Monday before we got things going again. I was almost glad something did happen Sunday to help pass the day.

The good people of The Hills got quite a surprise Sun night when I went to church for the first time. I went to the Knox, but I doubt if I'll go back again. There were about forty people in church and among them were thirty-nine of the poorest singers that God ever put breath into. It was a crime the way they murdered those Hymns. I would have got up and walked out only the usher wouldn't give me back my two bits.

I've started doing a little cooking here in my humble abode, but until I get a few more dishes I don't think I'll be able to make a pie exactly like gramma used to make.

I'm sure looking forward to seeing you this weekend, darling. Hope nothing comes along to change my plans. Seeing you every two weeks is not nearly enough. I'm lonesome all over again a few minutes after I leave you. Guess I'll have to write to head office and see if they will buy me a private car. I think they should do something about it, because I can't do any work in Three Hills when my heart is somewhere else.

Well my darling I think I'll make myself a spot of tea and then take myself off to bed. If I put plenty of sugar in it I may be lucky enough to dream of the sweetest girl in the world. Good night my sweet

As ever.

Walter

Shortly before Walter's death in 1983, Evelyn found herself procrastinating over a final chore in her fall housecleaning. She complained to Walter about her failure to clean the bedroom drapes. After he died, she became solitary and inactive in her grief. One night she dreamed that Walter said to her, "Don't you think it's time to clean those drapes in the bedroom?" She believes that was his way of telling her to get on with her life.

BEDTIME STORY

*This letter from a wife, **Yolande Lafrance**, to her husband, Marcel Faucher, was written in French.*

Montreal, 27 Oct. 1965

My sweet adorable love,

You must have found me so lazy this week, but you must excuse me. I would have written sooner, but I would have been saying how upset I was about you-know-what, and I couldn't bring myself to send you such a letter. Now I know that I was right, because I would have worried you for nothing. My friend arrived this morning. I can't tell you how relieved I am. We were lucky, my teddy-bear – and in future we'll be more careful, right?

I hope that all goes well for my president this week, and that you do well in your exams. Your little girl has worked very hard, and it was all for you. You know, teddy-bear, I think about you very often, and sometimes I wonder what my life would be like if I couldn't think about you all the time. I imagine I'd feel that something was missing, that there was a kind of emptiness.

You know what? It's been a long time since I've worried that one day you might not love me any more, and abandon me. You remember how often I talked about that last year, and how afraid I was. This year, it never crosses my mind, it's as if I know that it's impossible. We love each other too much to leave each other. And you too, my loving little husband, you must be sure. Sure, absolutely sure that I love you too much to leave you some day.

I feel entirely committed to you, my teddy-bear, and that will never change. I thought about it so much, as I should, before committing myself that now nothing could make me turn away. Nothing – unless someday you cheat on me; I don't know how I'd react to that. But if you love me very dearly all your life, forever, you need never worry that I might leave you . . .

And yet for the moment I must leave you, because it's time for little girls to go beddy-byes.

Have a splendid weekend, my shaggy teddy-bear, my lovely teddy-bear, be good and above all be careful. I will think about you. I am sure that this weekend will do you a great deal of good.

Bye Bye – I kiss you on your two ears, on your nose, on your fur – Yum yum yummmmmmmmm –

Your little wife,
Yolande
X X X

PLANTE, THE POET

*Born in Shawinigan Falls, **Jacques Plante** had a thirty-year career in hockey as goalie for the Montreal Canadiens, New York Rangers, St. Louis Blues, Toronto Maple Leafs, and Boston Bruins. Hypochondriac, superstitious, phobic, and eccentric, Plante was an innovative goalie, one of the first to don a protective mask and to wander out of the crease to handle the puck. He liked to knit his own tuques and to read classical literature. On the road often during his marriage, he sent home poetic messages in French to his Swiss-born wife, Caroline Raymonde Plante.*

April 1, 1978

To My Beloved Wife

Rising this morning,
I would have wished, like a small canary,
To whisper to you in a very soft voice,
Of all that propels me toward you.

First, it is your brilliant eyes,
Which make me your lover,
Because a single glance from you,
Makes me shiver and drives me mad.

Your smile like the morning dew,
Comes every day to satisfy my hunger,
For all that emerges from you,
A word, a song, even a gentle sigh.

Your walk is a dance step,
That never loses its rhythm,
For ten years now I have been admiring you,
And as time goes by, the more I desire you.

Like a stripteaser, you slip from your clothes with grace,
And into my arms you softly slide,
Nights pass by as does the wind,
But each morning, we embrace lovingly in each other's arms.

Have a wonderful day and be happy,
Above all, do not have empty hours,
Think only that I love you,
And mostly that you are my queen.

Jacques

*Caroline lives in Switzerland, five minutes from the cemetery where
her husband is buried (he died of cancer in 1986). She visits his grave
almost daily. "I had twenty beautiful years with him," she says. "I'm
still in love and Jacques is still here, living in my house."*

COUNTING THE WAYS

At a loss for words, college student **Rick Beaver** *called on the heavy-
weights of English literature for inspiration to express his love for the
beautiful Patty Reuter. But Coleridge, Blake, Shakespeare, Longfellow
(and Nimoy and Schultz) failed him. In the end, he found his own
voice.*

[1982]

Dear Patty,

Hi. Probably heard of me before, Rick Beaver from "Kinesiology". I'm that short, light and plain guy who's been watching you for a while now. Well, don't feel bad if you haven't noticed me before. I usually go unnoticed by women as beautiful as yourself.

What I have to say isn't easy. In fact, I find it so hard to express verbally that I have to try to do so in a letter. How can I start to express myself and the very deepest, personal feelings I hold for you? I cannot. You cannot. Even Coleridge nor Blake, Shakespeare nor Longfellow, Nimoy nor Schultz, do not convey the feelings I have. Colridge says "To meet, to know, to esteem, to love and to part, makes up life's tale of many a feeling heart". Blake explains "I love thee as the mother loves the child". No Patty, what I feel for you goes too deep for words.

Words don't hold the desperation of love; the feeling of vulnerability and helplessness or lon[e]liness and solitude. Simple words cannot express peacefulness and content, or happiness and ecstasy. No, the way to tell you how I feel is in my eyes and in my touch.

I long to touch you, so gentle, so softly. And when I look at you, my eyes well up with the beginnings of tears. Tears that say how much I care for you. Your touch melts my hardened heart, breaks down the carefully constructed walls I've built around it. Your gaze speaks to me with eyes so deep they seem to bare the very soul.

You are so, so beautiful. Today I watched you from the other side of the cafeteria and thought how all other eyes must have noticed you as well. You really do have that light that shines from the face!

Patty, if I could tell you how happy you've made me and how good I feel with you, it could only be done with 3 easy words. I LOVE YOU! Browning says, "How do I love thee? Let me count the ways". I love you only 1 way. With all my heart and soul.

Love <u>Rick</u>

Rick and Patty are now married and live in Barrie, Ontario.

A SECOND CHANCE

*Two decades ago **Jane Richardson** broke up a couple of times with her boyfriend, Ross Atkinson, while they were students at the University of Waterloo. Two years after their last parting, she realized her mistake and just after graduation asked him back into her life.*

May 18, 1984

Dear Ross,

Yes this is me writing to you su[r]prising as it may seem. Its very important for me to communicate my thoughts to you right now and I thought a letter would be the best way.

I guess you are enjoying your holidays before starting back at school in the fall. I am doing likewise here at home – its given me lots of time to think and as I expected, you have taken up a large percentage of that time. I miss you Ross. You may scoff at this but at least respect my honesty in telling you so. I know Convocation is coming up pretty soon and it will pass by just as fast and with this will be the last time I see you until a class reunion sometime in the future. I don't relish the thought of seeing you the next time with wife and kids knowing that you and I might have had a chance together.

I know I have a lot of explaining to do for past judgements and decisions – this is one of the hardest things for me to do because its a reflection of my own faults. But this is something I would like to explain in person.

I . . . really valued the way you listened to what I said, the way I felt uninhibited talking with you, the way we could laugh so much together but most of all I valued the feeling of equality we had. I used to think these qualities were a dime a dozen in guys. I have since then realized how rare these qualities are and how I passed them up when I called it quits. I don't regret the decision I made two years ago – I have needed the time to realize what I gave up. I do regret how I went about it. It wasn't until I felt the pain I put you through that I realized how awful the experience was for you.

I was really glad to see you down in Florida. It was a pleasant but confusing feeling which I tried to keep to myself. I was really disappointed we didn't run into each other on our last day and the thought of only seeing you again at Convocation upsets me.

I really want to give it a try again Ross and I'm not looking at it in a temporary sense just to pass time. Please give me another chance – I know it can work for us.

See you Friday,
Love Jane

"The conclusion to this story was that we got back together," writes the letter's author, now Jane Atkinson. "We have been happily married for fifteen years and have a precious eight-year-old daughter."

A GREAT GRANDFATHER

*Throughout the 1990s **Robert Young** of Fredericton, New Brunswick, sent a series of letters across the continent to Amy Brannen, a granddaughter in her late teens who was living in Vancouver.*

Dear Amy,
"The clearest way into the universe is through a forest wilderness"
John Muir 1838-1914
Thank you Amy for wanting to see some of my writing. You represent my future. To ignore the past is to risk repeating it. Perhaps from my words you will see some of the whys in the world you inherit.

The above quote reminds me of our Celtic past. In Scotland, Ireland and Wales, the celts knew trees were sacred . . . The circle in the celtic cross represents the continuity of creation, you and I are very small but important parts of that circle . . .

We share the celtic cross. Do not hesitate to hug a tree it is our best friend and neighbour and protects our air, water, soil and climate . . .

Granddad

"earth laughs in flowers" Ralph Waldo Emerson 1803-1882

Many's a time Nana and I enjoyed a handful of daisies or dandelions presented to her by your mother or one of her sisters.

As a man I smiled – for the joy it gave me to see the reaction of the giver and receiver to this simple act.

Respect and dignity come from the thoughtful act. Money and power cannot buy, or produce, the fact of giving and receiving what is worthless in the eyes of the commercial world.

How wonderful of creation to produce flowers – the result of happiness in acts of creation. We celebrate creation every time we stop to smell – or pick and give – flowers. Because earth laughs in flowers.

Granddad

THE COWBOY'S FILLY

*In 1994 Darlene Kernot met **Dan Hauck** at a friend's wedding in Alberta. Darlene wrote that Dan was a "Calgary cowboy," tall, dark, and of course handsome. Dan pulled up his stakes in Calgary and moved to Winnipeg, where he and Darlene bought a home. A truck driver, Dan wrote cards and letters to Darlene every day while he was on the road. The couple were engaged when Dan wrote this letter.*

[September 1998]

Well soon to be Mrs. Darlene Hauck. I love you Darlene very much. You are really the the woman I want to be with. You got the biggest and warmest heart I have ever seen. Wow making up for lost time sure is fun. So relax dear. You got me for the rest of your life. You make loving you so easy. Your a good partner. Even better now that you know I am going to be your husband. Did I say I love you Darlene. You sure make me feel like I belong. Remember this. You are a wonderful woman and I know I made the right choice moving out to Winnipeg. I followed my heart and look what it got me. "You" It's been over three years now and look what has taken place. You sure put me on the right track. I guess you really want me alot. Well I guess it looks like you got me now. I am not turning back. I like what looks ahead for us now. You make me a proud man. It sure is a good feelin. You got one good handle on me and our future together. Your the real woman I want. As you probably already know that I cherish you. Also spoil you too. But your worth it sweetheart. What also make me feel good about us is a don't have to worry about you going for someone else. Your just not that type of woman. I really know how much you love me so I don't have to worry at all dear. I love you sweetheart. So after everything is done in Calgary we will go forth. Thanks to you this wouldn't be happening to me. Your wonderful. Have I told you lately how much I love you Darlene. You sure give me a comfortable feeling about myself. It adds less stress on the job I'm doing which is stressful as is lready. I hope your reading this letter very carefully dear. You always called me a cowboy from the West so everytime you think of me think "cowboy hug."

I love you my sweetness. Now you can bother me for some attention.

Lots of love
From your future husband
Dan
XXX OOO XX OO

Before they could marry, Dan died of a heart attack, at age forty-one.

FILIAL AFFECTION

Kathy Norstrom, of Armstrong, British Columbia, wrote: "This may not be the type of love letter you are looking for, but I suspect that there will be other readers, like myself, who have special letters from family members." **Kirk Duncan** *is her younger brother.*

September 6, 1998

Kathy,

I just got back from the mall after spending 20 minutes scanning the birthday card section. A card seems like such an insignificant way to acknowledge such a momentous occasion as a 40th birthday, but under the circumstances it will have to do. I had a few small chuckles at some cards and got a lump in my throat from others, however none of them truly reflected the way I feel about "my" sister.

It is impossible to sum up our 38 year relationship in a few words, but I will note a few thoughts that come to mind. It is not just the occasion of your birthday that reminds me of how important you were, and are, in my life. I am given daily reminders as I witness Heather and Sean's relationship grow. There is truly something special about having an older sister. Unfortunately Sean doesn't know how lucky he is . . . yet! I know how lucky I am. You were there to guide me and protect me as I stumbled through my early childhood. After all, you had 19 months more experience than I did (and still do!). Sure, there were picket fences that got in our way from time to time, butt (pun intended) I was always quick to forgive you. I also know that there were times when you wished I didn't exist, but I know you didn't mean it. Our childhood bond always strengthened in the face of adversity (an older brother) and we could always count on support from our biggest allies (Mom and Dad). As we got older though, the 19 months that separated us seemed to grow. There were times when the only thing we had in common was a surname. I suppose that is natural, but I did miss my big sister during that "stage" of life. Unfortunately (or maybe fortunately) I seemed to have lost all memory of my teenage years. I am reminded by pictures and "happy hour" stories that we were the luckiest kids in the world to have lived on Okanagan Lake. Oh how I wish I was more appreciative back then. I hope Mom and Dad know how thankful we are. I am just kidding about the memory loss, but the 70's flew by so fast that I wish I could do it all over again. In the 80's that 19 month gap seemed to shrink to nothing as once again you took me (and Laura) under your protective wing. Your little brother was growing up . . . and shacking up! How stressful it must have been for you. I remember the "do you know what you are doing" lecture you gave me. As it turned out, you had nothing to worry about.

Then it was my turn to worry about you. Not only did you leave me behind in Calgary and move to Rimbey, Alberta. You lived in a mobile home and started dating a younger man. Oh how I worried! Actually, Rimbey didn't seem too bad and the trailer was kinda cozy, but a younger man . . . is this the sister I thought I knew?? Then you brought this guy down to Calgary to meet your "little" brother. How stressful that was . . . for all of us! I knew my opinion meant something (didn't it??). What if I didn't like the guy. Well, you know how that story ends. Ray and I were like long lost pals. I was more worried about what would happen if the relationship didn't last. Ray is the younger brother I never had!!

Well enough about the past. You are turning 40! If it makes you feel better you can think of it as the 21st anniversary of your 19th birthday! (I saw that in one of the cards). I can't say too much about turning 40 since I am not far behind you. I do hope that you look to the past with a sense of achievement and to the future with excitement. Although we no longer have our surname in common, we do have fantastic spouses, the cutest kids in the world, wonderful parents and a great brother. It is nice that I can write this letter knowing that I see you often and speak to you frequently. Not all families are as close as ours. I am also glad to know that you and I and our respective families will always be close, after all Kathy, you will always be my big sister.

Have a wonderful birthday Kathy. I love you.

Kirk

LOVE REAFFIRMED

Fiona Bially and her husband, Chris, in Belle River, Ontario, were dealing with a career change and a brand-new baby when, approaching their second anniversary, Fiona felt the need to renew her commitment to Chris.

September 2, 1999

To my dear husband,

When I told you I would love honour and cherish you, I didn't mean only when times were good. I didn't mean until the passion of new romance had faded. I didn't mean only when we were healthy and rich. I meant I would love you with my whole heart every day, I meant that I would honour you always. I meant that I would cherish every single day and memory we have ever made and will ever make together. I meant it until the day God tears us apart and decides that our lives together on earth are over. But even then I know that you will wait for me; or I for you in whatever place waits for us after the life is through.

For the kind of love we share together never dies; only grows and grows.

Your loving wife,
Fiona

EVERY HOUR IS SAVED

*Susan Bigland-Witton, of Meaford, Ontario, is the widow of **Harry Witton**, the "Ulysses" of this letter. Harry was a professional photographer (and church organist and choir master) who was employed in the photographic division of Braun Canada when he met Susan, a teacher. She helped him create one of his slide shows, "Pineapple Paradise" (a portrait of six Hawaiian islands), which toured Canada for three years. In 1972 Harry described in a letter to Susan the special person he wanted in his life. In part, he wrote: "This woman would be the central point of my existence, and one for whom my daily goal would be to bring some undefinable magic into her life." After Harry learned he had cancer and that nothing could be done to arrest it, he wrote to Susan, beginning with a quotation from*

Tennyson's "Ulysses," a poem he frequently quoted, and mentioning Crows' Nest, their home in Meaford, and his cruiser, the Harry Karry.

June 27/00

"And of one to me little remains; but every hour is saved" thanks to the caring help of my Life Mate.

Many years ago I asked myself how I could have been so fortunate as to have found you, and that feeling has never left me. My life has been surrounded by love, warmth and support at every turn. The mutual interests we share and pursue have made every day special and are often relived now in my quiet times. Our adventures in Hawaii, Holland and Sweden; the perfect day with which we were blessed in Agawa Canyon. The many theatre productions enjoyed together and before or after dinners; the special meals at Crows' Nest – all have combined to make a life that many people must envy.

You spoke the other day about us sometimes living on the edge of the ridiculous brought to mind velcroing curtains on the Harry Karry. I'll bet that people who do that task with their clothes on don't have half as much fun! Then, the moments while we were trying to get music and words to time together for the slide shows, plus the excitement when the finished product finally hit the screens. All these played their part in producing a perfect life script . . .

Several nights ago I awoke – I presume after a dream – in which I had been criticizing myself for departing so soon and leaving you alone. Fully awake I realized that you would not hold with my feeling that way. I know that with the friends we have you will do well on your own. Remember, I will only be as far away as the next room where you may share again the happy memories of our life together.

Thank you for helping plan and carry out the things on my list. It is a heavy load physically and mentally for you, but is making the final steps for me so pleasant. I hope my arrangements are good enough to make things smoother for you.

I have had . . . some moments of weepiness when it hit on me that this would be the last time I would be seeing or doing something. Thankfully the memory of time spent previously doing these brought me back to a happy feeling. You were there to help make it right, as you will be up to the end.

I will not be around long enough to list all the good things for which you have been responsible. Will I have memory of them on the other side? Just in case not, am making the most of reliving them now.

Some recent 'flash backs' were the 'Love Is' notes, and the incredible valentines, also the countless hours enjoying the closeness, touch and feel of each other. I can only hope that your life was enriched and made better by being with me as has mine with you and can only repeat again "how could I have been so fortunate?"

This letter has been written and rewritten in my mind but time tells me it should be put to paper while I am still able. Also debated was if it should be left in the S.D. [safety deposit] box or presented now. The latter was chosen as I would like to know that you are fully aware of my feelings about you and our life . . .

All my Love

Ulysses

Harry was seventy-nine when he died, on November 17, 2001, twenty-nine years to the day after his first assignation with Susan: "Although watching a loved one's body succumb to the ravages of cancer, and, even though I was emotionally and physically exhausted," Susan wrote, "it really was an honour and a privilege to be present to send 'Ulysses' on his final voyage . . . 'beyond the utmost bound of human thought.'"

A WONDER TO SHARE

*In the spring of 2000, after both had recovered from divorces, **Randolph Parker** and Johanne Brodeur were introduced by a friend. Randolph is an artist on Saltspring Island, British Columbia; Johanne is head of Music Therapy at the Victoria Conservatory of Music (a ferry ride away, on Vancouver Island). Although they spend weekends together, they live apart. Johanne wrote: "One day our lives*

*might be united on a daily basis but until this day comes, letters will
continue to play a magical and essential role in our love."*

09 January, 2001

My dear sweet Johanne,

6:12 a.m.
Darkness wraps itself around the studio
It is silent yet loneliness does not dwell here
The warmth of the studio bathes my spirit
You fill my memory
Photos of you here and there
A thousand little memories of your visit and our time
together makes me long for you, wonder, marvel and smile
Thanks goes out to the mysterious void that surrounds me
The first music of the day is by Harold Moses
Drums, voices, waves, wind, splashes of sunlight, heart
beats and spirits
The familiar routine, water in the plastic containers, brushes
felt, palette set out and breathing
The sound of a weeping ethereal viola brings you close to me
Brings my thoughts to your house, to your room and to
your bed
There is a special drama about this life that I love to
breathe in and you are now part of it
You have brought me love, affection, wonder, joy, beauty,
sweet memories, passion
Your warm body, hugs and a simple touch
You have also brought me yourself, the complex self, part
woman, part child
A strong spirit
Mingled with a radiant light
A light from a thousand candles burning in your own temple
In the temple is a softness, a place of self healing and a
place with pain

When we are together we mingle our spirits and bring the
    soft inner self to each other
We each have within us a realm of beauty that is a wonder
    to share
Thank you Johanne for inspiring me to think and feel this
Love, Randolph

AS LIFE MOVES AHEAD

*Nicholas Beresford was twelve when he died after a year-long strug-
gle with acute lymphoblastic leukemia. During his illness and after
his death, his mother,* **Susan Beresford,** *used the act of writing "to
empty the rooms in my head that fill with thoughts, memories and
the insatiable anguish that clamors for its due attention." She wrote
this letter to her husband, Frank, who was working out of town. They
live in Castlegar, British Columbia, with their first-born son, Frankie.*

Thursday, August 16, 2001

Hi Honey,
It is difficult when our grief and pain over losing our son goes in cycles.
For a time you have some relief and manage to keep the hurt from
taking over your heart and then you hurt so much and for so long that
you think you might lose your mind. I am also finding this time very
hard and I am not taking much interest in anything and find it hard to
get out of bed in the morning. At least I am home and even though I
miss you, I have familiar things and people around me. You are suffering more because you are working away from home and that is
always very hard by itself.

    I understand your sense of time slipping by and your urgency
at needing to be home with your family and not losing out on
the time when we could be loving each other. I got to thinking about
time and years and I discovered that I felt my almost 40 years was a
very long time. F-O-R-T-Y years! Count them, 1, 2, 3, 4, 5, 6, 7 . . .

it takes a while to count to 40. Most things that were manmade in the year 1961 when I was born wouldn't still be around in good shape and functioning. Cars, TV's, washing machines etc. are junked and in the scrap yard. Houses are being renovated or torn down and replaced. There are no animals still alive that were born in that year except some turtles, elephants and whales.

My point is that I have lived 40 years and I may live another 40 years. Your Mom is 82! Wow! That is a very long time. Your Grandma was 98! I don't think I want to live that long and have my boobs hanging down to my knees. Not a pretty sight. Anyway, what will be, will be and we need to take life as it comes because we both know we have no control over the future and the nature of things. And I am beginning to look at death as a friend that comes and takes all the pain and hurt away. And though I hope there is a heaven and I see sweet Nicholas and my Mom and Dad again, if there is no heaven, at least I won't be hurting and missing Nick anymore and I know that he has no more fear and is at peace.

Soon, we will be together with no plans of you leaving for work. Our lives will unfold the way it was meant to be as life moves ahead. Frankie and I will be here for you when you come home and I hope you can relax a bit until that time comes.

With much love,

Susan

THE FORGOTTEN WOMAN

Some letters cannot be sent; they are written to ease the pain of the writer, as was this one by **Me**, *a woman in Nova Scotia, who asked that her name not be used: "Rather I would like it to stand as the voice of the crowd – the wallflower crowd that is. There are lots of us."*

[2001]

Dear _____

I'm 60 now, my hands are twisted, face lined, breasts sagged, but the sparkle in your eyes, outshines the sun. With body bent and whitened head your smile yet stops my heart for long seconds and I remember when we were young and fierce.

There on that village street, I smile a tight little smile and wave and say hello to you and your wife, she whom you chose, all those years ago.

Time has eased my loss, diminished slightly that arresting heart pain that shortens breath and I pass on by. Sometimes laughing and talking together you don't even notice me. And that is as it should be between two who love. I'm much calmer these years and don't cry to see your clothes co-mingled on the clothesline, twisting and dancing together in the wind, as once we tangled in the bedsheets ourselves, all those years ago. Your sweat dropped and seared my breast. Unfortunately my breast has not quite been able to forget nor have I although I have tried, and tried and failed.

You seem happy enough, the two of you and your children. I keep busy and do my best and weep sometimes in the depth of night. Oh my no, not every night, not for years. Maybe the last time I saw you together at the dance it was. I gave that up, the dancing I mean. Now I read silly love stories and snivel at happy endings on Saturday nights when the music is loud. Perhaps next time, next life maybe you or someone might love me and hold me and want me. It seems a simple enough fantasy.

yours truly

me

THE MAGICAL ELLE

*On September 12, 2001, a day after the terrorist attacks on the World Trade Center and the Pentagon, **Frank Williams** kept a first date with Catherine Mitchell. Both lived and worked in the Lower*

Mainland of British Columbia. They had arranged to have coffee but kept talking for three hours that evening. They fell in love. Catherine spent the next few weeks alternately horrified by the aftermath of September 11 and euphoric because of Frank. At Christmas his present was accompanied by this letter, which she called "the most beautiful thing" she had ever read.

[Christmas 2001]

Catherine

When I first started thinking about what to get you for Christmas I was full of great ideas . . .

I was going too get you a really good umbrella – to protect you from rough weather

I was going to get you a cookbook that had the world's best recipes – to enrich your collection and culinary options

I was going to get you that special edition Barbie – to join your other lovely ladies

I was going to get you a little silver lighthouse – to symbolize how I feel when the storms of my life surround me and I think of you

I was going to get you a toy or two from one of those adult shops – for, ah, well, you know . . .

I was going to get you an exotic candle – to represent the light you bring into my world

I was going to buy myself a bottle of the perfume you wear – so I could pull it out of my pocket, like an addict, and take a quick shot whenever I need to be reminded that you are out there somewhere and I will be with you again

I was going to get you a crystal rose – because of the elegance and beauty you have added to my days

But when I was actually out shopping, I could find no satisfaction in any combination of these things. My budget was too restricting and whatever blend I could conceive seemed contrived and much too sensible. I wandered and wandered through the malls and stores and wondered what to do. Then, just before a mild desperation was setting in, in an obscure corner of an uncharted mallway, a little voice called

to me. I followed it and was surprised by what seemed a strange man-
ifestation of something I still cannot name. The little thing spoke to
me quite clearly in that it said, "I am the gift that you must acquire
and present. Buy that box over there and hide me in it. I am all you
need and I promise I will whisper in Catherine's heart. I will tell her of
your love. Do not doubt me. Buy me now before that woman behind
you discovers me, or that brain of yours analyzes me into oblivion."

I did what I was told. I hope you like it. I hope it was telling the
truth.

Love

Frank

*The gift was a ceramic elephant nestled inside a leopard-cloth box.
Elle, the elephant, now watches over Frank and Catherine in their
new love.*

THE ART OF THE ORDINARY
"No time for repining"

M ost Canadians spend their lives outside the orbit of dramatic events – the great upheavals, wars, and other disasters that prompted so much of the correspondence in this book. And yet the small diurnal dramas – local incidents, happenings at home, the frictions of the workplace – can also inspire fascinating letters. It may be that the letter-writers are living their lives in special places. That they bring intriguing backgrounds to otherwise commonplace activities. Or that they offer distinctive perceptions or write stylishly in describing the everyday.

Joan Bond of Steinbach, Manitoba, described good letter-writing in a letter she sent us: "It isn't a laundry list of facts, but a blending of emotion and intellect, like a rose unfolding its petals, revealing intimacies. A good letter isn't just weather coverage and carefully composed rhetoric. A good letter offers revelation and reflection about personal triumphs and tragedies; it shares news – all those trivial tidbits that mean so much. It is writing as if you were talking, as if the recipient was in the same room. 'Is grandmother finally over her cold?' 'Did Dad really make a pizza with anchovies?' "

Novelists shed light on the universal by rendering the particular. The best letters achieve the same thing. Strong Buffalo, a Peigan rancher who sailed across the Atlantic in 1895, described his journey in unaffected prose that suddenly lets the reader view the world through native eyes. The art of the ordinary is to transcend itself, and the letters in this chapter add that extra something to daily pursuits, making them extraordinary. As Joan Bond observed, "The hand-written letter carries such emotional weight, far heavier than any Canada Post scale can weigh."

FORLORN CORRESPONDENTS

*In 1851 the twenty-three-old **Sandford Fleming**, a brilliant Scot who had spent six years in Canada, was making a name well beyond his expertise in science and civil engineering. He would one day be knighted for his many contributions: overseeing the engineering surveys for a transcontinental railway; supporting a telecommunications cable across the Pacific; and fathering standard time zones around the globe. A summary of his diary for February 24, 1851, notes: "Breakfasted at Ellah's Hotel with Mr Ruttan and Hon^{bl} James Morris, Post Master General, designing Postage Stamp for him . . . Engraving, sketching & drawing for Mr Ruttan." The stamp was the famous Three-Penny Beaver, Canada's first postage stamp and the first anywhere to portray anything but a head of state. Ironically, for a fellow intimately linked to the mail, Fleming seems to have been a reluctant correspondent – as his wife, **Jeanie Fleming**, pointed out three years later.*

Peterboro June 14th/54

My dear Sandford

I have been long in writing partly because I did not think you deserved a letter sooner, & partly because I have been very much occupied in nursing a sick child. Why were you so tardy in writing your last letter? Are you weary of answering my poor attempts? Or what is the matter. I had almost made up my mind to give you a good scolding. As it is I feel very cross. You do not know how anxiously I look for the arrival of your letters. And what a disappointment it is when I have to wait day after day for them. You might I think find time to send me a line or two oftener than you do for I cannot help feeling anxious when you are longer than usual in writing unless I know that you are to be away from home.

I do not approve of your keeping company with such companions as the one you mention having had on your way home from Collingwood . . .

Believe me
dear Sandford
very affc^{tly} yours
<u>Jeanie</u>

A decade and a half later it was Sandford who was feeling forlorn about a lack of correspondence.

Ottawa 27th July 1868

My dearest Jeanie

I have been looking for a letter for some days but as yet I have not received one I may get one this morning Knowing the difficulty I experienced myself in coming here I need scarcely be surprised at letters taking a long time. I got rather impatient yesterday and telegraphed to Bingham about 3 o clock in the afternoon. About 7 o clock I had a reply that all well at home. This was satisfactory but I think with you, when one is very hungry for news from a distance a letter seems to satisfy the appetite more than a telegram. I say that without undervaluing the latter in the slightest degree. This is mail day and I am writing you before breakfast lest I should get so busy through the day that I might not have time to write a decent letter . . .

Your afftn husband
Sandford

FAREWELL TO BYTOWN

Irish-born **Lord Dufferin** *– Frederick Temple Blackwood – was Canada's governor general from 1872 to 1878. He had been a lord-in-waiting to Queen Victoria and a member of William Gladstone's Liberal cabinet before becoming the third post-Confederation representative of the Crown residing in Canada. Much preferring Quebec City to Ottawa, he was the first governor general to establish a vice-regal residence there, having the old British military fortification of the Quebec Citadel restored as his alternative abode. From Quebec, he wrote the Dowager Marchioness of Ely, Lady of the Bedchamber to the Queen.*

The Citadel, Quebec

Aug 14/72

Dear Lady Ely,

I had not halftime enough when I wrote to you to bid you good-bye or to tell you how sorry I was to think how long a time it might be before I saw you again.

It will be very nice of you if you would sometimes remember me and write us a letter of the current gossip.

We had a very prosperous passage across the Atlantic though we commenced proceeding by running down a brig and encountering a heavy gale of wind, during the course of which, two passengers repaired to my cabin at midnight and called upon me as Governor-General of Canada to "do something"! The conclusion of the voyage though not less eventful proved more auspicious, as it included a birth, a baptism, a marriage, and a honeymoon each of the four ceremonials being conducted with equal publicity.

We found the most blissful weather on our arrival[:] clear skies, no rain, a bracing atmosphere, & Highland air. Both Lady Dufferin and myself are delighted with the climate the people and the country . . .

The only residence provided for the Governor-General is at Ottawa, which on account of the heat, is uninhabitable during Summer, everybody flying to the banks of the St. Lawrence. I had already sent my children to a bathing village called Riviere du Loup, and it is there we have been passing the last few weeks. I have had a little yachting and have caught my first salmon, but being anxious to be more in the world I have made them fit up a deserted barracks in the citadel of Quebec. I have hung a wooden balcony out of the windows, from which we can drop biscuits on to the decks of the ships in the St. Lawrence hundreds of feet below. We have run a broad deck along the whole length of the topmost bastion. From this quarter-deck walk the view is unequalled, the broad river stretching away on either hand. On one side the shining tin-sheathed spire, and towers and roofs of the City clustering up towards us, & on the other the silver stream of the St. Charles circling round the northern walls of the lower town, while beyond there stretches a splendid breadth of corn fields and woodland interspersed with white villages and villas to where the picturesque outline of the Lorentian Hills bounds the view . . .

Please give my humblest duty to Her Majesty and perhaps you would ascertain for me whether She would wish me to write her from time to time an account of Her subjects and her Government in this Country.

Ever yours affectionately
[Dufferin]

TORONTO THE SPIRITED

*British immigrant **William Davies**, writing home to a friend in the same decade, was a Toronto businessman who dealt in meat and vegetables, butter and eggs throughout North America and in England. With his Baptist puritanism, he represented the citizens who then inhabited Toronto the Good (a nickname minted in that period during the reign of reform mayor William Howland). It was a homogeneous, overtly moral city, where strict Sabbath laws were observed well into the 20th century.*

Toronto June 15, 1876

My Dear Friend

. . . I have my business in such shape now that if I had only 3 or 4 children and they not any ties here, I should try to get a partner to take hold of this end & I w^d live in England . . . But I am not sure that it desirable, even if practicable – from what I hear & read there is so much drinking there that I think young people are in greater danger there than here. Among professing Xtians here intoxicating liquor is very little used and tho' I am not a total abstainer I am very nearly & I think it is the duty of Xtians to shew their disapproval of the custom by leaving it nearly or quite alone where it is not needed. Yesterday I was looking thro' a paper called the Grocer & was surprised to find how much of the advertising space was taken up by puffs of whiskey, brandy, wine, nourishing stout &c, and the same will apply to the correspondence & articles in it which shews what a prevailing & pervading habit it is. I think the sale of wine & spirits by Grocers & Chemists has had a good deal to do with it. It is a peculiarity of the liquor trade the more is offer'd for sale & the more convenient the package, the more is used . . .

In Ontario at the last sitting of the Legislature an act was pass'd which has very much circumscribed the sale of liquor, and of course, as might be expected, has created a tempest among those who have been deprived of their licenses & among the brewers &c &c. Some here are sanguine enough to agitate for & believe in prohibition, but I do not think public opinion will be ready for it in this generation. By the way, when I was in Portland, Maine, where a prohibitory law is in force, I staid at a medium hotel, quite respectable as the phrase goes, and people were constantly coming in week day & Sunday & visiting a back room where they could get what they wanted. This I think is worse than where the "drinking is according to law." I am not sure that many do not drink because it is against the law, a spice of danger & contrariness about a thing has attractions for some.

There is sitting in Toronto now the General Assembly of Presbyterian Ch. They have got a knotty job on hand. 1 of their number, a very popular man in Toronto, preach'd a sermon some months ago in which he gave his views on future punishment & hinted at restoration. This was published by the press all over the Dominion & by many of the secular papers he was much applauded. It is an important sign, I think. Those of whom there is the least suspicion of godliness are most in his favor . . .

Yours very sincerely
Wm Davies

MUFFLED OARS

*The son of a tugboat captain, **Wallace Ross** of Memramcook, New Brunswick, was already a strong oarsman at age fifteen. He competed on many Canadian courses, including Toronto Bay in 1877, when he lost to the great Edward Hanlan. Financially, 1880 seems to have been a very good year for Ross: he won the grand single scull event at Providence, Rhode Island, for a hefty three-thousand-dollar prize and was the stroke on a fours team that took the New England championship. He then went to England and won second-prize money in the prestigious Hop Bitters' Race and more cash in the race with Trickett on December 5. This half-apologetic letter is to Bertha Amelia Steele – twenty-four years old and working in Lynn, Massachusetts, possibly as a servant or housekeeper – who may have been his girlfriend.*

Putney London
Dec 18th 1880

Dear Amelia pardon the liberty i take but i thought i would drop you a few lines for old aquantince sake you will remember when i bade you good bye that night in Lynn that you promised me one of your Photos and i would like very much to have one as i am compelled on account of illnes to stay here some time i have had a very hard time of it over here this time i was in splendid health when i first came over but i caught a terriable cold and it settled in my throat and i had to go to a Doctor and have a operation performed which was very painfull but otherwise i have been a very good winner as i have won over three thousand Dollars here i got second prize in the Hop Bitters Race which was fifteen hundred and i won two thousand when i beat Trickett if i had been well i would have won something like five thousand Dols but that is no use when you have not got your health Mr. Hanlan is staying in the same house with me only for that i do not know what i would do i sometimes lay all day in bed and do not see anybody i know when i was in St John i called at your house but i was surprised to find nobody there i saw your sister Emma and she told me that you only went away the day i got home i do not know of anything to write that would interest you so i will close hopeing to hear from you soon i remain yours

very truly

Wallace Ross

C/o Sportsman Office
Ludgate Hill London

According to his obituary, Wallace won the world championship against an English oarsman in 1884 but lost the title two years later. He ended his career by giving exhibitions of broadsword exercises and training racing crews.

THE DEACON'S DOG

*The Reverend **Ned Harris** was a freshly ordained, twenty-three-year-old Anglican deacon from Prince Edward Island when he came to assist the stodgy rector of Mahone Bay, on the Nova Scotia coast, in 1864. He wrote home every few days, recounting the challenges of his parish, including this report of an encounter that his dog, Col ("Colin Harris"), had with a local politician.*

Mahone Bay
Sept 5 1887

Dear Mama,

. . . Friday afternoon I took a turn down the street, Col following. But he got away from me somewhere and I came home without him. After tea I went down the street again, where Mills asked me if Col was here. I said I had not seen him for a while. Then he said, Cora Zwicker saw Colwell (a man in Edwin Kaulbach's office, who last election was a local candidate) take Col by the back of the neck, put him in the coach, and start for Lunenburg holding him. My hair pretty nearly stood on end. I made for the hotel where Mrs. MacDonald corroborated the charge: Colwell lifted a dog into the coach. Others saw it and knew it was Col. I then hesitated – whether to send a constable after the rascal, or go myself. Foolishly I decided to go myself, and hurriedly got my horse and started off for Lunenburg (this was about eight o'clock, the coach had left at five). As I sped along, nursing my wrath, about a mile upon the road, in the dusk, all at once my eye caught Col now beside me, and looking up as he dashed along to keep pace with me, as if to say, "Here I am." Of course, I was astonished, stopped and got out to have a look at him.

Then two men came along from before me, who said Col had come flying along past them from the direction of Lunenburg. It was then quite evident that Col had escaped and made at once for home.

Well, I came back rejoicing at having Col, but disappointed that a constable had not hold of Colwell. I sat down and wrote a stinger, but thought I would not post it until I got cooled down. So next morning I started for New Germany, only getting home Sunday evening. On getting back I learned that the driver of the coach had told Colwell it was my dog. Col jumped out from him three or four times, but he insisted on stopping the coach (he being the only passenger) and capturing Col once more. When opposite Greenwood's at the entrance to Lunenburg he again jumped. The Greenwoods, who know Col well, saw Col jump from Colwell, and watched the performance. Again stopping, he requested boys near at hand to chase

Col with stones in order to make him follow them. Thus he was driven in towards town. Some one there said it was my dog, but he told them that the dog kept running away from me, and that I was tired of being bothered with him, so he had got him. Where or how Col escaped at last I do not yet know. But, good old fellow, he did not take long to get home.

Then this morning came a letter from Colwell apologizing, not for <u>stealing</u>, but for taking by mistake my dog. He is greatly grieved to think a rumour is spreading like wild fire over the Bay and Lunenburg that such a <u>big</u> man as he stole a dog, to actually call it <u>stealing</u> startles him. He begs me to hush the gossip up, and when he <u>sees</u> me offers to explain how he took a dog which he did not know was mine.

The real explanation is that he was <u>drunk</u>. And so was the driver of the coach. But if a man will drink, especially a man in his position, he deserves to be punished when he commits such crimes as theft. However, I fancy he will not again lay hands on Colin Harris, who is now well known all over the country . . .

Love to all, kisses to your children.

Your loving son
E.A.H.

CHECKERS CHAMP

Stephen Leacock – who became Canada's most famous humorist, as well as a professor, political economist, and historian – was attending Upper Canada College in Toronto as a fourteen-year-old when he wrote (with the odd mistake and ink blotch) to his father, then a land agent in Winnipeg. The lighthearted tone belies the fact that Stephen's dad, faced with tough times as a farmer, became a heavy drinker – and that three years later, Stephen, fed up with his father's abuse, threatened to kill him if he ever returned to the family farm.

June 28/84

My dear father,

The little ones all started for the lake this afternoon; they went this morning but they missed the train. The party were 8 in all, carrying about 10 trunks and some 1/2 dozen dogs & cats; In order not to be late they went to the station about an hour early, and, true to their orders not to go on to the platform, they sat patiently in the car for the best part of an hour before the train started. Of course they forgot some of their luggage. Miss Wilson headed the young Israelites and Miss Bertha made an able second. There will be probably be a notice about in to-morrow's mail headed "Departure for happy hunting grounds" or something of that sort. Do you remember the fuchia which you got for mother at a butcher's shop on Queen st? There are 76 buds on it now & the Italian primroses & violets are doing well.

I got some checkers down town and Mother & I played three games; I beat her in all of them, but she says it was only because she got stupid at the last, or the baby cried in the middle, or she thought that king was a common, or something of that sort.

Mother wants me to tell you that it was not the children's fault that they missed the morning train, as they were all up at half past four, in fact they hardly slept at all, and their trunk had been packed about a week before.

Mother was out in the yard for the first time yesterday and had the pleasure of beating me in a game of croquet; she put in down in her diary (at least its very likely) in red letter capitals. Yr affec$^{t/n}$ son

Stephen B. Leacock

THE OXEN KNELT

James Caswell was a storekeeper in Palmerston, Ontario, when his brothers in Saskatchewan persuaded him to pack up his wife and six children and homestead at Clark's Crossing, near the new city of

Saskatoon. **Maryanne Caswell,** *the oldest child, was fourteen in April 1887, when the family set out. Her letters to her paternal grandmother fulfilled her promise to record the adventure.*

May 8, 1887

Dear Grandma,

(Here we are in Clark's Crossing.) First day was Sunday. We were awakened from our promised long sleep, that there was no room to move till we had folded our bedding. We dressed and were shown how to fold and put our bedding out of the way.

Uncle John made flour porridge. Aunt Patience fried eggs in lard with bread. We had breakfast. After helping to wash the dishes and learning how to feed calves from a pail in which we were to coax the calf to drink after inserting our fingers in its mouth, we were glad to sing hymns to Aunt Patience's playing on the organ she had brought from Cherokee, Iowa.

By and bye, Martha and I, wearying for mother, stole quietly as we could to Uncle Rob's where the others of the family had slept and were to stay until we had our own shelter, as it might be.

The ravine was lovely in its dips and curves deepening to the river, the water pleasantly gurgling on its way in the evening shadows . . .

Uncle Rob's house is of small, white upstanding poplar logs, plastered and whitewashed, two large rooms, bedroom and pantry. Uncle Rob has made a bed-sofa, stool and sideboard for the parlor, very pretty cut-work and comfortable. He has not been with the government telegraph company since the [Riel] "Rebellion." He, it was, sent the message from Duck Lake of the rebellion to General Middleton in the east. While out repairing the cut telegraph line he was taken prisoner by the rebels and placed in a cellar in Batouche's house in the village of Batoche. Later he was liberated through the intercession of Louis Ross, a half-breed who was also taken prisoner with him while repairing the telegraph line.

Next week was a busy one for each of us. Father sowed his White Russian wheat on his last year's breaking; the peas, oats and flax on

Uncle Joe's land. I was shown how to handle the oxen, to harrow a good seed bed while father sowed from a big bag tied round his waist. All went well till I came to the end of land, turning too short the harrows tipped up on the oxen's back, frightening them into a run. I hung on to the rope halter shouting "whoa" till father came to release the harrows, explaining the serious effect to us if the oxen had gotten out of control. My hands were burnt with the rope. Mother made a salve of Balm of Gilead (black poplar) to heal my blisters.

With willing help and hindrance, we assisted mother to plant the roots of rhubarb, currants, strawberry, iris, and others we had brought with us from Palmerston. The garden seeds got under the ground. Our food to prepare, the care of Andrew and Mabel, many new chores to learn, the wandering cattle to herd as they wander far, and helping father get ready for a trip to Moose Jaw (for supplies), gave us no time for repining and wishing we had stayed at Heath's out from Moose Jaw, or, as Mr. Alexander tried to persuade father, remained nearer the railway . . .

Love from all of us,
Maryanne.

[Christmas 1887]

Dear Grandma,

A Mr. George Barley stopped overnight on his way to Prince Albert. He has a team of mules. He has built a round stone house on his homestead about ten or more miles upriver. Says he built it round so there will be no dirt in the corners. He has been trying to arrange with father to work with or for us next spring. Wears his hair long and does not shave. Says Jesus wore his hair and whiskers as he does and that is the style for him.

The river was frozen over. Gladly we went with father for a load of wood and to do some measuring of the river from bank to bank to locate a likely place for a railway bridge when it comes, as we are not far from "MacKenzie's survey". Father's friend, Mr. Archibald Young of Toronto, has written him for this information. We felt quite elated and important to do this and made our first winter picnic of it.

We built a fire while father selected and cut the trees, then we lopped off the smaller branches and helped load the sleigh. When the water was boiling in the camp kettle we put in a pinch of tea, toasted our frozen sandwiches of bread and cheese stuck on sticks over the coal. After refreshments we started our measurements across up and down the river each trip until we had covered several miles. Father later sent his measurements to Mr. Young. An acknowledgment came from his son at Upper Canada College to say his father had passed on. The loss of his friend was a great blow to father . . .

We made some Christmas cards to send to our relatives and friends in Ontario. We peeled and dried some birch bark off some of the wood pieces from the river bank. We selected our best pressed and dried flowers, that had retained their coloring, pasting them with egg white in a pleasing arrangement or design, sometimes stitching them. The spring flowers and autumn made the best showing but we are anxious to display the variety that grew on the wild prairies, so each family got different flowers and colorings. It was a problem to get white paper to wrap the finished cards for mailing so we wrapped them in yellow-brown building paper for security, and note paper for addressing. We were complimented on the results, so we are making some for our walls . . .

For Christmas gifts we had not any (like simple Simon) but we exchanged some of our treasures and put them on a bare poplar tree, decorated some Chautauqua books Uncle Alex or A.K. had sent us with his usual Christmas letter. "May the Lord bless you and keep you and make his face to shine upon you and do you good."

For dinner we had a cherished wild goose stuffed with potato dressing seasoned with wild sage, vegetables, of course, suet pudding of grated carrots, flour and dried saskatoon berries boiled in a cloth.

Mother allowed us some hoarded sugar for taffy, flavoured with wild mint. Some of our pop-corn popped but not much pop in it. We danced on the threshing floor and in the evening played hide-and-seek and did some story reading by lamp for a treat as coal-oil is five dollars a gallon at Saskatoon.

At midnight Christmas Eve we girls went to the stable to see if the oxen would kneel as father said they would or did on Christmas Eve. We had never had the opportunity until now. When mother followed us out to the stable the oxen knelt for a second, as they got up they were disturbed. See?

We missed you and our old friends, Grandma. Everyone sends love.

Maryanne.

WILDLIFE REPORT

Leon Ladner, a lawyer who articled with Sir Charles Tupper, Canada's sixth prime minister, became a member of Parliament from Vancouver and then formed one of that city's most prestigious law firms, Ladner, Carmichael & Downs. In 1892, though, Leon was a mischievous eight-year-old writing his absent father from the family home in the Delta area.

Canoe Pass
December 23rd [1892?]

Dear Papa.

I hope you enjoy your self down there. We are all very well to-morrow is examinaition day and the fifthclass had to fix the school and the fourthclass and thirdclass had to clean the papers out of the yard and the second class went home. and I saw a woodpecker on the tree and I saw Edward at his place and I told him to get his gun and to shot him and he said no and I tooke my slingshot and shot at him and the third or fourth time I shot at him & shot a rock at a him and it hit the tree and bounced and very near hit him and then I went on and I saw the buggy and went home. how long before you will be coming back because mama said she was coning back in six weeks.

does Violet have mush fun with aunt dollie because she was so excited
when she left here. Edward is sitting in a chair and is a sleep and Ida
is netting a little mat. and Ellis is gone to the choir practise and I dont
no when he will be back. and Allie is writing a letter to Eddie. I hope
you have a good time at Christmas and you will get some nice things.

Edward shot a musk-rat and he was chewing at the ground and
put a pretty big hole in him if he did not put sush a big hole in him
I would skin him. everything I know of is all right. I got a report I
rank first in a class of five and Allie rank third. Ida took some
Chinajars and put some sage and put it on and painted them red and
they look very pretty. our school got out before the other school
and I went to see the the boys and girls sing and to speake and so
the first boy that spoke a piece it was Ralph and I forget all of the
others. and wa[s] Violet glad when she got at Aunt Allie's because
when she left here she was in a rush a big hurry to get there and she
was rushing to get her shoes and coat a and everyhing else. has Uncle
Walter shot any rabbits yet or squirrels. Your loving son.

Leon Ladner

OVER THE BIG WATER

*The arrival of the Canadian Pacific Railway on the western prairies
in early 1880s galvanized the growth of ranching in the foothills of
southwestern Alberta, attracting a variety of men and women to
raise cattle for a hungry British market. Among them was* **Strong
Buffalo,** *a member of the Peigan tribe in the Blackfoot nation. A
rancher, he had a big herd of cattle and by 1895 a burning desire to
complain to Queen Victoria about injustices to his people. He paid
his own way on a voyage to England with the local Anglican missionary. He never did meet the queen, but he had a fine time, as he
described it in this letter to his friend Jerry Potts, a celebrated Metis
warrior and a scout and guide for the North-West Mounted Police.*

2 Hanover st.,
West Hartlepool, England,
Jan. 16th, 1895.

Dear Mr. Potts, –

When I got to Ottawa I went to the Parliament Buildings and saw the room where Parliament meets, and sat down on the throne. I also went and saw a meeting of women. I stayed 6 days in Montreal. At Halifax I stayed 4 days.

We sailed on the Saturday. On the Monday it blew very hard. The water came over the boat, and all the dishes fell off the table and were broken. The big water was as big as from Elk River in the north to Sheep River in the south. We were ten days and nine nights in the ship : the ship was very big – there were almost 500 people in it. The ship was as long as from the Mission House to Bear Trail's house ; ship went very quickly.

We have been here in England four weeks now.

I have seen where they make iron. First I saw some iron like stone. Then I saw them melt it. I could not look at it without blue spectacles. I saw them pour melted iron like water. I saw a big hammer as heavy as 25 sacks of flour. I saw them roll thick lumps of iron out till they were thin and flat like boards, and I saw them cut iron with a knife just as easily as I can cut bread.

I saw white men conjuring, but I cannot tell you all now. I will tell you when I come home. I saw a woman lay two eggs. She was only as far as from your house to the kitchen away from me.

I saw some elephants ; they took a gun and fired with their trunks.

I saw a man take his head off and hold it up in his hand, and the head spoke to us. I was close by.

Here in England there are a great many houses. I have seen houses one of which would hold all the Bloods, Blackfeet and Peigans.

This island is as long as from Elk river in the north to the Big river in the south.

I went into a school and there were as many children in it as all the North Peigans, men, women and children.

I have been into the churches here. They are very big and many people go into them. I have spoken twice. A great many people came to see me. They clapped and stamped, and seemed very pleased.

I want you to tell my friends all I have written to you. Tell Bear Trail and Little Wolf. I have been buying some things for my wife. Things are very cheap here. Tell Bear Trail I have got some pictures for him, but not very many yet. I have not yet seen any chiefs ; we have just been resting. In a week or two I am going up to London, and I may see some there.

If the old Peigan chiefs were to come over the big water they would die with fright. When the big ship rolled they would think they were going over, and they would ask the sun to save them, and then their wives should make a sun-dance.

Shall be glad to have a letter from you, telling me all the news.

Strong Buffalo

BRIDAL BEDLAM

Maude Estelle De Long of *New Germany, Nova Scotia, was a twenty-year-old when she relayed the local gossip to her cousin, Etta Palmer, who was studying at the Lunenburg Academy.*

New Germany, N.S.
March 14, 1897

My Dearest Cousin:
Well, I was pleased enough to get your nice letter . . .

Our sleighing is about spoiled. We were up to Springfield Friday evening and dear, dear, such a time! It makes my heart palpitate to think about it. We got the invitation about a week before. There was plenty snow then but it commenced to rain right away and by Friday the roads were pretty nearly bare in New Germany . . . You can imagine the gentle scraping along over the gritty road . . . It was quarter past three when I got home and it poured all the way. You may imagine I felt <u>sweet</u> or <u>soft</u>, I don't know which after that <u>soaking</u> . . .

. . . Myrtie has been out to Bessie's on a visit. Bessie has got a little boy. There is a Miss Silver teaching at Foster Settlement in the lower school-house from Lunenburg and Susie Dunn has the upper school. Susie was out to see her beloved Osborne a few weeks ago. I would like to write you a real long letter but I feel so sleepy from my Springfield trip, I will have to go to bed. Now write to me as soon as you can like a good girl.

Lots of love,
Maude

P.S.

We had great fun the night Uncle Enoch got married. We fastened bells to the feather bed and put a lot of bells behind the bureau, fastened a string to them and put it out through the window and after they went to bed, the boys got hold of the string and rattled the bells for about 10 minutes. I tell you it was fun.

BRANDED

John Ware was an ex-slave who at the end of the American Civil War left a plantation in the southern United States and eventually became Alberta's first black cowboy. Around 1890, after working for cattle companies, he began ranching on his own spread near Sheep Creek; a decade later he settled near Brooks. This letter, dictated to his daughter Nettie, is likely one of the few the illiterate Ware ever wrote.

Millarville May 4th 1898

Dear Sir

I wont to get my brand recorded 999 on left ribs for cattle and 9 on left shoulder for horses John Ware Sheep Creek, and I wont to get DC on left side and hipe [hip] for cattle treasfer [transfer] from me

to Miss Nettey Ware. can Robert Ware brand † get this brand for
cattle on left side and hipe.

I am sending bil of sail to show you that DC brand belongs to
me it is recorded in the Old brand book in Courtney main please
return bil of sail to me I inclose One Dollar for treasfer.

your truly John Ware
Millarville P.O.

*When he died five years later in a riding accident, hundreds of friends
attended his funeral, which suggests that John Ware was held in high
esteem.*

THE COW BOMB

*Early in the 20th century a Methodist minister's daughter from
England named* **Monica Hopkins** *and her childhood sweetheart-
cum-husband, Billie, ran a cattle and horse ranch and a small coal
mine on their land near Priddis, Alberta, just southwest of Calgary.
She wrote regularly to family and friends back home about life in a
log cabin amid the Rocky Mountain foothills – including this anec-
dote about their hapless hired hand, Jenks.*

Enmore,
Priddis,
August, 1910.

Dearest Gill:
Helene and I are in the kitchen trying not to let our laughter be heard
outside where a loud voice can be heard issuing commands and where
our laughing would certainly not be appreciated at the moment. Later
on Billie will enjoy the joke but certainly not now.

I'll have to start at the beginning and tell you all the sad events
that led up to this amusing ending. Jenks is in trouble again! Bad
trouble too. Yesterday he left the gate open leading to the mine, a
thing that he had had impressed upon him that he must not do, and

our cows went through and wandered down to the mine buildings. There one of them spied a box of delicacies and ate quite a large quantity before she was discovered and driven off. It was gunpowder! I don't know what gunpowder is made of but anyway it killed the cow. Would you believe that cows would be such fools? She lived about 12 hours and passed away on a little knoll about two hundred yards away from the house where she still is, or what remains of her, waiting to be removed to some spot on the range where she can pollute the air without our smelling her as well!

Billie was furious naturally and nearly fired Jenks there and then, but it is a mistake that can easily happen. Indeed at one time or another we have all left that gate open, only fortunately without any bad results. This time we were not so lucky. Jenks wept and promised such good behaviour in the future if only he could stay on that Billie cooled down and after another lecture told Jenks he would give him another chance. But if he ever found that gate open again, "heaven help Jenks." On his part Jenks assured Billie that his actions in future would be exemplary, or words to that effect, and scurried off to clean out the stable as a good start as he need not do any chores after supper. You could almost see the faint glow of the halo!

This evening at supper Jenks said apropos of nothing, "I'd sure like to stick a knife in her." At first we couldn't think what he meant then we realized that he meant the cow who has swollen to gigantic size, the gases in her having made her almost circular.

Billie, with whom the affair still rankles, said off-handedly, "Well, why don't you?" and thought no more about it. While Helene and I were washing up the supper dishes and Billie was smoking his pipe outside, he called us to "come and see what that silly fool is up to now." We looked and there was the noble Jenks seated on top of the rolling carcass looking for the exact spot to dig his knife in. Being very near sighted, his face was only a few inches above the spot where he intended to strike. Before Billie could yell to tell him to stop, Jenks struck!

It was hard to see what exactly happened but the animal exploded. Liquid, gas and bits of decayed flesh flew in all directions, but most of it spattered over our hero who was bounced off the carcass and rolled down the knoll. When he could regain his feet he simply flew towards us but even before Jenks reached us the most awful smell preceded him. What Jenks would be like we daren't think. Billie rushed towards him shouting, "Stop right there!" and told him to get down to the creek and wait for him. Billie shot into the house and collected some rags, disinfectant, old towels, and some string. I couldn't think what the string was for but now I know, for Jenks is standing up to his waist in water stark naked and tying strings to his clothes which are to soak in the creek anchored to bushes on the banks. There they will stay until they are clean and the smell leaves them, if it ever does! Meanwhile, Billie is on the bank giving orders in a most indignant voice; we have just heard, "Rub that soap (the dogs' carbolic soap) all over your head and then rub it well into the cloth and keep on rubbing it." This produced more laughter from Helene and me. Billie's last injunction was, "You'd better go to bed and if you smell tomorrow you'll have to have another bath."

Well, you can't say we don't have excitements out here. Now I must go and see what my spouse is doing, and tell him not to do it. I have just caught sight of him, handkerchief to nose, on his way up to the scene of the explosion. I only hope I won't have to give <u>him</u> a bath! . . .

Monica

A BEER-AND-COLLINS BENDER

Bob Edwards – Robert Chambers Edwards – was the black sheep of an important Scottish publishing family who escaped to Wyoming and then, in 1894, to western Canada. In Calgary he launched the Eye Opener, *a "semi-occasional" newspaper that satirized the likes of the* CPR, *land developers, and politicians. Some failed to see his humour: Alberta's premier sued him – unsuccessfully – when Edwards described the province's three biggest liars as "Robert Edwards, Gentleman;*

Honourable A.L. Sifton (premier); and Bob Edwards, Editor of the
Eye Opener." He fought a futile battle against the bottle ("I am a
Prohibitionist. What I propose to prohibit is the reckless use of
water.") He wrote this letter to a nurse who once saved his life.

CALGARY EYE OPENER

R.C. Edwards, Editor and Proprietor

Calgary, Alta., Feb.7, 1915

My dear Miss Ross,

. . . If you only knew how I dread <u>starting</u> to write a letter! I keep
putting it off, until the letter is never written at all. That I am sitting
down now to write this one, is perhaps the most astonishing event of
my life. Every other line I have to stop to pinch myself to see that it
is really me . . .

I saw Mrs. Johnston yesterday. She was looking fine and was in
her usual high spirits, though complaining that she missed you terribly. She spoke about seeing Dr. Birch to offer you a position as one
of the nurses to look after the health of school children, but while I
did not discourage her in this brilliant scheme, I did not encourage
her, as I don't think such stupid work is in your line at all. You better
stick it out in New York until times revive here . . . And here it might
be appropriate to remark that I have been on only one (beer) bat
since you left. Was all right again in three days. I haven't touched
spirits (outside of a stray morning Collins) since that memorable
occasion when I died and came to life again – or rather was <u>brought</u>
<u>back</u> to life again. I shall never forget what I owe you for your great
work that time. The scare has done me good . . .

I want to tell you a funny thing in connection with that bat I got
on some time after you left. It was only a beer one, but it had a solid
foundation of Collinses. I commenced to <u>wither</u> on a Saturday and
forgot to lay in enough beer to last me over the Sunday. I had half a
dozen quarts, but drank 'em up in no time after I had gone to bed.
About 2 in the morning (Sunday) I woke up and hunted around for
a drink. The only thing I could find was a bottle of unfermented port
which Mrs. Cook, the woman who looks after my rooms, had

brought me in a present some weeks before. I started mopping up the stuff, for I was awfully thirsty, with the result that I became sick and had a vomiting spell, leaning on my elbow out of bed and removing the port from my stomach into a basin. Of course I occasionally missed the basin and saturated the edge of the sheet with a dye of bright red port. It was a bloody looking sight. Finally I grew so weak & sick that I deemed it prudent, in case of collapse, to get up & dress and go to a hospital. It was all I could do to dress, floundering about in a forest of empties. When at last I had on my coat & hat I went out & slammed the door. Then I discovered I had forgotten my glasses. I at the same time discovered that I had lost my keys and I couldn't get back into the room. You remember that step ladder that stands outside my door? Well, I took that and busted in the glass panel, enabling me to reach in an[d] open the Yale lock. I got the glasses & hied me over to the Western hospital, no one being any the wiser. On Monday morning old Mrs. Cook arrived as usual at eight o'clock and was alarmed to see the glass part of the door busted in. She peeped in and saw I wasn't there. So reaching in her arm she opened the door & went in. The rooms bore a striking resemblance to Louvain the morning after the Germans sacked it and she feared something had happened to me. Glancing towards the bed her eye lit on the bloodstained sheet and her worst fears were confirmed. A tragedy had occurred. Some evil persons had broken in to my rooms and murdered me <u>sure</u>. People in the neighbourhood tell me that poor Mrs. Cook was running around like an old hen with its head chopped off . . .

Am still in the same old rooms and lonesome as the very devil. Am thinking of investing in a dog this spring. So long. Bob

MUCH BAD LUCK

The legend of Fernie is that a native chief showed a white prospector the location of local seams of coal in return for the prospector's promise to marry the chief's daughter. When William Fernie reneged, *the chief placed a curse on the coal-mining community of Fernie, founded in southeastern British Columbia's Elk Valley in 1898. The curse seems to have worked: a mining explosion in 1901 killed 128 men; a blaze burned out most of the business section three years later; a forest fire nearly destroyed the city in 1908; and a river flooded the place eight years later. Among the more than three thousand residents driven out of their homes in the 1908 inferno was Fernie's fire chief, **D. McDougall**, whose wife was in hospital at the time. He wrote to a creditor in 1916, the year of the great flood.*

FIRE DEPARTMENT

D. McDOUGALL, CHIEF

CITY OF FERNIE

Fernie, B.C. Feb 12th 1916

W. T. Danby Esq.

Clayoquot B.C.

Dear Sir

your kind & much welcomed letter received yesterday I was very much gratified to get a letter from you containing so much news . . . yes since I left the West Coast I had much bad luck, but the worst of it all was the loosing of Mrs. McDougall it nearly broke my heart. Poor Dear Soul, but such are those disappointments – of which we have no control. I am still at Fernie & am getting along as well as can be expected, I got the boys up here with me. The little girl is at Victoria with Mrs. O'Leary her aunt. The boys are going to school & getting along very well . . .

Concerning my account I admit that I should have paid you on this, I assure you that I had not forgotten you. But owing to Circumstance I have been unable to send you anything up to the Present Time. the morning after the fire of August 1st [1908] I found myself Without a Dollar & every thing that I possessed gone up in smoke & Mrs. McDougall dying in Cranbrook Hosbital. I managed to get her to Victoria where she died three months after. When I returned from Victoria after burraying her, I found myself owing Six hundred Dollars to Hosbitals Doctors & Undertakers which was a

Hard Proposition stearing me in the face. But I am glade to say at the Present time that I have this amount Very nearly Paid off. Therefore I will be able to send you some the first of march hoping this explanation will cause you to understand the reason why my acct. have not been paid before now. I hope that I will be able to Pay you in full in the near future . . .

I Remain yours Sincerely
D. McDougall
Fernie B.C.

LAST ORDERS

The year that McDougall wrote the above letter, a former resident of Fernie named **Emilio Picariello** *was running a hotel in Blairmore, Alberta, when that province passed a Prohibition law. The Italian-born Picariello soon became a bootlegger, bringing contraband spirits from British Columbia and the neighbouring state of Montana. In 1922 a provincial police constable shot Picariello's son Steve in the hand after accusing the sixteen-year-old of transporting liquor. His father and the family nanny, Florence Lassandro, later confronted the constable, who was killed in the ensuing melee. Picariello and Lassandro were tried in a high-profile court case – in which doubt was raised about their guilt – and sentenced to be hanged on May 2, 1923. The night before he died, the father of seven children wrote to his wife and family.*

[May 1, 1923]

Mrs. Picariello
Blairmore
Alta Box M
My Dear wife and childrin
I expect this well be the last letter I will be abel to write to you and the children

I go to the scaffold to morrow morning as an innocent man, and I am prepared to meet My Maker. I hope that you and the children will live good and happy lives to gether and that we will all meet again. According to the will you have already from me you are the sole exciutrix until Steve our Son be comes of age and then you will both become trustees. And I wish that they will get an equal share.

I want you to know that I do not owe any body. I want you to know that Mr. E. Gillis as already had 500.^{00} from me and I consider I have over paid him for work that he had never done, all others lawyers are paid in full.

I want you to know that I did not authorize dr. Oliver to attend any body professionally out side of our own Family. I want you to remember all the people I have helped at different times they have forgotten me now and dont come to help or cheer me

I will say good bye with love to you all children til we all meet again and may God Bless and keep you all safe kis all the children for me

Your loving Husband
and Father
Emilio Picariello

HORSE OF A DIFFERENT COLOUR

*After moving to Manitoba from Connecticut, **Martin Kartzmark**, a machinist, took up market gardening on forty acres at St. Andrew's, north of Winnipeg. His daughter, Elinor, born just months after this exchange of letters with **George Camplin**, still lives on the family farm.*

Lockport Man.
March 2nd, 1926

Mr. Kartzmark
Dear Sir
I am herewith submitting a claim against you for Twelve Dollars, for Hay eaten & destroyed by your horse, on Lot 86 If I do not hear

from you within seven days I shall take the necessary proceedings to collect the above damages.

Yours Truly

George Camplin

RR No 1 Wpg

Mar. 7. 1926,

Winnipeg R.R. #1.

Mr. G. Camplin.

Dear sir,

I received your letter last Tuesday, about a horse eating and destroying hay of yours on lot 86. all the horses I own have been in my barn, and have not been running at large.

If it is a roan horse you are referring to it belongs to a party by the name of R. Nagengast cor of Thames & Tecumseh Sts Winnipeg. If this does not explain matters sufficiently to you and you wish to take proceedings against me, hop to it.

Yours truly

M. Kartzmark

THE FIRE-DEVIL

Frans van Waeterstadt was one of hundreds of Dutch immigrants recruited after the First World War to populate farms and work in the forests of Canada, particularly in Ontario. Van Waeterstadt farmed and logged in the fire-prone northern bush, where he was working when he wrote (in Dutch) to a newspaper back home.

8 December, 1928

To the Editor

Leeuwarder Nieuwsblad

"To the bush! To the wonderful green bush!" I sang those words many times before I'd ever worked in a bush. Now I don't sing those pretty sentiments anymore. Oh no! I know darn well that our bush isn't all that wonderful and certainly not green. Practically every pine and spruce has been robbed of its green attire. The long, thin trunks stand straight up, candle straight and bare to the very tip top. Even more are lying flat on the ground, unable any longer to withstand the screaming north wind, because their tough burly strength was taken away by time or fire.

Fire! The most dangerous and insidious enemy of Northern Ontario. Fire annually ruins hundreds of hectares of Ontario's beautiful tree splendor and leaves behind a multitude of bare half-burned and fire-blackened stumps.

In this neighbourhood there have been a significant number of forest fires, but when the people talk about "the fire" then they always mean the one which put the population in peril and out on the street six years ago. Its origin was very innocent: a couple of hunters boiled up a cup of tea in the middle of the bush and afterward "thought" that their campfire was out. A little spark that remained smouldering, then some wind, a little bit of dry grass that caught fire, a blueberry bush, dry as a cork after a hot Canadian summer that caught on fire very easily, then the surrounding pitch laden pine trees. Finally, up went a blaze, swept ahead by an evergrowing fire storm which burned everything to the ground in a path which was five kilometres wide and almost forty kilometres long.

Not only the bush burned flat. Sparks were driven through the air and fell on a little pile of hay that had been left lying in a field around a farm. That little pile of hay blazed up and the wind took it and blew it ahead and let it fall on the roof of a house or barn. As I said, the summer had been hot and dry and the houses were built of wood and covered with tar paper. Where a spark landed there was fire. The poor farmer who, with his wife, had chopped a few acres of ground out of the ancient forest, at a cost of an incredible amount of sweat, and who was so very happy and proud of the house, which he himself had built out of wood which was sawn out of his own tree trunks or had been built up with the rough logs, that poor farmer saw his home-made estate burn flat to the ground in a flash.

Some were barely able to save their own lives. In groups, they fled to some deep ravines where the ground was still slightly damp. They lay there for hours, their faces buried in the cool moss, while above their heads the flames and sparks were whirled in a terrifying, wild blast through the air. Everyone took his turn to expose his face and eyes to the scorching smothering smoke and heat in order to extinguish the sparks which were falling on his companions' clothes.

People told me much more about the terror which a forest fire brings with it; much more than I could describe in one letter. The blackened stretches of burned forest give me an idea of what it was like.

However, the bush is not the only easy victory for the fire-devil. The poverty-stricken, poorly built wooden houses are a constant fire hazard. They often don't even have a brick chimney, a hole in the roof lets the stove pipe through, and in the evening you can see the sparks of the blazing wood fires come sweeping lustily out of and around the pipe. When it's so bitter, bitter cold in the winter, it's so pleasant to throw an extra chunk of wood in the stove and stoke up a fine, cosy, hot fire. The stove becomes red instead of black, and even the pipe glows from top to bottom. Then there's danger, terrible danger.

Our nearest neighbour, that means a half a mile from us here, came home thoroughly soaked one evening about three weeks ago after he'd walked in the rain for an hour and a half. The man is as poor as a church mouse and he probably had no other clothes to put on the following morning. Anyway, a fire was quickly started in the stove and within a few minutes the man's pants and jacket were on the line to dry. Before he went to bed, the stove was stuffed with dry pine so that the fire would burn long enough to dry the clothes. In the middle of the night the woman of the house woke up. The attic, where the whole family slept, was full of smoke and the flames were licking along the walls in the corners. Fire! The five children were awakened and everyone fled to the stair-opening in a frenzied haste. There were no windows in the attic of the self-built house and the stair-opening was terribly small. A ladder, which had a few missing rungs, had to be used by everyone trying to scramble downstairs. Most of them got downstairs. Not all. When I came to look in the morning, they had just found what was left of the four-year-old youngest child in the hot ashes. A wooden house, the inside walls of thick cardboard, no chimney, the attic an absolute trap and then the fire.

A week ago, another house, a couple of miles from here. The attic, another trap. A small window in that one, about big enough to let a cat out. The husband and three of the nine children so badly burned that they had to go to the hospital. The man has now succumbed.

That's two fires in the last three weeks in this neighbourhood. I haven't been here a year yet, but there have been almost a dozen fires.

Fire! The most dangerous and stealthy enemy of the people in Northern Ontario, the land of forest and poorly built wooden houses.

Frans van Waeterstadt

UPWARD BOUND

Russell Bruce left his wife and children in Vancouver to log in the forests of British Columbia. At the time the previous letter was written to a Dutch newspaper, Bruce wrote to his wife from a camp about sixty-five kilometres east of Vancouver.

R. Bruce
Allco, Camp 3, BC
Aug 24, 1928

Dearest Hazel,

Just a line to let you know that I have arrived here OK, and having gotten one day in. The camp is on floats on Stave Lake and we pass the BC Electric dam on the way up. The Camp is nine miles above the dam. Good camps and board. This evening there was chicken for dinner done up like the red hen also corn on the cob – lots of it. The board is above the average but "oh gee gosh" the hills are steep. I climb straight up for about half an hour and then it leans over backward for about a thousand feet and I learned to walk as a fly does across the ceiling. The best part is that I <u>can</u> climb "and not be weary" and work is easy now. Quite a difference believe me.

I am going to write a few letters tonight, Hazel Dearest, so am making this short. Just a note for you and the kiddies.

I left my pen at home and it is rotten to be without just now. Hoping this finds you all OK.

Yours always with love and kisses,
Regards to all. Camp 3
Russell

GREY OWL'S MOTHER

Archibald Belaney, born in Hastings, England, in 1888, hid his roots so well that he was universally accepted as an Indian – part Scot, part Apache – named **Grey Owl.** *Belaney guarded this personal fiction, believing it advanced the conservationist causes he promoted. In 1935, as the author of several books, he was invited to lecture in England, including his home town of Hastings, where he wasn't recognized. Later he was approached by his own mother at a book signing. He refused to acknowledge her – perhaps to protect his persona, perhaps to punish her for having left him as a very young child to be raised by his stern Belaney aunts. This undated fragment of a letter seems to have been written to Anahareo, his Iroquois wife. The "wee Reptile" is Shirley Dawn, their daughter. Grey Owl's mother had remarried and was using the name Scott-Brown and is likely the Mrs. Brown mentioned here.*

[after 1932]

. . . melt the beeswax, & pour into it, whilst liquid (but not too hot) an equal amount of coal oil. Soak the moccassins thoroughly, using a stick, & hang them up to drip. When dry (about 5 minutes) take a knife & scrape off the coating of wax, inside & out. It is a messy job, but they are real waterproof, soft, & <u>not slippery</u> . . .

How is the wee Reptile? I wish I could see her, but it is hard to get in & out of here without you stayed a couple of weeks, & took a chance on Bill when he goes, which is not often.

Mrs Brown has tried to get money from the Literary Society (whoever they are) in England in my name, claiming to be my mother! I wrote & told her they had informed me & to lay off as I would contest the legality of the so-called adoption & told her to look up that Leonard son of hers. She thinks I am a millionaire having written one book, & claims the credit, saying she inspired the book!!! Mr. C & Mr. G. M. D. (F & O) are still fighting as to who discovered me (not to be mentioned) & some lady poet has written claiming my work for the British Empire, even tho I am an American; my oh my; all the stirrings over nothing. But heres worse, or better. Two old maiden ladies living in some part of Scotland, have written me thru Country Life, & claim to be first cousins or some kind of cousins of my fathers side of the family. It seems genuine although they do not know my uncle (McNeil) but seem to have heard of him. They are called "Belanys of Mac-" something or other, & are very old, & are very proud of me, & dont want anything except to know me as they have independent means of their own, although not rich or anything. They have a letter from Buffalo Bill which they treasure very much in answer to an enquiry as to his (my fathers) whereabouts time he was in the old show, in which he speaks very highly of my dad. Yes, I must get that letter of old man Codys about him, or a photograph of it. Anyway, I have written the old ladies I believe they are the real thing.

Funny how things turn out. No doubt we will find that you have inherited your warlike spirit from the Duke of Buckingham. Perhaps our daughter is the rightful Queen of Scotland, or an apache Princess who knows what next will be heard . . .

Give my love to the Pig & one X . . .

With best wishes
Archie

Belaney's true identity remained hidden until after he died in Canada in 1938.

PAY THE PIPER

It sounds like an opera. **Norma Piper** *was a Canadian soprano whose family lived in Calgary when she made her debut in 1930. George Pocaterra was an aristocratic Italian who had spent nearly thirty years in Alberta working as a cowboy and then operating his own dude ranch. After the death of his father, George returned to Italy, where he met Norma, who was in Milan to work with a voice coach. Norma was poor and proud (and arithmetically challenged), while George was rich. In the four brief acts of this work, she sang and reprised an appealing aria to her dear daddy, Calgary dentist W.A. Piper.*

Milan, Italy,
Via Ampère 40
October 7, 1934.

Dear Father: –

I was very glad to get your letter of September 18th., containing local news, but sorry about the deplorable condition of the crops in the Youngstown district.

Received Jack's $25.00 which was very welcome as my finances are rather in a deplorable condition . . . Had it not been that I had been assured of $500.00 for Sept. 15th, I would not have been able to face the necessity or the humiliation of asking Mr. Pocaterra for a loan until my money arrived for he had spent a good deal of money on the summer vacation, as he was determined to stand the biggest share of the expense.

At present I have only enough money for October and then I shall have absolutely not a dime left. Again for your perusal my un-reducable expenses are per month:

Pension and piano –	650 lire
Mastero	800 "
Italian lessons	<u>130</u> "
	1550 "

This does not take into account clothing and I do my own laundry, but occasionally there is drycleaning to be done. Tips to the maid, car fare. It is quite a distance to the masters and one is not supposed to exert oneself physically immediately before exercising the voice. I do a great deal of walking in the afternoon and at times in the early morning and sundays. The $75.00 per month just about takes care of the masters charges. I am really in a terrible state now as Mr. Pocaterra will be leaving this month. I cannot ask him for any more money, until I can show him that there has been money deposited to his credit in Calgary. Now Father, I would like you to try and place yourself in my position. A girl in a foreign country, where I have made alot of friends but where I cannot possibly expect to be able to raise any funds, without materially hurting my position. In such matters old countries are extremely strict . . . Please forgive me dear and try and understand my position, which has caused me to write in such a strong manner. I am sure you will see how it is with me here dear. I love you dearly, you know that, and I want to make good for your sake and the rest of the family and friends. Now with my dearest love.

Norma.

Oct.12/34

Dear Father, –

. . . Have now finished "L'Elisir d'amore" and am going to start "Don Pasquale". Today at lesson I sang [the] whole opera from the first note to the last all from memory. The voice is getting more beautiful every week . . .

I am thoroughly convinced that I am going to be a first class artist. My biggest booster and my hardest critic is George. He helps me a great deal with the pronunciation & expression & is absolutely certain that I am going to be a marvelous artist.

Otherwise he wouldn't be assisting me as he is. If my chances were not 100% he would have married me months ago & taken me away.

By jove! but he is a fine chap! . . .

Much love,
Norma

Oct.18/34

Dear Father,

. . . I hate to talk so seriously but see that I must. Sweet words and talk of "don't worry" are all right, but they don't buy food, and you can just imagine the position of any girl in any country without funds. You know how life is dear. I am sure you can realize what an uncomfortable position I am placed in . . .

If I do not have 2000 lire ahead for emergency, and sufficient money at the end of each month to pay all the expenses for the following month, I shall appeal to the British Consul for my return fare to Canada and come home.

If my family or my country cannot possibly raise the money that is necessary for my keep here, we will have to bid good-bye to our dreams.

This is the <u>last</u> time I shall write to you dear in this manner . . .

With fondest love,
Norma

Nov. 7/34

Dear Father, –

Poor dear. I am terribly sorry that I have to give you all this worry about my finances. It make me feel terrible to have to write such horrid letters, but what am I to do? I surely appreciate the 600 hundred that came the other week . . . My career is a sort of joint

partnership in which every one shares. Every one will share the glory
too when that time comes . . .

So glad you are feeling fine

Heaps of love

Norma

Nov.12/34 XII.E.F.

My dear, dear Father, –
Your three wonderful letters received today. What a sweet feeling of
love and happiness they caused to flow into my heart. It is wonderful, wonderful to have such a splendid, ideal Father. I shall never be
able to repay you for all the love you have lavished on me.

I am so tremendously thankful that the financial business has
been so well arranged. I wish it were not necessary to have help from
my loved ones but there is nothing I can do just yet to avoid it. But
oh what an incentive it gives me to work hard . . .

I must leave you now dear for a little. I thoroughly appreciate
your dear words and send you my fondest love.

Lovingly

Norma

*Two years later Norma and George were married. When the Second
World War cut short her operatic career, which he was managing, they
returned to Canada. Norma taught voice in Calgary until the 1970s.*

A FASCIST FUNERAL

*Two other young Canadian women were studying in Italy in 1934.
Nineteen-year-old* **Eleanor Bone** *and her twenty-one-year-old sister,
Grace, from Belleville, Ontario, were spending a year in Florence at
the Villa Donatella, a finishing school run by an Englishwoman
named Miss Penrose. (Eleanor had been expelled from Branksome*

Hall, a private school in Toronto.) They had sailed over on an Italian liner, the Rex, abrim with 350 charming young Italian Fascists who had won a trip to the United States in a contest organized by Italy's dictator, Benito Mussolini. On board, the men became the sisters' dancing partners. Eleanor wrote this letter to her parents.

Saturday, Oct 27. [1934]

Dear Mother and Daddy –

How are you all. I was just thinking of you as I was having my bath, a few minutes ago, and decided it must be about time for afternoon tea at home, and I was wondering what you had been doing, and what had happened since we left. We have only been gone two weeks, but it feels like a year to me. I suppose it is because it is such a complete change . . .

Today Mussolini came to Florence to help bury the bodies of the 35 Fasci[s]ti who died for the cause of Fascism when it first started, and which formerly reposed in the Duomo, and were being moved to the Santa Crocè (?) Cathedral. So we were wakened at 6.30, I wore my vagabond [hat?] and navy blue woolen suit & oxfords & my rain coat, as it was a cold dismal day. My shoulders ached all day, which made me very unhappy, I think it is neuralgia.

Anyway we got under way at eight and you never saw such a sight. The streets just milling with blackshirts, beginning with little boys, some not any older than five, right straight through to the old bleary veterans that had fought with Garibaldi! We were absolutely pop-eyed. We got outside the Piazza del Santa Crocè, but were not allowed to go through, because the commissaire would not give his consent. As we were standing there, and Mamselle was talking to three handsome officers the one officer kept turning and looking at me, and finally Mamselle called me over and the officer said he had seen me on the Rex, but that he hadn't had a chance to speak to me, as there were so many students already. So we had a nice little chat, and then he left, and the officers said we could go through, so I guess he had told them we weren't going to throw any bombs, or anything.

The square was line, upon line of fascisti and it was really a marvellous sight. There were no plain clothesmen at all, and no women. We had reserved windows overlooking the square near the cathedral, but seemed to be the only people looking on. After nine o'clock every street into the square was closed, and the streets were all guarded straight thro' with the soldiers as they were so afraid something would happen to Mussolini.

We stood there from 8.30 till half past one before Mussolini arrived, and we were all starving, and aching from head to foot, but the fascisti students were very entertaining in the square beneath, and the time did pass quickly. Mussolini finally did arrive most unexpectedly from a side street in a little car, & most of the girls missed seeing him, but I happened to be looking that way and saw him at once, before the police guard closed in on him and hustled him into the cathedral. Then the most appalling & spectacular parade of soldiers and more soldiers passed across the cathedral and in behind him, it must have taken an hour before they all passed, and the coffins of the 35 fascisti, with their names on the coffins.

The ceremony was broadcasted in the square and was very short. As each coffin came in Mussolini called out Camarate – and then the man's name and the kettle drums rolled three times, and a volley of shots were fired, and pidgeons would wheel around the cathedral and the assembled fascisti would all raise their arms and yell "presente". Finally Mussolini strutted out from a little lane beside the church, and I almost fell out of the window trying to see him, which I did for a couple of seconds while he gave the fascisti salute. Then every one rushed at him, roaring and yelling, and the soldiers rushed at the mob, & Mussolini got in his car & drove away. The people over here simply worship him, and you begin to think he is a demi god yourself after a while. His picture is plastered all over every store, on the streets, in the papers & everywhere.

We finally got back to the school about 2.30, and I slept all afternoon, as my shoulders hurt & I had a headache & felt too miserable to be pleasant. At half past six, Miss Ramage took some of us to see

Ponte Vechio & Ufizzi galleries illuminated, and it looked very beautiful. Then we came home and had dinner . . .

Heaps of love to Jamie and all the family –

Eleanor.

Eleanor's daughter, Stevie Cameron, recalls that the sisters were brought back home earlier than planned "because they fell in love and their parents wanted to erase that danger."

A WOMAN'S WORK

Rit Wengel, a university-educated Danish governess, came to Canada in 1925 to wed her beau, Paul, who would prove to be an unfaithful, parsimonious husband. After a lonely period on a Saskatchewan farm, she returned to Denmark during the Second World War but came back to move to the West Coast with Paul. His refusal to give her more than basic support forced her to seek labouring jobs in the fields and factories. For decades she corresponded with a Saskatchewan family, to whom she sent this letter in 1948.

p.t. Chilliwack
4 July 1948

Dear Mrs. Miller!

. . . Now you better hear about the work. I came back June 26 and started with 42 other women to work in a cannery in Abbotsford. It takes an hours drive in a truck over partly rough roads and it is <u>awful!</u> Work starts at 9 1/2 o'clock [p.m.]. We sit on a small round "plate," while ever moving tables loaded with berries pass; they have to be cleaned for leaves, rotten stuff e.t.c. 12 women to the table. After a while the world seems to go around and around wherever you look, your legs cut to pieces o[n] the edge of the seat and your back to be pinched by hundred devils; but there is still let us say 3 hours left before 1/2 hours rest for lunch at 1 1/2 o'clock [a.m.]. After that we climb up to this mind-inspiring work for another 5 <u>or</u> 6 hours work <u>without</u> rest at all. It is cold there as the berries have to be kept cold and when we at last are released in the morning we can't hear the birds sing for our chattering teeth. So we ride back to Chilliwack, try and clean away some of the dust and dirt, go out shopping, get a few hours sleep and I start picking raspberries and sweat as much in the sun as I froze during the night. I cannot keep up both any longer; don't know which to drop as the night-shift pays the best; but I feel dizzy and fearfully dull, so I suppose I shall drop that.

You ask why I do it. I just get enough from Paul to pay rent and by careful planning food. Whenever I mentioned stockings or shoes or the like in Victoria he said "This is no time to buy that." Keeping up that attitude means, that time to do it will never come for me, so unless I go to Paradise or join a nudist-club I must find some way to provide, the most necessary things myself . . .

Dear Mrs Miller you do keep up my trust that there still are a few – a very few marriages that survive storms and sickness and bad times, and last till death them do part – <u>even</u> in this country. That is how it should be. Craigs & Mary will be like that too. Love to you both from

Rit W.

Rit Wengel and her husband were still married when she died in 1959 of complications from an ulcer.

REGAL SUIT

After the Second World War, Canadians returned to a renascent Europe to study. In 1950 **Eric Nicol** *was a naive young Vancouverite attending the Sorbonne in Paris – until he got a call from a Canadian friend, a comedian named Bernie Braden, to write the pilot for a BBC radio series in London. Leave Your Name and Number was an overnight success (as would be their next series, Breakfast with Braden). Nicol moved into a flat with three attractive women, one of them a Canadian-born friend named Margaret, who had a posh Mayfair*

accent. At thirty, unexpectedly successful in his career as a scriptwriter,
Nicol wrote these letters to his parents in British Columbia.

3/6/50
15 Crompton Court
Brompton Road
London S.W. 3
England.

Dear Folks,

. . . I'm tossing pounds all over the place, spending money like blood,
which for me, as you know, is a drastic loosening up. For one thing,
I've ordered a new suit. Since I have not had a new suit since 1947,
this might not seem too frivolous a gambol, but wait. I let Margaret
take me to the sons of her tailor, who turned out to be in the West
End, and whose shop had the air of awful drabness that means get
ready to be soaked. The two young tailors welcomed us (Marg came
along at my behest to make sure I got pants with the suit and avoided
other natural blunders), and said, "Oh, yes, you're the gentlemen
Mr. Douglas Fairbanks said would be in." You can imagine with
what flushed babbling I confessed that I didn't know Mr. Douglas
Fairbanks. Luckily Margaret was able to produce a name that softened the stiffness of their manner, and we all started looking at bits
of cloth, none of which looked big enough for a suit for me, certainly not a suit that I could wear in public. Marg and I had already
decided in a general way that I should have a grey suit, but she
wanted something dark enough for London while I wanted something light enough for Banff. The tailors wanted something that
would get rid of us. Finally one of them brought out a couple of
bolts. One was a light grey, very fine herringbone, which I liked and
decided to have. Then he let me have the second bolt: the price. Price
upon delivery, including zipper: 37 quid. By paying on the export
plan, in U.S. dollars, I cut this down to 30, or about $87 U.S. I need
hardly say that this was more than I expected to pay, but I felt the
honour of the senior dominion was at stake, so I nodded speech-
lessly. I was immediately set upon by three different little men, like

Gulliver by the Lilliputians, trying me down, up and sideways with tapes and uttering mysterious sounds to each other, amongst which I could distinguish only general approbation about my chest and pungent silence about the length of my legs. They asked me a good many mutually embarrassing questions about the American-cut suit I was wearing (the old blue which now fits me like a maternity smock), such as was I addicted to flaps on the pockets and did I always wear braces. I tried to give the answer that was expected of me, adding materially to the confusion. I shall not be surprised if the fly proves to have both buttons <u>and</u> zipper, and five watch pockets.

As we were leaving I expected the tailors to say something about a deposit, and sort of hung around waiting for them to remember to ask me, thereby giving our exit every bit as much awkward shuffling as our entrance. Not until I was walking light-heartedly towards Piccaddily did Margaret remind me that the difficult part of dealing with an English tailor is getting him to accept you socially as worth his label. As for paying for the suit, he hardly expects it, and if you pay on time or anything like it he is liable to be offended at such an abrupt termination of your association and never make you another one . . .

10/6/50

Dear Folks,

. . . Was summoned by my tailors for a fitting last week. As I entered the shop I noticed for the first time the royal crest on the window. Benson and Clegg are by appointment to Guess Who? Oh, after this Woodward's simply won't do. Anyway, they had the suit all sewn together with white thread. I got into it, and after reaching the verdict that I was disproportionate they tore the suit to pieces before my very eyes. First one sleeve, then the other, then the collar, and finally a lot of horsing around in the crotch. It was straight out of something written for Jimmy Durante. After they had the suit in rags they smiled gamely and said they'd let me know when they were ready to take another shot at it . . .

23/6/50

Dear Folks,

. . . My tailor called me in again this week. This time they didn't bother putting it on me. They just brought it in and tore it to pieces immediately. I know that they now firmly believe that I change shape, like the bladder fish, according to season or sudden sounds. They're trying to find my maximum size and build the suit around that. The little tailor who has to do all the work (the others stand and watch horrified) didn't actually break down, but I could see that his lip was trembling, and I shook hands with him before I left, giving an extra squeeze to buck him up a bit . . .

7 July, 1950

Dear Folks,

I have just come back from a fitting at my tailor's. I have lost count of how many fittings I've had now. All I know is that the two young fellows in charge aren't in the shop any more. They've fled to Cornwall, the rockier part, leaving the little old fellow who holds the trousers off the floor so that I have to high jump into them. I think we're gradually closing in on me, though. Today there was a distinct glint of hope in the old boy's eyes as he fitted the padding over my shoulders. Just has to move one button about an eighth of an inch, he says. After that I get to pay for it. Exciting, eh? And I never know when I may meet the King coming out of the dressing room in his drawers. That's almost worth the extra money, if you talk about it to enough people, as I intend to . . .

Well, I must away to my scribbling board and another knock-up with nonsense. Tell the mountains to get spruced up, because local lams home.

Doink . . .

Eric

Not unexpectedly, Eric Nicol would go on to become a popular columnist in Canada and win the Stephen Leacock Medal for Humour three times.

GEORGE WOODCOCK, HOMESTEADER

George Woodcock was born in Winnipeg in 1907; his family moved back to England shortly thereafter, his father having failed as a farmer. George, a pacifist, worked as a market gardener during the Second World War. His real passion was words: he wrote poetry, edited a literary magazine with an anarchistic bent, and ran a pacifist publishing house after its editors were charged with sedition. By 1949, the author of a dozen books, he returned to Canada with his wife, Ingeborg, to farm on Vancouver Island. He wrote this letter to his friend Herbert Read, the eminent English editor and critic.

Sooke Post Office,
Vancouver Island,
British Columbia, Canada
13th July, 1950

Herbert Read, Esq.,
Stonegrave,
Yorkshire, England.
Dear Herbert,

It was very good to hear from you, though we were both greatly disappointed to hear that we have to wait until next year before we might see you here. I had intended to write you much earlier, and the only explanation for my delay lies in the vast press of work at this time of the year. Sometime before the winter sets in we have to complete the foundations, walls, floors, roofs and windows of the final extension of our house, as well as stuccoing the outside – everything, in fact, that is needed to make it weatherproof so that we can work inside when the bad weather sets in. Then we have had to keep our garden going sufficiently to grow enough vegetables for the summer, and potatoes, onions, beans, peas, tomatoes, etc., to store and bottle for the winter. We have also put in a few gooseberries, black currants, boysenberries, cultivated blackberries, and a fair sized rhubarb bed. But we've not so far gone in for livestock, partly because we find them a great tie – potentially – which would prevent our travelling about at all easily, and partly because even here it is doubtful whether we would find the effort financially worthwhile, unless we grew food on a large scale. We have put in some sunflowers and maize as an experiment, and if the crop is large enough we may try some chickens over the winter in partnership with a neighbour.

From the standpoint of Walden economics, I suppose we have done fairly well. Our acre of land costs us two hundred dollars; the long frontage has a lane running beside it, down which, owing to the proximity of a power station and a reservoir in the hills behind us (feeding Victoria), we are lucky enough to have electricity and water facilities. So far, we have spent about eight hundred dollars on the house, which has given us one large room, twenty by sixteen, complete, except for top floor, with a brick fireplace, and I hope to put in the floor next week. Then there are a kitchen, a bathroom and a bedroom-study, all in various stages of finish, but at least usable. To fit these out completely will cost perhaps another six hundred dollars, which will include stucco. Afterwards we shall build a studio and a study, which, since their finish will not have to be so elaborate and will not include appliances of any kind, should cost no more than four hundred dollars. So that for two thousand dollars, or about seven hundred devalued pounds, we shall have built a roomy, rambling and sufficient house.

There does still remain the financial problem. Fuel is easily obtainable. All last winter we got by on a pile of odd pieces from a local sawmill which had been dumped on our field, together with some sawdust which we used for fertilizer and mulching, and I think what is left will cover the next year. After that, we shall just have to go and cut our own wood. Then we do get some fruit and milk, even occasional eggs, by bartering for vegetables. But groceries, electricity, water and bus fares are dear by English standards, and there is still lumber to be bought for the house. However, the last month we have been picking strawberries, earning anything from fifteen shillings to two pounds a day each, according to the weight of the crop, and I have been getting quite an amount of radio work recently. The CBC is trying to infuse some interest in literature into Canadian life, and I have managed to persuade them to put on some pretty serious talks on people like Silone, Orwell, Malraux, Greene, yourself, and am now presenting a series on the classic Russian novelists. Finally, when the broadcasting is not sufficient, I can get work as a builder's labourer in Victoria, digging ditches for what seems to me, still, the fantastic wages of thirteen pounds a week.

At times we both get a great deal of satisfaction out of this life, and at times we are really painfully nostalgic for European amenities and for the company of our friends. Here one has hundreds of cordial acquaintances, hearty and first-name-calling, but few real friends to whom one feels any depth of attachment or any inclination to open oneself. And I find at times an insatiable desire to see an ordered landscape, or to look at an old, lived-out building, no matter how ugly. On the other hand, the almost frontier uncouthness here is really fascinating in its way, and there is something exhilarating about the fluidity of life, the way in which people shift from job to job, from trade to trade, loggers one year, fishermen the next, carpenters the next, and perhaps undergraduates or clerks. And we get a great deal of pleasure out of such things as hummingbirds, garter snakes, deer, raccoons, and our occasional fleeting glimpses of cougars or of bear tracks.

I may get a commission for a travel book on the coast up to the Yukon, and am thinking of a book on the art and life of the coast Indians. I wonder whether, apart from Ruth Benedict and Boas, much has been published on them in England. It would really make a fascinating subject, if a publisher could be found. However, I haven't even started on it.

Write whenever you can. With greetings to your family from us both,

Ever,

George

Woodcock went on to become one of Canada's most distinguished men of letters, writing scores of books of history, biography, and literary criticism and editing the journal Canadian Literature. *He died in 1995.*

THE LIFE OF BRIAN

In the early 1950s **Brian Moore** *was a recent Irish immigrant to Canada who had left a reporting job with* The Montreal Gazette *"to become a serious writer." To support himself he wrote two paperback thrillers under his own name for Harlequin, the Canadian publisher better known for its romance novels, and another pair under a pseudonym for the U.S. Gold Medal line. Meanwhile he was completing his first non-genre novel,* Judith Hearne. *The British publisher André Deutsch was considering publishing it when Moore wrote him this letter.*

June 12. [1954]

Dear Mr. Deutsch:

I received a letter from Miss [Diana] Athill yesterday in which she suggested that you would like to talk to me about my novel and my future plans. Unfortunately, I leave Paris for Montreal Monday June 14, by BOAC and will only be in London airport for an hour between planes.

I therefore thought I would write you a letter telling you something about myself and answering some of the questions which, I imagine, you would put to me in the event that you decide Judith Hearne is worth the trouble you envisage in selling it.

I am 32 years old and was born and educated in Ireland. I am at present a Canadian citizen having lived in Canada for the last six years. In the intervening time I did a lot of travelling, working for the British Government, UNRRA and for some Irish newspapers. I have been in seventeen countries and have lived in Poland, France, Italy and England. I have always wanted to write but only got down to it seriously three years ago when I sent a short story to the New Yorker and was encouraged to continue by Hollis Alpert, one of the editors. One of my first short stories was published by Northern Review, a Canadian little magazine. At the time, I was working as a reporter on the Montreal Gazette and I decided that I would have to give up journalism if I wanted to become a serious writer. I also decided to find some way of making enough to live on which would leave me most of my year free for the work I wanted to do. So I wrote two Canadian pocket books and sold them and also wrote some short stories for the American slicks. Willis Kingsley Wing agreed to become my New York agent and in that first year of "commercial" writing I sold stories to the American Magazine, Lilliput, Weekend, Bluebook . . . this s.s. [short story] writing proved to be too time consuming, so I wrote another pocket book under an alias and it immediately sold to Gold Medal Books for an advance of three thousand dollars. I wrote it in two months and this left me with the time and money to write Miss Hearne.

Gold Medal were very keen on the book which they plan to bring out in July and have assured me that I can do them one a year. This means that for two months work I have ten months free to work at the serious writing which interests me. In addition, my wife has an excellent job. So I am for the time being free from the economic pressure which, as you know, forces many serious writers to work at fruitless chores.

Miss Hearne is my first novel and you are the first British publisher it has been shown to. It is perhaps a "joyless" book, but it is one which has been in my mind for a very long time and which I feel I had to write. I chose a difficult type of heroine, I admit, but I wished to avoid the autobiographical type of first novel and I feel very strongly that if you write you should progress in each book, not repeating yourself, but tackling new problems each time. James Joyce has been my main literary influence and Judith Hearne is a Joycean type of book. I tried to show, in a dramatic form the dilemma of faith which confronts most non-intellectual Catholics at some time or other in their lives. Certain movements in the book follow the ritual of the mass and the problems and questions raised in it <u>I am sure</u> are ones which will strike an emotional response in Catholic and ex-Catholic readers. The problems are also typically Irish and, I am certain, would cause a lot of comment, most of it hostile, in both Northern and Southern Ireland.

It is also a book about a woman, presenting certain problems of living peculiar to women. I wrote it with all the sympathy and understanding that I am capable of and I think that among the people who have read it so far, no woman has disliked it. I think it is a book for women to read because they understand the viewpoint and for my own sex, it is an effort to help men gain a greater understanding of women like Miss Hearne.

I make no apology for its being about an uninteresting woman. Miss Hearne is meant to bore and irritate the reader at times. Real people do. There's far too much of a vogue at the moment for books about one eyed men, whores and other assorted weirdies – for phony sensationalism – which I feel has little or nothing to do with life as it is lived by most of us.

Whether Miss Hearne is published or not, I plan to start my next book in July. It will be a different book and the main character will not be "uninteresting." But that is because, as I said earlier, I feel a writer should not repeat himself and should set himself new problems with each book he writes.

Politically I'm neither right, Left or centre. I've been all of them at times and have found flaws in all three. I lived for two years in Poland – 1946-1947 – at a pretty unique time in that country's history but I never wrote about it. I believe very strongly that the business of propaganda for or against should be kept out of the novel which is an emotional form of sharing of experience – not a political pitch.

I am an ex-Catholic – Jesuit educated – and you might say that I'm a sort of Graham Greene running the other way. As this is an emotional and important thing to me, I expect it will color whatever I write in the future.

I am also Irish – one of a new generation of Irish exiles. The middle classes have been going out of Ireland in the last twenty years for the first time in the country's history. I am interested in the Irish and Irish exiles, particularly the Irish Americans. I am interested in what makes them lose most of their qualities and grow lumps and covers of corruption when they are faced with the American scene. I expect that I will be writing about this in my next book.

This is all I can think of telling you for the moment. There will certainly be other questions you would like to ask me in the event that you decide to publish Miss Hearne. I work a full day at writing and I intend to continue.

I hope you do publish it because I believe very strongly in the book and I hope that it will have a wider interest than you perhaps imagine. I also think that it should sell pretty well in Eastern Canada because I worked up a fairly good name while I was with the Gazette and the book would certainly be widely reviewed and mentioned there.

My Montreal address is 4525 St. Catherine Street West, Montreal. P.Q.

Sincerely,
Brian Moore

OUT OF AFRICA

*From the mid-1940s to the mid-1960s Einar and Muriel Neilson oversaw "Lieben," an informal but fruitful artistic oasis on Bowen Island, near Vancouver. Some of Canada's finest authors, artists, and intellectuals visited Lieben (German for "to love") to gain inspiration amid four forested hectares above a rocky beach. One of the Neilsons' friends was **Margaret Laurence**, a Manitoba writer who* *went to Africa in 1950 with her civil-engineer husband, Jack, to live in the British protectorate of Somaliland and later on Ghana's Gold Coast. Laurence had begun to write short fiction but had not yet produced the novels, such as* The Diviners *and* The Stone Angel, *that would make her a literary icon. She wrote this letter to the Neilsons.*

> c/o Chief Engineer, Port of Tema,
> P.O. Box 1, Tema, Gold Coast,
> W. Africa.
> 7 Oct 55

Dear Muriel and Einar:

The worst effect that the tropics has on one is the gradual loss of memory, and when you start out with a bad memory, as I did, what is left at the end of a tour is precisely nothing. I regret to say I cannot remember whether or not I wrote to you telling you that we were expecting another child, or when I wrote to you, if at all. Anyway, I will attempt to catch you up briefly on what has happened to us this tour. Most important, our son David was born Aug 9. He was 8 lbs 12 oz at birth, and now at 2 months is quite a robust lad. He is a dear little boy, and looks very tough and aggressive. Actually he seems so far to have quite a good nature, being full of the joy of life as long as he is full of milk as well. We are quite lucky in that both our kids have had as babies quite a simple character – they cried when hungry, and that's about all. As they say in pidgin English, 'palaver finish'. Jocelyn has taken to David remarkably well, although for the first month she was incredibly naughty and rebellious in other ways. She has always been very gentle with him, but showed her resentment by arguing incessantly with us. I wonder if anyone achieves the perfect parenthood laid down in the books? I know I don't. I would try to be loving and patient with her, and would succeed in being so until she asked for the 150th time <u>why</u> she had to come and wash her hands before lunch – then I would explode and roar like a regimental sergeant major – usually with surprisingly gratifying results. However, she has simmered down now and is a little less lethal than before. Her most difficult (and perhaps most endearing) trait is that she always has a ready answer – one can never beat her to the draw, so to speak. Jack one day got a bit annoyed after he'd told her about a million times to stop doing something, and he said to her, "If you don't stop doing that, I shall have to give you a good crack". To which she replied, "You can't crack me – I'm not an egg!" She is at an interesting age – frantic to know everything. Jack taught her to count to five, and the other day he wrote the numbers 1, 2 and 3 on her blackboard for her. She came rushing to me, shouting, "Mummy! Come and see what clever Daddy can do! It's very wonderful! He can draw a three!" . . .

I hope the ebony head reaches you in good condition. It is quite a nice one, I think – it is the head of a queen, with the traditional head-dress, done in brown ebony. All the wood used in carving these heads is the so-called "brown ebony" – it is blackish, but if you look carefully you will see that it is streaked with dark brown.

We will be going on leave on Oct 16, and will be in London for 3 months, at the very worst time of year. We still haven't got a flat, but are hoping we shall be able to find something that is heated. English houses and flats are notoriously cold. We shall be returning here for one more tour, at least, and after that we don't know. We may return to Canada, but it is likely we won't do that until Jocelyn is of school age.

Must go now. Hope you are both well. Please write sometime when you have time, and I will try to be better correspondent in future.

Love from us all,

Peg.

A WOMB OF ONE'S OWN

Lieben was a creative catalyst for Malcolm Lowry when he was writing the first draft of his final novel, October Ferry to Gabriola. *Earle Birney, the dean of Canadian poets in the 1960s, wrote his first novel,* Turvey, *there: it won the Stephen Leacock Medal for Humour*

in 1950. Birney spent weeks at a time at Lieben, writing, entertain-
ing his mistresses, and cataloguing the flora and fauna of the land
lent him by his friend, Einar Neilson – to whom he typed (mistakes
and all) these letters of friendship.

[September 17, 1961]
. . . Einar, I do hope you are feeling better. Muriel told me something
about your headaches. I do wish you could work out some sort of
compromise between "no 222s" and "22 222's" or whatever it is. I
think you should ask a doctor whether that amount of 222s mightnt
be harmful,and try tapering off rather than suddenly cutting off and
feeling what must amount to withdrawal pains. I worry about you
and wish to christ I knew how to help or what to say. This I do know
– that you shouldnt let yourself get depressed about your own life
and your future. Muriel sais you wrote her something about "crawling back into the womb of Bowen". My friend, it may be a womb,
but it's a womb with a view, such as few men have ever created. We
all have to have wombs to crawl into because it's not us that's mad
but the cockeyed world; the madenss is a collective thing and we can
only keep individually sane by keeping as much out of the collective
society as possible (I mean, the bourgeois-collective society, "collective" in the acquisitive sense).You have a found a way.Of course you
pay a price for it – you havent become a captain of industry or a har-
rassed professor with stomach ulcers, or a bullying politician or a
psychopathic peddler of soap or snow. You've remained Einar Neilson,
a man who has more friends and well-wishers and admirers than any
man I know; a man who has created a place of peace and beauty in
the time of war and ugliness,and shared it with marvelous generosity
with those who needed it most,and who have been helped in turn to
go about their own creation. Einar, this is a wholly admirable and
unique thing you have done with these years of your life; you have
created not only something physical, but a symbol,a way of living
which has been both balm and stimulus to hundreds of other people.
Dont think cheaply of it or of yourself; think only of how to carry it

on,how to work it out practically so that you dont have to live away from Bowen to earn the money to maintain Lieben . . .

And write me. I wont try even to say thanks,because the word is too small for the wonderful summer you have given me.

LIEBEN
27 May 64

Dear Einar,

Interim report on stewardship. Everything going swell. After nearly a week of rain,now have days like midsummer,with fresh cool spring nights. Mr. Cat flourishes. And I? I begin to live again, that slow wonderful return of calmness Lieben has always brought me, plus,this time, a gradual feeling of healing in my ravaged stomach. So far I've had little spirit to think or write – a feeling of disgust at the intellectual world still pervades me,after the worst winter I've ever put in at that university – whose "leaders" get more corrupt and autocratic and stupid every year. I wd. quit all teaching at once if I could afford to,but my pension doesnt start for another five years, I cant even get an advance loan on it,and so I must go on working.

And you,my friend? I hope your stomach is healing too,and that the airs of Banff, or Field,or wherever you actually are by now, are proving spring-like at least . . .

So far have spent most of my time and energy happily on the Lieben surrounds. Cleared out the trail to the spring,and up to the Nooky Nooks.Raked and trimmed the trail to the road. Dug all the rotting cedar sections out of the salal and am drying them in the sun. Those already dry,in and around woodshed, I've made into kindling and stacked for the winter.Also stacked up the alder chunks for the winter.Am meantime getting my own fuel for fireplace out of the fallen loose wood scraps in nearby woods,so you'll have a good supply of wood still – or at least there'll be a good supply left by first of July,and by then presumably there wont be much need for a night fire.It's been down to 35 at nights lately. I weeded the flower bed by the woodshed and it looks grand: those black tulips and the white rockery flowers. I sickled down the grass to the incinerator and rescued some rotting wood by the old wheelbarrow,dried it and stacked it in the woodshed for the winter. Mowed the terrace lawns,sickled the lower terrace,weeded the flower borders,got the dandelions etc. out of the lawns. Etc. It's been good to get back to working with my hands,and sleeping at nights. Tomorrow, who knows, I may write a poem again.

Love. Let's hear from you.

Earle

SLAUGHTER WEEK

Susan B. Peters, the daughter of Russian Mennonites who emigrated to Canada, was educated in Alberta in the 1920s and 1930s. After the Second World War Susan volunteered with the Mennonite Central Committee in Europe. In 1956, having earned an education degree from the University of Alberta, she went north to teach Inuit and Dene children at Reindeer Station, a settlement established in 1932 to introduce reindeer farming to northern Canada. During her time there she wrote scores of hurriedly typed letters to friends and relatives.

Reindeer Station,
NWT., Canada
Nov.4,1956.

Dear Elma –

Hi!How are you and all the good people in Newton, Kansas? Are you surprised to hear from me, and then from a place so very high up north? Yep, I went and did it what I have been wanting to do for a number of years – went to the Northwest Territories to teach "little"Eskimo and Indians.

You will find Reindeer Station at 68 43' N., 134 07' W. (look up in your old Geography text what that means) on the map. It lies on the east channel of the Mackenzie River, about 60 miles from the mouth , MacKenzie District, Northwest Territories. It is the headquarters for the reindeer industry; has a private commercial radio station and a trading post. The Hudsons Bay company has a store here as in so many outlying posts of Canada, for they were the first ones to come this far north. The company was established in 1620 [in fact, 1670] and ,at one time,owned just about all of Canada.

There has never been a school at this settlement. Some of the children have attended the Mission school at Aklavik, or have taken some correspondence courses. At any rate – it's quite a mix-up as far as grades and ages are concerned . . .

I had quite a time making them see and understand that they must come to school on time. This is not hard for them to do as they live only a few steps from the school, in fact, closer than I do. They still do not understand why this is necessary, but they are on time. When the bell rings, they start running until they get here. A few times I had to go and get them, now they come . . .

Some years ago the Eskimo here had no reindeer. Then the government hired some Laplanders to bring a herd from Alaska, I believe. It took them 5years to bring them across, and a lot of hardship was suffered by the people, also many of the reindeer perished. But now a number of herds have been established, some of them owned by the Eskimo themselves. The government sells the herds to them on easy and long terms, so that anyone, who has any ambition and a long-range view can become an owner,e.g.the natives only, not the white people. These herds were brought in solely for the purpose of giving the natives a ready supply of meat.

In two weeks the annual slaughter of the reindeer will take place at this station. A certain number of the government owned herd is killed every year, and the meat divided up among the natives. The schools of the NWT also get a supply of meat which is used for hot lunches for the school children during the winter months . . . Just mentioning it in the letter , made me hungry for it, and I shall go and have a slice of cold roast which I had for dinner. Come and join me.

Before the slaughter, the families of the herders will be brought in to the station. They are with them during the summer and live in tents. For the winter, they move into Reindeer Depot, where they live in log cabins. With them will come in some more pupils, who will go away again in spring. I wonder if I ever shall have a well-ordered school, with pupils attending regularly and passing every year. But that is almost too much to hope for . . .

In a few years this whole settlement is supposed to be moved to New-Aklavik or East Three (E.-3) as it is called here. There the government intends to build a 15-room school and a two dormitories to hold 500 children. This is to prevent the children to leave school when their parents go hunting or trapping.

Today we heard over the news that the first CPA (Canadian Pacific Airline) has come in to Aklavik. It brought 1000 lb. first-class mail. They will go for it from here next week by snowmobile which travels on the river. When I say "the first plane" I mean – the first plane since the river froze over this fall. There is a time when we get no mail, sometimes for two months, and that is in spring at thawing time and in fall at freezing time . . . All summer and fall the mail comes in by pontoon planes which land on the water . . . The other day we went "jigging" that means fishing through holes in the ice. You have just an ordinary stick with a short string and a bent nail for a hook on it. This you gently move up and down through the hole, and in no time you have a fish. But you must be very quick and jerk the fish out the minute it bites, otherwise it will escape as there is no barb on the hook. The fish one can catch are from 1 ft.-5 ft. long. Some of them are good to eat, like the white fish, others not even the sledge dogs will eat unless they are cooked. Even our dogs here are spoiled . . .

Greetings to my friends in Newton . . .

Susan

Reindeer Station, N.W.T.
Mar. 30, 1958

Dear Rudy:

. . . This week was Slaughter week again as they had not finished killing all the reindeer, they had intended to kill. On account of the flu, the kill in fall was started rather late – in December – and by the end of the week it was too dark too see when shooting the animals. The animals are all being herded together on top of the hill. The herders get them "milling" around e.g. a bunch is herded together, then they start going round and round. The next group goes round and round this first , and so on. This is all done very quietly. You can hear a faint: Ough,ough (pronounced like the German sound "Ö", the short Ö, like in the word: Götter. Several herders choose the animals they want to shoot. These are being shot while the herd is milling around. Other herders skin the dead reindeer and often draw them right there, and also dehorn them. This killing and skinning goes on at the same time. Then the bombardier is driven up, and long, stout rope tied to the rear of it, and then the reindeer carcasses are tied to rope at intervals. A string of about half a dozen carcasses are being dragged down the hill to the slaughter house, which is about half-way down. There the heart, liver, and heads are being examined by government veterinarians. The men finish skinning and drawing the animals, then they are hung up and washed, and finally are hung up on racks outside to freeze. After a few weeks the people haul them to the missions, schools and the Hudson's Bay trading places, where the meat is sold for 55¢-65¢ a pound. I get mine for less than that . . .

Writing about meat makes me hungry, so I shall fry some for my supper . . .

Susan

SEND MONEY

In the late 1960s **Steve Vigneault** *was attending college in Montreal and trying to figure out how to survive financially away from home. His mother thought he should be able to get lunch for half a buck. His grandmother wanted proof of his expenditures. This letter to his mother was written in French.*

Hauterive, Montréal, 14 Oct. 1968

Mother,

I was glad to receive the $25.00. Father sent me $10.00 last week and I have just received another $10.00 from him. I'm going to pay $10.00 for my laundry and that only leaves me $25.00 because with last week's money I had a suit cleaned for $3.00, my blue trousers shortened for $1.00 and I had breakfast and now all I have is the $25.00 you have sent me.

I am not doing any judo because the outfit costs $20.00 and I'm not doing any typing because I wouldn't have enough time to study.

Right, I want to explain something to you: my meals.

At the moment, I have lunch and dinner but never enough to satisfy my hunger.

Lunch does not cost ¢.50, that's impossible here. If you don't believe me, call the college. First, soup with bread and butter = .20¢ 2 scoops of hamburger with potatoes = .80¢ a dessert = .15¢.

So that is $1.15 for a complete lunch, not .50¢ + .10¢ for a glass of milk.

When you can't stand the thought of another mouthful of hamburger, you can buy minute steak = $1.25 or something else. I forgot also that at our age, we need milk, which costs .10¢ a glass.

Breakfast on average is .75¢ if you order 1 milk, 2 pieces of toast with jam, a bowl of cereal. 1 egg = .40¢ So here's what it all means:

Complete lunch per month at $1.25 each	$37.50
Dinner...	$37.50
Breakfast............. at 75¢.........................	$22.50
	$97.50

I just hope that you believe me and that you're not like grandmother who always needs proof. If you want, telephone the director, Alphonse Trottier. I'm not such a liar that I'd steal from my parents!

I admit there are some thieves in the college, but I can't do anything about that: I hope to receive my loan from the government, that's what it is for. Now this is how I manage to feed myself: I don't order any soup, or milk, or dessert, or breakfast. I eat hamburger with potatoes and water. Sometimes there are less expensive items

on the menu, like chicken salad or Chinese food or an omelette with
1 slice of ham: when that happens, I order soup or a dessert as well.
I'm not saying all this because I'm angry, but because I want you to
know that I am really not trying to trick you out of your money and
that I'm making sacrifices too.

So here's what it costs me each month, by depriving myself of
breakfast, milk, soup, dessert, etc . . .

Lunch per month at 80¢	$24.00
Dinner per month at 80¢	$24.00
No breakfast	00.00
	$48.00

What happens is that after dinner I play indoors hockey or hand-
ball and after the game I'm tired and I am hungry and thirsty. So I
buy myself a soft drink and some pastries, and then I don't have any
money left because I spend it on the pastries and the soft drink and
sometimes when I am hungry I eat breakfast and pay with money
meant for my lunches and dinners.

Don't forget that I also need soap, toothpaste, mouthwash, Halo
[shampoo], deodorant, shoe polish, pens, graph paper, letter paper,
stamps, a clothes brush, envelopes, combs, rulers, white lined paper,
glue, scotch tape, all the little things that taken together are quite
expensive.

What I need now is 2 of the Walter Foster series of learn-to-draw
books, No. 18 about faces and No. 96 about nudes, which you can
buy in an artists' supply store like downstairs in Dupuis or in Omer
Desserres. Second, I need .05¢ coins from 1967, 10 of them, for .20¢
each at Dupuis. They're for M. Arthur Coulombe who kept me for 1
week in Baie Comeau. That's really urgent because it's a month since
I promised him that they'd be arriving from one week to the next.

I wanted to tell you how things work this year at college but I
have other letters to write and it is 1 in the morning. I'll write you
later and reply also to the letter from Léo. I'm sorry, but I just don't
have time. Thanks again.

Til later,
Steve

SPEED, DARING, AND BIG BUCKS

John Masters was a partner of Canadian Hunter Exploration, which Peter C. Newman once described as "Alberta's most successful discoverer of big-game gas reservoirs." The American-reared Masters and his Canadian partner, Jim Gray, were mavericks who in the late 1970s ignored the received wisdom and decided that Canada was not running out of natural gas; they believed sizable gas fields were still to be found in the West. In 1976, after six dry holes, they discovered the enormous Elmworth Deep Basin area along the Alberta/British Columbia border. Masters wrote this letter to Alf Powis, president of Noranda, the multinational conglomerate backing Canadian Hunter.

[1978]

Dear Alf,

We have 200,000 acres posted [for sale] for April 6. We have got to hit that sale like a ton of bricks . . . whatever we pay, the land can only increase in value . . . The April sale is where we have to lay it on the line. That will be our last chance.

In a way, the March sale was good for us. We got the best tract, just barely, and we learned a helluva lesson. In this business, you never stay ahead of the game for long. The rest of the industry is too smart and too rich for any one company to stay out in front.

I must tell you what is beginning to show clearly from the results of the January, February and March sales in Alberta and B.C. First, the strength of the sales is obviously building. Many more companies are bidding on many more tracts. Experienced landmen can sense this at the sales, like brokers at the stock exchange. The hum of business turns into a roar. Our landmen are seeing dozens more men at the sales, carrying bundles of bid envelopes. The per acre price at the last B.C. sale was the highest in history. It did not result from a few spectacular bids, but a solid, healthy price on nearly every tract offered.

We can still buy acreage out on the plains, I am sure. <u>But any acre we can buy in the next six months will never be cheaper</u>. In one year, Alf, this will be a different ball game. It will be dog eat dog, the kind of competition I knew in the U.S. We'll still make money, but it won't be stealing like we've been doing.

In the Deep Basin, we have not yet seen any appreciable competition. I think that means the following: companies are rapidly picking up the log analysis idea, but no one has collected enough information over the whole area to put together the regional picture. This is a conceptual problem. It is impossible to know when it will flash on some widely experienced geologist. He'll be ignorant one day, but in the middle of the night he'll suddenly understand the whole thing. We know that Amoco understands the entire concept in the U.S. Rocky Mountains, but incredibly, they do not yet recognize its application in Canada. They will, sure as hell. Shell should also pick it up soon.

The only thing we can do is speed up acreage buying as fast as possible. Once the big boys are onto the idea, then watch out. They will brush us aside like a fly.

I must tell you in the strongest terms: the incredible opportunity that has been Noranda's is fast disappearing. With the acreage we have now, we are a major company, but we can double this in the next several months. By the end of this year, we may have to be pretty selective about where we try to compete.

At the risk of being terribly presumptuous, I submit that <u>the most important corporate decision you and I may ever make will be how much money we can get for acreage buying in the next six months</u>.

We are blasting ahead on the assumption that somehow you will find the money for us. What is done in the next several months will lay the foundation, huge or only big, for the future company.

Our directive, as we understand it, is to bid heavily at the B.C. sale, even if we go over the budget, and then figure out a solution later, either by bank loans or selling some to a partner. This method is entirely satisfactory to me. We can get back inside the budget later.

I apologize, Alf, for being so 'pushy' about this acreage money. But, in my whole experience, I have only one time previously seen a major exploration move that so clearly needed to be done – with speed and daring and big bucks. The other time was Ambrosia Lake. I laid my career on the line to McGee that it was the right thing to do. I feel the same way about this. The Deep Basin acreage is an absolutely unique opportunity to make a giant gas company.

Let's charge . . .

John

Masters was right: Canadian Hunter became one of the country's major independent gas producers. In 1998 Jim Gray succeeded his partner as president, and in 2001 the U.S. giant Burlington Resources bought the company for $3.3 billion cash.

DEAD LETTER OFFICE

*The federal Post Office Department became Canada Post, a crown corporation, in 1981. The idea was to streamline operations and improve service – and even, if possible, to make a profit. The new company branched into competitive courier and e-mail services, introduced more convenient postal outlets, and turned a profit approaching $100 million a year. Along the way, though, it had to divest itself of many uneconomic post offices across the country. Some were in and around outports in Newfoundland and Labrador. One post office was in St. Joseph's, a town near the head of St. Mary's Bay, on the southeast coast of Newfoundland. **Joseph Dobbin** wrote this letter to the editor of* The Evening Telegram *in St. John's.*

[March 19, 1988]
I am dying and this is my last request, so could you please publish my letter.

It is my wish before my demise that my history be seen in writing.

I was born a long time ago, so long I cannot recall the exact day. I may even have been the brainchild of Simon Solomon. Research shows, though, I was here as early as 1851 . . . Sometimes I came by coastal boat and sometimes I came overland.

The Careys at the head of Salmonier directed me to my patrons in the early 1850s and many an enjoyable ride I had on the gigs of their fast horses. I can recall splendorous winter scenes on the route from Holyrood to St. Mary's.

In the year 1857 I found a permanent home at St. Joseph's in the home of Bridget McCormack. Life was glorious then. I could fill a book if I had a mind to. Marconi's success at Signal Hill, the loss of the Barbara Barr, Father Enright's coming to St. Joseph's, the ss Home taking the boys to the war, berry picking on the harbor Road, Father Shea . . . Oh the essays which have passed along my pages.

My office, "The Office," which I am affectiona[te]ly called, was always a labyrinth of conversation. The lobby, especially during the holidays, vibrated with the voices of young and old alike. Sarah O'Neill gathering news for her column, talk of the new arrivals, news from the young men overseas, talk of Fr. Gough's ordination, of what the Baby Bonus was going to mean, little whispers of gossip, all scenes from the lives of the people I've loved and served.

Bridget and Elsie McCormack, Ellen Gough, Richard Daly, John McCormack were my [caretakers] over the years. They were good people. God bless them all. The ladies Gertie and Anna who will be at my side till the end (March 31, 1988). God love them also.

To some young student of Folklore at Memorial University, write my story sometime. You're sure to get an A.

Be kind to my executioners though. Remember the famous words uttered so long ago: "Father forgive them for they know not what they do."

Adieu!

The Post Office of
St. Joseph's, Salmonier

IDEAS AND IDEALS

"What of the Soul of Canada?"

Jeffrey Scouten, a Vancouver lawyer, was approached in 1996 by the editor of the local bar association's journal to open a public dialogue with a Québécois counterpart on the subject of national unity. What most appealed to Scouten was the opportunity to do so by letter. "In our fast-paced world," he said, "we've lost the advantages of letters, where ideas get exchanged in slow-motion form and you can let them sink in and digest them."

Many Canadians use letters to the editors of newspapers and magazines to address the issue of what makes Canada Canada. One such correspondent is the Quebec-bred newspaper baron Conrad Black, who readily fires off letters to declaim his already-omnipresent views. When John Ralston Saul criticized him in 1985 for coveting *The Daily Telegraph*, Black responded with the longest letter ever published in that London newspaper (in brief, he wrote: "I am not interested in the fatuities of journalists").

Pierre Trudeau rarely wrote letters to the editor. On one occasion, however, he was the soul of wit and brevity in questioning *The Globe and Mail* about the disappearance of political columnist George Bain, who had quit in 1973. Jack Kapica, editor of *Shocked and Appalled*, a collection of letters to that newspaper, said that "despite an announce-ment of the move, the post shortly delivered the following letter": "Sir: Where's Bain? P.E. Trudeau Ottawa".

The most prolific and, in subject matter, most catholic writer of letters to the editors of Canadian newspapers was Eugene Forsey. The research director of the Canadian Labour Congress, member of the Canadian Senate, and constitutional expert composed hundreds of letters over sixty years on themes ranging from the abuse of the English language ("hopefully . . . means, 'in a hopeful frame of mind'") to the threat of separatism ("perhaps we are not such mind-less jellyfish, as Mr. Lévesque takes us for").

While no one has supplanted Forsey as epistolary pundit, there are contemporary pretenders to his throne. How do editors decide which of their letters to publish? As Robert Fulford, the former editor of *Saturday Night*, explained: "An element of cunning is involved: the editor gets to know after a while what letters will provide more letters, possibly better ones. The editor also realizes that there are a few correspondents (Forsey above all others, in my lifetime) whose contributions are more valuable than those of paid employees. The editor takes good care of these people, not necessarily running all of their letters but certainly responding to anything they send. What the editor wants most, of course, is not balance but an interesting feature; fairness has only a little to do with it, I think."

But perhaps the purest form of the letter of ideas is the personal communication between friends or colleagues. No pressure, no twenty-second sound bites, no editor lopping off your last three paragraphs. Such correspondence allows the writers to explore their thoughts at length and at leisure, to describe their lives and careers and the motivations that propel them. For expressing ideas and ideals, nothing (as a Canada Post commercial once put it) says it better than a letter.

This chapter differs from the others in one significant way: the letters are grouped thematically under larger headings and appear chronologically within each section.

IN DEFENCE OF CANADA

TO BE A NATION

*The concept of Canada has always been under siege, from within and without, even before Confederation. **Goldwin Smith**, an Oxford University don, was an early proponent of free trade among nations. He later taught at Cornell University and in 1871 moved to be near family in Toronto, where he lectured Canadians on why they should pursue commercial union with the United States. While still living in England in the early 1860s, he wrote a series of public letters to a London newspaper urging the Province of Canada to end its dependence on the Mother Country and to stop worrying about annexation by Americans.*

[March 21, 1862]

TO THE EDITOR OF THE "DAILY NEWS."

SIR, – If any Canadians have been offended, as it appears some have been, by my first letter to you on the subject of Colonial Emancipation, it is the fault of The Times, not mine. I send to you, whose motto is open councils, a letter obviously intended as a contribution to English discussion, but which, when read entire, could not be thought disparaging to the Colonists . . .

But my argument is that timely separation, while it is good for both parties, is especially good for the Colonists. They have a fresh start in the world, with a heritage of modern liberty and civilization, unencumbered by the feudalism which still presses, and will long continue to press, on the energies of the Mother Country. Their destiny, as it is the last gift of Providence, is probably higher than ours, if they will only go forward like men to meet it, instead of clinging, like frightened children, to the skirts of the Old World.

What is it that the Canadians hope to gain by remaining a province? What is it that they fear to lose by becoming a nation?

We have given them all that we really have to give – our national character, our commercial energy, our aptitude for law and government, our language, with all the stores of wisdom and beauty which it contains, the memory of an illustrious origin, and a bond of affection which will not lose its force when the Governor General ceases to exercise his nominal role. We have given them the essence of our constitution – free legislation, self-taxation, ministerial responsibility, personal liberty, trial by jury. The accidents of that constitution – the relics of a feudal mould in which it was wrought – we can no more give them than we can give them our history or our skies. Do they, or any of them, desire an hereditary aristocracy? . . . I find it difficult to soar to the poetic conception of a fire-new Canadian monarchy with Colonial lords of the bedchamber and ladies in waiting; but I find it still more difficult to soar to the conception of a Canadian peerage, with the Duke of Montreal, the third perhaps from the creation of the title, begging like [Byzantine general] Belisarius for an obolus [copper coin], or whistling on a costermonger's cart . . .

Or, to descend from these refined and airy speculations to those which are more vulgar and substantial, do the Canadians hope that this country will always go on paying for their army and navy? If they do, I believe they hope too much from the sufferance of even the English people . . .

If, then, the Canadians have nothing to hope from continuing a dependency, have they anything to fear from being a nation? . . .

They dread annexation to the United States. But I submit that their greatest, and in fact their only, danger of being annexed arises from their position as a dependency of England. That England will someday get into a war with the Americans is only too probable, were it only from the antipathy which our aristocracy naturally feel to the model republic, and which has so signally broken forth since the commencement of the [American] civil war. And in case of a war between England and the Americans, Canada, as an outlying dependency of England, would no doubt be placed in jeopardy. But is there any reasonable ground for presuming that the American people are so extravagantly ambitious and so outrageously profligate as, without provocation, to invade and annex an independent nation? . . .

. . . Such people may of course be goaded into war, and even into conquest, by insulting them and making military demonstrations on their frontier: but it is not likely that, if they are left to themselves, their military ambition will ever disturb the world . . .

I rather doubt the judgment of the Canadians in these matters, because I see that some of them are animated by a childish antipathy to the Americans. Their reliance on the protection of England encourages them to give vent to this antipathy, which may some day lead them into acts of folly, and consequently into disaster . . .

I am, &c.

GOLDWIN SMITH

THE MOTHER COUNTRY

*Schoolteacher, newspaper publisher, tanner, politician, author, and Tory loyalist – a friend of Sir John A. Macdonald – **William Kirby** lived in Niagara-on-the-Lake, Ontario, in the late 19th century. He wrote, among other books, a popular historical novel,* The Golden Dog. *At the time of Confederation in 1867 he began a correspondence with the renowned English poet Alfred, Lord Tennyson by sending him a patriotic song he'd composed ("Canadians Forever"). "Most heartily do I echo both the watch-word of the song, and its burden," Tennyson replied. Three years later, Kirby reported to Tennyson.*

Niagara, Canada, May 27 [1870]
. . . During the last two months events have occurred which have vastly increased the danger of a serious misunderstanding between Canada and the mother country. The utterances of the Premier [lawyer John Sandfield Macdonald] and others in parliament have been interpreted to mean that he regards the connection of Canada with the empire as of a temporary character; and the cold, almost contemptuous, manner in which the colonies are alluded to has galled

our spirited and loyal people, who, by a pardonable provincial vanity, think they merit a tone of more sympathy and appreciation from her Majesty's ministers . . .

We have no fear of the Fenians overrunning any extent of our territory. They will be speedily driven out where they are. We expect an attack on this frontier, but they will be repelled. But you may imagine, sir, that such a state of things is ruining our country, and preparing men's minds for desperate changes in our political relations. That Fenian attack will give an increased momentum to the colonial question, and will, I fear, bring on a political crisis. If England is desirous of warding off the coming crisis she may yet do so, but only in one way. Let her appeal nobly to that sentiment, which Mr. Adderley despises. Let her Majesty repeat in such words as would spring from her Royal heart the noble sentiment uttered by William IV. , 'Canada must neither be lost nor given away' – words which became the motto of Canada in 1837, and [were?] more strength to us than 10,000 men. Let the Imperial government show its sympathy for the outraged feelings of Canadians, and acknowledge its unity with us by offering to share the tremendous costs to us of this foreign attack upon British territory and the British flag. Should they do that, the public feeling would subside at once, and Canada would cheerfully and gladly believe itself to be once more a valued and integral part of her Majesty's dominions.

This invasion took place on her Majesty's birthday [May 24], which we were all celebrating far more than you do in England itself; and the day was chosen in order to make the insult more flagrant against our Queen. Pray excuse this long letter. If my words may do one atom of good I shall be happy. – I remain your obedient servant,

9 p.m., 27th.

An attack on this frontier (Niagara) is expected to-night. It may be a false alarm, but our bugles are sounding the assembly, and our men would infinitely rather fight than turn out for nothing. From the temper they are in it is more than probable that they may cross the frontier, and pursue the foe into the United States territory, and at once raise the question from a provincial matter to an international affair that cannot be blinked by England.

It is a vexation to us to read the remarks made by Mr. Monsell [an Irish member of the British Parliament] and others in the House of Commons. Instead of expressing in honest English their sense of this national insult they send a chorus of compliments and congratulations on the alacrity displayed by the president of the United States [Ulysses S. Grant] in issuing a proclamation against the Fenians. Of the spirit that backs up the proclamation you may judge. Upon the Niagara frontier, forty miles in length – with Buffalo, a teeming focus of Fenianism at one end – that government has not to-day more than forty United States soldiers to enforce that proclamation. That government never did and never will interfere to stop aggression in Canada until it has been tried and failed. Then it will make a show of suppressing what has already beeen suppressed by our forces.

We are truly ashamed that John Bull should let himself be pulled by the beard and kicked by the Yankees, and then like a Chinese who has received the bastinado [torture by caning the soles of the feet], humbly thank the mandarin who so carefully teaches him his place and corrects his manners.

I doubt I encroach on your time and patience by these remarks; only the importance of the subject will excuse them I know.

Wm. Kirby

AN INDEPENDENT NATION

*In late 1915 the remarkable **Talbot Papineau** was in hospital in France, where he had been serving as an officer with the Canadian Expeditionary Force during the First World War. Recovering from acute bronchitis, he managed to write the rough draft of an open letter that later became a stirring defence of a united Canada. Papineau was born in Montebello, Quebec, between Montreal and*

Ottawa, and in character and sympathies he was an intriguing cross between his French-Canadian father – grandson of the radical Quebec patriot Louis-Joseph Papineau – and his English-speaking, American-born mother. One of Talbot's cousins was another of Louis-Joseph's grandsons, Henri Bourassa, a Quebec nationalist who founded Le Devoir. Finishing his letter while back in action, Talbot Papineau responded to Bourassa's argument that French Canadians should not serve in a war between two imperial powers.

In the field,
France, March 21st, 1916

My Dear Cousin Henri,

I was sorry before leaving Quebec in 1914 not to have had an opportunity of discussing with you the momentous issues which were raised in Canada by the outbreak of this war.

You and I have had some discussions in the past, and although we have not agreed upon all points, yet I am happy to think that our pleasant friendship, which indeed dates from the time of my birth, has hitherto continued uninjured by our differences of opinion. Nor would I be the first to make it otherwise, for however I may deplore the character of your views, I have always considered that you held them honestly and sincerely and that you were singularly free from purely selfish or personal ambitions.

Very possibly nothing that I could have said in August, 1914, would have caused you to change your opinions, but I did hope that as events developed and as the great national opportunity of Canada became clearer to all her citizens, you would have been influenced to modify your views and to adopt a different attitude. In that hope I have been disappointed . . .

Let us presume for the sake of argument that your attitude had also been adopted by the Government and people of Canada and that we had declared our intention to abstain from active participation in the war until Canada herself was actually attacked. What would have resulted? One of two things. Either the Allies would have been defeated or they would not have been defeated. In the former case Canada would have been called upon either to surrender unconditionally to German domination or to have attempted a resistance against German arms.

You, I feel sure, would have preferred resistance, but as a proper corrective to such a preference I would prescribe a moderate dose of trench bombardment. I have known my own dogmas to be seriously disturbed in the midst of a German artillery concentration. I can assure you that the further you travel from Canada and the nearer you approach the great military power of Germany, the less do you value the unaided strength of Canada. By the time you are within fifteen yards of a German army and know yourself to be holding about one yard out of a line of five hundred miles or more, you are liable to be enquiring very anxiously about the presence and power of British and French forces. Your ideas about charging to Berlin or of ending the war would also have undergone some slight moderation.

No, my dear Cousin, I think you would shortly after the defeat of the Allies have been more worried over the mastery of the German consonants than you are even now over a conflict with the Ontario Anti-bi-linguists. Or I can imagine you an unhappy exile in Terra del Fuego eloquently comparing the wrongs of Quebec and Alsace.

But you will doubtless say we would have had the assistance of the Great American Republic! It is quite possible. I will admit that by the time the American fleet had been sunk and the principal buildings in New York destroyed the United States would have declared war upon Europe, but in the meantime Canada might very well have been paying tribute and learning to decline German verbs, probably the only thing German she could have declined.

I am, as you know, by descent even more American than I am French, and I am a sincere believer in the future of that magnificent Republic. I cannot forget that more than any other nation in the world's history – England not excepted – she has suffered war solely for the sake of some fine principle of nationality. In 1776 for the principle of national existence. In 1812 for the principle of the inviolability of American citizenship. In 1860 for the preservation of National unity and the suppression of slavery. In 1896 for the protection of her National pride and in sympathy for the wrong of a neighbouring people.

Nor disappointed as I am at the present inactivity of the States will I ever waiver in my loyal belief that in time to come, perhaps less distant than we realise, her actions will correspond with the lofty expression of her national and international ideals . . .

But there was the other alternative, namely, that the Allies even without the assistance of Canada would not have been defeated. What then? Presumably French and English would still have been the official languages of Canada . . . In fact Canada might still have retained her liberties and might with the same freedom from external influences have continued her progress to material and political strength.

But would you have been satisfied – you who have arrogated to yourself the high term of Nationalist? What of the Soul of Canada? Can a nation's pride or patriotism be built upon the blood and suffering of others or upon the wealth garnered from the coffers of those who in anguish and with blood-sweat are fighting the battles of freedom? If we accept our liberties, our national life, from the hands of the English soldiers, if without sacrifices of our own we profit by the sacrifices of the English citizens, can we hope to ever become a nation ourselves? How could [we] ever acquire that Soul or create that Pride without which a nation is a dead thing and doomed to speedy decay and disappearance.

If you were truly a Nationalist – if you loved our great country and without smallness longed to see her become the home of a good and united people – surely you would have recognized this as her moment of travail and tribulation. You would have felt that in the agony of her losses in Belgium and France, Canada was suffering the birth pains of her national life. There even more than in Canada herself, her citizens are being knit together into a new existence because when men stand side by side and endure a soldier's life and face together a soldier's death, they are united in bonds almost as strong as the closest of blood-ties.

There was the great opportunity for the true Nationalist! There was the great issue, the great sacrifice, which should have appealed equally to all true citizens of Canada, and should have served to cement them with indissoluble strength – Canada was at war! Canada was attacked! What mattered then internal dissentions and questions of home importance? What mattered the why and wherefore of the war, whether we owed anything to England or not, whether we were Imperialists or not, or whether we were French or English? The one simple commanding fact to govern our conduct was that Canada was at war, and Canada and Canadian liberties had to be protected . . .

Could you have been here yourself to witness in its horrible detail the cruelty of war – to have seen your comrades suddenly struck down in death and lie mangled at your side, even you could not have failed to wish to visit punishment upon those responsible. You too would now wish to see every ounce of our united strength instantly and relentlessly directed to that end. Afterwards, when that end has been accomplished, then and then only can there be honour or profit in the discussion of our domestic or imperial disputes . . .

. . . You and I are so called French-Canadians. We belong to a race that began the conquest of this country long before the days of Wolfe. That race was in its turn conquered, but their personal liberties were not restricted. They were in fact increased. Ultimately as a minority in a great English-speaking community we have preserved our racial identity, and we have had freedom to speak or to worship as we wished. I may not be, like yourself, "un pur sang", for I am by birth even more English than French, but I am proud of my French ancestors, I love the French language, and I am as determined as you are that we shall have full liberty to remain French as long as we like. But if we are to preserve this liberty we must recognise that we do not belong entirely to ourselves, but to a mixed population, we must rather seek to find points of contact and of common interest than points of friction and separation. We must make concessions and certain sacrifices of our distinct individuality if we mean to live on amicable terms with our fellow-citizens or if we are to expect them to make similar concessions to us. There, in this moment of crisis, was the greatest opportunity which could ever have presented itself for us to show unity of purpose and to prove to our English fellow-citizens that, whatever our respective histories may have been, we were actuated by a common love for our country and a mutual wish that in the future we should unite our distinctive talents and energies to create a proud and happy nation.

That was an opportunity which you, my cousin, have failed to grasp, and unfortunately, despite the heroic and able manner in which French-Canadian battalions have distinguished themselves here, and despite the whole-hearted support which so many leaders of French-Canadian thought have given to the cause, yet the fact remains that the French in Canada have not responded in the same proportion as have other Canadians citizens, and the unhappy impression has been created that French-Canadians are not bearing their full share in this great Canadian enterprise. For this fact and this impression you will be held largely responsible. Do you fully realise what such a responsibility will mean, not so much to you personally for that I believe you would care little – but to the principles which you have advocated, and for many of which I have but the deepest regard. You will have brought them into a disrepute from which they may never recover. Already you have made the fine term of "Nationalist" to stink in the nostrils of our English fellow-citizens. Have you caused them to respect your national views? Have you won their admiration or led them to consider with esteem and toleration your ambitions for the French language? Have you shown yourself worthy of concessions or consideration? . . .

At this moment, as I write, French and English-Canadians are fighting and dying side by side. Is their sacrifice to go for nothing or will it not cement a foundation for a true Canadian nation, a Canadian nation independent in thought, independent in action, independent even in its political organisation – but in spirit united for high international and humane purposes to the two Motherlands of England and France?

I think that is an ideal in which we shall all equally share. Can we not all play an equal part in its realisation?

> I am, as long as may be possible,
> Your affectionate Cousin,
> Talbot M. Papineau

Bourassa replied in another open letter, in French, which criticized Papineau for writing in English and argued that Canada, as "a nation of America, has a nobler mission to fulfil than to bind herself to the fate of the nations of Europe or any spoliating Empire . . . To speak of fighting for the preservation of French civilization in Europe while endeavouring to destroy it in America, appears to us as an absurd piece of inconsistency." But in English-speaking Canada and in England, where The Times *reprinted almost all of his ten-thousand-word letter, Talbot Papineau was celebrated as a Canadian patriot. He died in battle at Passchendaele in 1917. Canada lost a potential political giant who was Trudeau-like in his erudition, charisma, and leadership qualities.*

ANOTHER COUNTRY

Of the eight hundred or so letters to the editor that **Eugene Forsey** *wrote during his long career with the Canadian Labour Congress and in the Canadian Senate, his most impassioned often concerned the future of Canada. In* The Sound of One Voice: Eugene Forsey and His Letters to the Press, *J.E. Hodgetts wrote: "As an unabashed monarchist and dedicated believer in political institutions inherited from Britain, Forsey fought strenuously to preserve what he considered to be the symbolic hallmarks of a True North strong and free, attached to, but independent of, the British Crown." This letter appeared in* The Globe and Mail *on December 23, 1963.*

[December 1963]

... If a large number of Canadians do in fact feel we should join the United States, and if we are not to be governed by mere feeling ... then it is high time our leaders started giving the populace some instructions on the differences between the two countries.

One of the fundamental differences is that the United States is a country of one language and one culture, Canada a country of two languages and two cultures ... If we could all get it firmly into our heads that both the British and the French traditions are basic in the Canadian tradition, and that to remove either is to destroy ourselves, we might at least have some better notion of what we should lose or gain by annexation.

A second fundamental difference is in our systems of government. They are both forms of democracy, but otherwise as different as chalk is from cheese. The Americans have a presidential–congressional democracy, modelled on the early Eighteenth Century British Constitution. It is a proof of their genius that they manage somehow to manoeuvre this political sedan chair through Twentieth Century traffic with astonishing success. We have monarchical-parliamentary responsible government democracy modelled on the late Nineteenth Century British Constitution, and steadily modernized to meet new problems. Joining the United States would be, politically, reactionary, in the proper sense of the word. It would be going back, not, indeed, 'to Methuselah,' but to a system of government which the British peoples outgrew nearly two centuries ago. We should have to adjust ourselves to a whole series of quaint practices, fraught with meaning for Americans, because rooted deep in American history, but a veritable obstacle race to anyone else ...

If these fundamental differences between Canada and the United States seem high-falutin' and academic, there are others, less fundamental, but important, which are not open to that reproach. We have family allowances; the Americans have not. We have non-contributory old age pensions; the Americans have not. We have hospital insurance; the Americans have not. We have a national system of unemployment insurance; the Americans have not. We have Workmen's Compensation; the Americans have nothing like it. Perhaps some of the people . . . interviewed might not have been so glibly annexationist if they had realized the solid benefits they would lose by union. My old Scots tutor at Oxford used to say that there were two ways of wanting a thing: Really and un-really. If you really want it, you are willing to pay the price; if you are not willing to pay the price, then you only un-really want it. I suspect that a good many Canadians who say they want union with the United States only un-really want it.

Eugene Forsey

ON BEING A BACKWATER

Marshall McLuhan, the University of Toronto communications theorist, gained a global reputation after publishing Understanding Media *in 1964. Four years later he sent this first of numerous letters to the minister of justice and new leader of the Liberal Party of Canada – only four days before Pierre Elliott Trudeau became prime minister. It was the beginning of a friendship that endured until McLuhan suffered a stroke in 1979 that left him speechless.*

[Bronxville, N. Y.]
April 16, 1968

Dear Pierre Trudeau:

It was a piece in the Toronto *Telegram* by Douglas Fisher and Harry Crowe that emboldened me to drop you a note. The piece was entitled "Good Will for Trudeau, for a time".

The men of the press can work only with people who have fixed points of view and definite goals, policies and objectives. Such fixed positions and attitudes are, of course, irrelevant to the electronic age. Our world substitutes mosaics for points of view and probes for targets. Knowing of your acquaintance with De Tocqueville, I can understand why you have such an easy understanding of the North

American predicament in the new electronic age. The U. S. A., in particular, began with the latest technology, namely, printing from movable types. The dynamics of that process inspired and permeated the entire industrial and social establishment that grew so rapidly and consistently between 1776 and the present. Any "backward" country tends to enjoy the advantage of starting with the latest technology, so that in the electric age, all the countries that missed the 19th century and its mechanical orientation can now speedily adapt to electric technology without endangering any literate and mechanistic backlog of achievement, e. g. Russia, Japan, etc.

French Canada never had a 19th century. May this not be increasingly a basis for its great advantage over English Canada? Never having had the intense specialism of a mechanized consumer economy, French Canada retains its bond with oral cultures and their total field approach. The all-at-onceness of electric data is not only organic and inclusive but reshapes the entire imaginative lives of highly literate communities. The TV generation, for example, is almost oriental [in its] involvement in the inner rather than the outer life. This means, naturally, a total loss of goal orientation in the old sense. The outer space programs thus in many ways represent 18th-century rather than 20th-century orientations.

I have always felt that one of Canada's greatest assets was its being a kind of "backwater". Never having been totally involved in current trends it has been able to enjoy a flexibility that is now rare. The rigidity of commitment of all powers that were great in the 19th century confronts them with anarchy as they attempt to readjust to the total field awareness demanded by the speed of electric information. The de-Romanizaton of the Catholic Church is only one instance of the decentralizing effects of electric information on older bureaucracies. By the same token the liturgical revival is that kind of involvement and participation that goes with the simultaneity and coexistence of electronic experience.

At present I am studying the American political developments, noting the utter conflict between Policies and Images as it concerns the candidates. May not the same thing happen here as in Canada recently? The old political professionals simply exhaust and liquidate themselves by going through the old motions, making room for quite unexpected candidates at the last moment.

Like most Canadians, I am delighted that it happened that way for us and that you are to enter into this complex new role.

With most cordial wishes and prayers,
Marshall McLuhan

COMMON GROUND

A contemporary version of the Papineau–Bourassa debate (pages 278–84) unfolded in the mid-1990s on the pages of the Vancouver Bar Association's journal, The Advocate. *Editor Tom Woods sought two lawyers – one French-speaking in Quebec, the other English-speaking – to exchange views on issues of national unity. Jacques Tremblay of Quebec City has strong sovereignist sympathies, and* **Jeffrey Scouten**, *a Vancouver-based lawyer, has an abiding love for a Canada that includes Quebec. "Our correspondents are not lawyer/politicians," Woods explained in introducing them to his readers. "They are ordinary people – busy practitioners who lead busy lives." They also proved to be eloquent debaters about the fate of a nation, as this letter from Scouten revealed.*

[Spring 1997]

Me Jacques Tremblay, avocat
Pothier Delisle
3075, chemin des Quatre-Bourgeois
Bureau 400
Sainte-Foy, Quebec
G1W 4X5
Dear Jacques:
I have stolen a day off work and am writing to you this time from my home on Bowen Island. The sun is out and my daughter has just

brought me a little pot full of daffodils that she harvested out of our garden. It is luxuriously warm outside, and the kids left to catch the school bus this morning without their sweaters. Living on the coast, it's hard not to gloat that spring arrives so much earlier here than it does for you in the East . . .

You spent a good deal of your last letter talking about the concept of a "partnership" between Quebec and Canada. I can certainly see why Quebeckers who hope for independence find this concept so appealing. It offers all the benefits of autonomy and enhanced social vigour that you believe sovereignty would bring, together with the protective cushion of a preferred economic relationship and other links with Canada. I was also impressed by [Concordia University] Professor [Guy] Lachappelle's remark about the "moral and philosophical obligation to create a new Quebec-Canada solidarity". This indicates a respect for the present and historical affinities that exist between Quebec and the rest of Canada, which is something you yourself have referred to several times. On the surface at least, the partnership model seems to offer an attractive formula for Quebeckers who yearn for independence to have the "best of all worlds".

I appreciate that the architects of the sovereignty movement are still thinking through the mechanics of how a partnership with Canada would work in practical terms. The devil, as you say, is often in the details, so I will be interested to learn more about this from you down the road. I do have a couple of initial reactions to the idea, however, that you may want to take away and think about in the meantime.

First of all, it seems inevitable that any new "partnership" arrangement between Canada and Quebec would have to involve breaking the family-like bond between us that I keep talking about. Doing this, I am afraid, will strike right at the heart of those intangible elements of civic pride, sense of heritage and national identity that I mentioned in my first letter and that are so vitally important to me.

On a more practical level, any split between us, whether accompanied by a new partnership arrangement or not, would certainly diminish Canada's international stature significantly. We would drop in the eyes of the world from a respected major power to two smaller, less influential ones. A unilateral decision by Quebeckers to separate would also destabilize relations among the remaining parts of Canada in ways that I am not sure many Quebeckers appreciate. "English Canada" is not one cohesive, monolithic entity, after all, and it is hard to predict just how the imbalance of power that would arise in the wake of Quebec's departure would affect the willingness and ability of the remaining parts of Canada to coexist.

Given all that is at stake for us, I frankly cannot shake the uneasy feeling that sovereigntists seem prepared to sacrifice the rest of us to their own ambitions. I am sure you do not intend it this way, but you should understand how all of this looks from my point of view.

Apart from severing the tie of civic togetherness between us, I also still have trouble seeing how a new partnership-based relationship would differ all that significantly in concrete terms from a looser fitting confederal structure. A partnership patterned on the European model, for instance, would still involve a common "parliament" to which Quebeckers would send elected representatives directly. The purpose of such an institution would presumably be to make rules and set policy in areas of interest and concern shared in common with the other regions of Canada. In general terms, this is essentially what our federal level of government does now. One of the key assumptions that appears to underlie both the partnership concept and our current federal system is that Quebec and Canada are interdependent in many ways, and that we mutually gain by cooperating to make the most of that interdependence. In what ways, I wonder, is a partnership an inherently better vehicle for managing that interdependence? . . .

The psychological dynamics of the conflict between French and English Canada, unfortunately, are complex and deeply rooted. As bleak as the situation sometimes seems, however, I am still optimistic that the cycle can be broken and things can be put on a more positive footing again. I believe there is still a reservoir of good will in this country. We saw a glimpse of it last summer during the Saguenay flood disaster. The question is how to tap into it and harness it in resolving the current conflict over our future.

You said something in your last letter that has stuck with me. You said "the wind will never blow in the right direction for the person who does not know where he or she is going". In truth, I don't think Canada has a clear vision of where it wants to go right now. Until recently, it seemed to get along passably without one. I think the close referendum result in 1995, however, has changed that. Since that time, there has been an explosion of seminars and conferences held, papers written, speeches made and action groups formed in which Canadians outside Quebec have thought carefully about who they are, where they are going and how Quebec fits into the picture. There is more going on in English Canada in this vein, therefore, than you might think.

My own hope is that the rest of Canada will seize the present opportunity to define a set of national objectives for itself which will catalyze all of its citizens, including Quebeckers, to work together with the same passion that Quebeckers feel toward building their own society . . .

I do think there is a way to by-pass the media's message to debate our respective futures (whether together or apart) more constructively. I believe the key, however, lies in crafting a well-designed *process* for engaging individual citizens and perhaps their leaders to explore these questions in a thoughtful and systematic way. This has been a weak link, in my view, in our past failed efforts to develop a public consensus around issues of constitutional reform. Without an overarching process of some sort to guide the search for common ground, I think we are bound to remain immobilized by conflict and indecision . . .

I look forward to hearing from you again.

Yours truly,

Jeffrey P. Scouten

IDEALS ON THE FIRING LINE

A FINE FREE COUNTRY

Letters allow correspondents the luxury of defending their philoso-
phies, especially when their values are being tested in the real world's
trenches. **J.S. Woodsworth,** *the Grand Old Man of Canadian demo-*
cratic socialism, was a Methodist minister and a leader of the "social
gospel" movement that surfaced in Protestant churches before the
Great Depression. He ministered to immigrant slum-dwellers in
Winnipeg, where he lived in a communal house; he strongly backed
workers' rights; and he resigned his ministry in 1918 to protest the
church's support of the First World War. Three years later, after
working as a longshoreman on the Vancouver docks and lecturing
across the country, he laboriously typed a letter to a woman friend
in China.

530 Main St.,
Winnipeg
Aug. 25th 1921

My dear Hattie:

A few days ago, mr. Geo. N. Jackson was telling me that some of my
friends in China had been enquiring after me, and also the explanation that he had given of my erratic career. It struck me that I should
have to try to find time to give my own version of the matter. Really,
it is quite a time since we had one of our old-time talks.

Well, you know that for years I was not orthodox and not altogether happy in the regular work of the church . . .

. . . We went to Gibson's Landing, a short distance up the Coast
from Vancouver. On this, our last [mission] field, we had a very good
year,but increasingly felt the widening gulf that separated our ideas
and ideals from those of the Church. Years before , I had seen the
evil of war and now I was supposed to preach this hideous thing in
th e name of the Prince of Peace! Further the Church was turned into

a Political Machine and we were expected to work for the Union Government [of Liberals, Conservatives, and Independents] – one of the most corrupt administrations Canada has ever had. My position became impossible,and I resigned. Strange that to remain true to my convictions I had to leave the associations that had been most deeply imbedded in my very being.

As I still needed outside work and had to make a living and knew that I would be ostracized, I went down to the waterfront in Vancouver and sought work as a casual laborer. It was a great experience. I thought I knew something of the problems of labor, through my long years at All Peoples Mission ,It was a different thing to stand outside in the rain waiting for a job/or to spend the quiet Sabbath day rolling oil barrels along a greasy deckwith the cold fog all about one.After awhile I got into the Union and in time became a fully qualified Longshoreman

Then it was time to move on. So after nine months ,I set off on a lecture across the country. By good fortune,or bad, I landed into Winnipeg in the middle of the great general strike of 1919. That strike has been entirely misrepresented.I know the inside details intimately Without hesitation,I say that there was not a single foreigner in a position of leadership,though foreigners were falselyarrested to give color to this charge. One poor man who was arrested by mistake – a returned soldier was nearly railroaded into an insane asylum, as you Chinese say,"to save the face" of the officials. There was absolutely no attempt to set up a Soviet Government.The money which was said to be coming from Russia in large quantities was a collection of 250dollars raised by some miners in Alberta to bring a lecturer from Winnipeg. It was charged that the attempt was to overturn the Government by force yet not a single gun was discovered from Nova Scotia to Prince Rupert! In short it was the biggest hoax that was ever "Put over" any people! Government Officials and the Press were largely responsible. Of course some of them were quite sincere but absolutely hysterical.In the South End where Mother lived people [were?] guarding their homes with rifles against imaginary monsters, whilethe flesh and blood strikers,were some of them holding what can best be described as great revival meetings and praying for strength to hold out for another week for what they believed [were?] their rights.

It was a curious situation. Yielding to fear the public permitted all sorts of illegal and unjust acts in the name of law and order. British subjects were denied the right to trial by jury; illegal arrests and searches were madeand fundamental liberties denied.

When I came first,I thought that possibly I might do something to bring about a settlement,but that was impossible. I'm not saying that the strikers did nothing wrong. A/strike is a serious weapon, but I do say that the strikers kept their heads far better than the business men.

Anyway, when [William] Ivens was arrested,in order to suppressthe paper of which he was Editor . . . Mr. F. J. Dixon Member of the Provincial Legislature and I felt it our duty to carry on the paper: we knew what was likely to happen as an unscrup[u]lous lawyer had been vested with almost unlimited powers. After a week,I was arrested on a charge of seditious libel and the paper suppressed/ Dixon baffled the police and kept the paper going from a place of hiding untilby a turn of events Ivens was released on bail and back on the job, so we did not miss a single issue!

How desperate the authorities were may be imagined fromthe charges brought against me. One was a conciliatory letter which I wrote on the urgent advice of some of the leading business men in an attempt to bring about a settlement. The second was a quotation from Rt. Hon. Arthur Henderson. The third charge – the gem of the collection – was a quotation without comment or application from the book of Isaiah – and credited to Isaiah! Dixon went before a jury and was acquitted. the Government simply did not dare to bring on my case. I could have made the whole performance very ridiculous though to be sure that would not have saved me with the spirit that then prevailed. Of course ever since I've been a very bad man! For a year,I was followed by police and detectives at every meeting.Never before had my speeches [been?] so carefully reported! Had quite an escapade when I out-witted the Provincial Police of Saskatchewan who themselves had been conspirators in kidnapping a labor organizer! Life has still some zest for anyone who sides with Labor!

WhenLucyreceived the news of my arrest, she w as teaching school She sent Grace home and with the help of our friend,Mrs. Dr. Inglis, (Dr.I. formerly a Medical Missionary: now an ardent "Red") Grace gathered together and secreted my books and papers. In all parts of Canada houses were being illegally raided by the mounted Plolice Force,by the way, at that time under the department presided over by our friend N. W. Rowell. Five months later when I got home, Grace, the sole custodian of the secret of the hidden papers said – "Father, I've kept your things safe" and she proudly led me through the Garden,back into the woods over logs and stumps till we came to the carefully concealed cache. A Fine free country, this Canada of ours!

Well last September I returned to the C oast once more and we moved into Vancouver. We bought a house in Kitsilano.We think it a fine location ,just a few blocks from the beach and near to public and high-schools . . .

. . . [In Winnipeg] I am working in connection with the "Labor Church". We have a central theatre meeting and half a dozen suburban branches. During the week I conduct six group study classes in industrial history and economics. Now , how/is that for a history up to date?

. . . Our plans are very indefinite. I am "blacklisted" and must take whatever work offers for the time It's not easy financially and any thing but pleasant to be separated from the family; but we will not give up the fight before we are forced to do so. To an outsider our course may seem erratic but it is really right in line with the work of al[l] the previous years.The idealism of today has largely passed from the churches – at least so we think.We are confident that time will vindicate our position.

Forgive me using the Type-writer. I'm only a beginner but even at that you can read the letter much more comfortably.

With kindest regards to Wesley and other friends in Western China

Yours Sincerely

J. S. Woodsworth

WHITE SEEK GRACE

Dr. Norman Bethune has long been a heroic figure in the Chinese communist pantheon, where he was known as Pai Chu En – White Seek Grace. *He served China's cause during its war with Japanese invaders in the 1930s. But even before going into battle there, the well-born Bethune had earned his stripes as a labourer-teacher with Canada's Frontier College, a stretcher-bearer in the First World War, a member of the Royal Navy, and an inventor of numerous medical devices. His disenchantment with the dollar-driven concerns of western health care led him to join the Communist Party and then, in 1936, the anti-fascist forces in the Spanish Civil War. In Spain he created the first-ever mobile blood-transfusion service for troops. Two years later he was in China, performing operations in the field and teaching medicine on the run. This letter was written to an American friend and fellow thoracic surgeon, Dr. Louis Davidson, of New York.*

On the Border of N.W.Hopei,China,

Chin-Cha-Chi Military District,

August 15, 1939.

Dear Louis:

It seems such a long time since we last met and so much must have happened to you. It has certainly happened to me. These last months (nearly two years) now, have been very full, so full that I hardly know where to start to describe them to you. So this account will be a disconnected one at best. But I am anxious that you should receive one letter at least of those I have written you, for you never received them as I have had no reply. That is what I have come to accept, more or less irregular [mail]. It takes at least five months for any letter to reach me after it has arrived in China. I calculate that I get only one in 25. Books and periodicals are even worse, I have received none in one and a half years. My reading consist[s] of a year's-old San Francisco paper used as wrappers for sugar, tea and cakes by merchants. I am thoroughly conversant with the goings on of the "smart set" and the vagaries of Hollywood, but of anything of importance, I know less than an Arctic explorer. He, at least, has a radio. I have none. It was three months before I knew that Madrid had fallen.

. . .The work that I am trying to do is to take peasant boys and young workers and make doctors out of them. They can read and write and most have a knowledge of arithmetic. None of my doctors has ever been to college or universities and none has ever been in a modern hospital (most of them have never been in any hospital) much less a medical school. With this material I must make doctors and nurses out of them – six months for nurses and one year for doctors. We have 2300 wounded in hospitals all the time. These hospitals are merely the dirty one-story mud and stone houses of out-of-the-way villages set in deep valleys, overhung by mountains, some of which are 10,000 feet high. We have over 20 of these hospitals in our region which stretches from Peiping in the north to Tientsin in the east, south to Shih Chia Chuang, west to Tai Yuan. We are the most active Partisans area in China and engaged in very severe guerrilla warfare all the time.

The Puppet Government set up by the Japs seem to work in a sort of fashion in the cities. In the countryside they are complete flops. Our own local governments are the only ones recognized by the people who pay their taxes to them. Japanese taxes are pure and simple robbery and extortion – capricious, uncertain and based on the simple gun-man principle: How much have you got?

We must help these splendid people more than we are doing. We must send them more money and more men. Technicians of all kinds are badly needed: doctors, public health workers, engineers, mechanics – everybody that knows some technical specialty well. Last year, I traveled 3165 miles of which 400 miles were on foot across Shansi and Hopei Provinces. 762 operations were performed and 1800 wounded examined. The Sanitary Service of the army was reorganized, three text books written and translated into Chinese, a Medical Training School established.

It's a fast life. I miss tremendously a comrade to whom I can talk. You know how fond I am of talking. I don't mind the conventional hardships – heat and bitter cold, dirt, lice, unvaried, unfamiliar food, walking in the mountains, no stoves, beds or baths. I find I can get along and operate as well in a dirty Buddhist temple with a 20 foot high statue of the impassive faced, gilded god staring over my shoulder, as in a modern operating room, with running water, nice green glazed walls, electric lamps and a thousand other accessories. To dress the wounded we have to climb up on the mud ovens – the k'angs. They have no mattresses, no sheets. They lie in their old, stained uniforms with their knapsacks as pillows and one padded cotton blanket over them. They are grand. They can certainly take it.

We have had tremendous floods this summer. It's been hellish hot and muggy. Rain for two months coming down like a steady shower bath turned on full.

I am planning to return to Canada early next year. I must leave here sometime in November and go 500 miles on foot over to Yenan. From there by bus – I hope – to Chung King and then by bus to Yunnan in the south to get another boat (a freighter to Honolulu to avoid Japan) then another boat to San Francisco.

I want to raise a guaranteed $100 (gold) a month for my work here. I am not getting it. They need me here. This is 'my' Region. I must come back.

I dream of coffee, of rare roast beef, of apple pie and ice cream. Mirages of heavenly food. Books – are books still being written? Is music still being played? Do you dance, drink beer, look at pictures? What do clean white sheets in a soft bed feel like? Do women still love to be loved?

How sad that, even to me once more, all these things may become accepted easily without wonder and amazement at my good fortune.

My health is pretty fair – teeth need attention, one ear has been completely deaf for three months, glasses for eyes and correction, but apart from these minor things and being pretty thin, I'm O.K.

Goodby, Louis, I'll be seeing you soon,

Beth.

Bethune died three months later, of blood poisoning.

A MAD AFRICAN WAR

Dr. Lucille Teasdale was born in Montreal, got her medical degree from the University of Montreal, and married Dr. Piero Corti, an Italian pediatrician, in northern Uganda in 1961. They took over a missionary dispensary and built it into a university hospital recognized throughout Africa. Piero and Lucille devoted their entire professional lives to St. Mary's-Lacor Hospital and the Acholi people of Uganda, who revered them for their courage – particularly during Idi Amin's dictatorship, when most foreigners left the country. Lucille wrote this open letter to her friends.

Gulu 27-5-1979.

Dear friends,

It is one week that we have been liberated by the Tanzanian troups, and we just started to relax. Today, sunday, we are thinking of all our friends scattered around the world and maybe anxious to have news about Lacor. So we took the decision to write this "collective" letter in english because this is the language that almost all our friends can understand.

It is impossible to remember all the sad and the terrible events – and the laughable ones – that happened during the last two months, because you can imagine that we were so overworked that we had no time, nor the feeling, to write a Journal. We will just try to give you some ideas of what the war was in Gulu.

The invasion of Uganda by the Tanzanian troups and the Ugandan Liberation Front (later) started in December, but up to the end of March it was for us so far away that we could not even think that it could reach us in the North . . . Then on the 11th of April Kampala was taken by the Tanzanians, and the terror started in Gulu.

Gulu was a very important army & air-force base: all of a sudden the officers of Amin's army left the town to take away their families to Sudan or East Nile Province, leaving behind thousands of soldiers with plenty of rifles, grenades, machine-guns etc. For one week those soldiers – mixed with the many running away from the front-line – became bandits, going around in groups, shooting, stealing, and destro[y]ing all government and private buildings in Gulu: Post Office, Government Hospital, Bank, Police station, the Prisons... were looted, and the prisoners left free. They even raided the mission Institutions, especially looking for cars, lorries and other properties of value. The Bishop'[s] House was actually assaulted by successive groups, with much stealing and destruction. They probably would have killed the Bishop, but he barely escaped, hiding in the toilet for the whole night, until Piero and two Sisters went to rescue him the day after, luckily reaching the house between two groups of looters. They brought the Bishop to our house, where he remained for one and half months. During the first three weeks he did not move from his room, locking himself in and opening only when we brought food three times a day. During that week the soldiers respected only our hospital – because we were treating so many of their wounded – with the exception of the second day, when they invaded the hospital compound and succeeded in stealing the old lorry, putting also three bullets over the door of the italian sisters house . . .

Fortunately, after that week, some of the Amin's officers came back to Gulu and did their best to establish some kind of control, and putting a few soldiers at every mission po[i]nt for protection. – By then most of the population had escaped and gone living in the bush, far away from the town and the main roads. Gulu was deserted and devastated – a g[h]ost city –, as we realised a couple of weeks later, when we finally dared to reach the Government hospital, where all doctors and paramedical staff had run away long before, with the remarkable exception of two nurses, a medical assistant and the anesthetist, who were going to look after patients for [a] few hours a day. Four of these patients, we brought to Lacor because they needed doctor's attention. Beside the soldiers cars, our ambulance has been the only one on the roads, between Lacor and Gulu for a few trips . . . but with a fully armed soldier well in evidence on the front seat!

During all this time the Out-Patient Clinics at Lacor were working very little, fortunately because we spent most of our time operating [on] wounded people. We had 60 major bullet wounds: about one third were civilians shot by army men, and the others were soldiers, usually shot by their companions. Only one of those wounded soldiers was a real war casualty brought all along from Bombo front and he was the only one shot by regular hard bullet (approved by the Geneva Convention). Amin's bullets were soft ones – against the rules of Geneva Convention – and doing terrible bone & soft tissue damage. Many of the wounds were in the thighs, and you can imagine that we were not organised to treat 10 – 12 open/compound fractures of femur. We had to improvise bone traction the best we could. – Then the situation became more difficult when the electricity was cut off (all together we were 3 weeks without electricity). The hospital had a small "stand by" generator, sufficient for Theatre and Laboratory work during emergencies in case of main electricity failure. Can you imagine Lacor hospital without electricity? . . . Fortunately Brother Bissin was with us and saved the situation: he organised transportation of all apparatus in the small shed of the generator and fixed everything to work, alternately, on the little electricity produced by the generator, with a line to the frigs for a few hours a day.

All the time during the first week there was shooting, shouting . . . Some cars even used machine gun bursts instead of horns to keep the way open while driving madly to escape: usually shooting in the air, but occasionally at people on the road or outside their houses (four people killed in a single two miles run in front of the hospital, one tragic afternoon) . . . Probably Lacor has been the only hospital in dangerous zone where all the african staff – more than hundred between Nurses and student Nurses – did not run away! . . .

Thursday 15th May . . . there was much agitation in the parking-lot of the hospital. We rushed there to see what was happening, and found a big bus with two or three soldiers who ordered to bring all their wounded recovered in the hospital to the bus: they wanted to bring them to West Nile. We said that some of them were not fit for traveling, but they ignored us, and started to scatter around to collect them. Such doing created more alarm and panic, so that even the femur fracture cases under bone traction liberated themselves from their pins and rods, and were carried to the bus. – About two PM they were gone and we went home for a quick lunch. Fifteen minutes later we were in the theatre to operate the abdomen case, who had also a broken ankle. – Piero wanted to do general anesthesia, but fearing some other invasion, decided for "continuous epidural", and went around after putting the catheter in. Then for four hours I patched up that patient, hearing shots from time to time. At 6 PM the real shooting started within the hospital compound. In the theatre we were in the dark, not knowing what was happening. Dr. Maria, Martn and myself brought the operated patient to the ward, and found all the patients terrorised, and all the Nurses gone, except one student-nurse. She stayed with us all the time and helped us to put all patients under the beds for protection. This we did in all the wards.

Still I did not know where Piero and the other male doctors were. Once the shooting stopped we all met and Piero told me what happened. A group of twelve cars full of soldiers, deserters and their families had stopped in front of the hospital to look for more cars and petrol to steal . . . Their leader wanted Piero to go and check in the cars that his radio was not there, and pulled him outside the gate. Once there he got suddenly mad at Piero: slapped him violently on the right ear and kicked him in the legs. Then he shouted that he wanted to kill him, but having no arms himself, he asked annother soldier for his gun. The soldier, having been treated by us only a few days before, refused. So the mad man run to his car to get his gun, while Piero (finally!) run back to the hospital. The mad one had time to shoot a burst of bullets, but missed. Piero got inside, locked the door, and hid in the small shelter of the gate-keeper. The man shot him again through the wire part of the gate and missed by a few inches, from two meters distance . . . (the wire having deviated the bullets). Then the mother of this man – a lady we knew as our patient – got out of one of the cars and started to shout: don't kill doctor Corti; don't kill doctor Corti . . . It seems that this was the way the Providence choose to save the life of Piero. In fact this mad man, leader of the band, was a well known killer, as we were told afterwards . . .

Today, Sunday, one week after liberation, I think it is the first time that we had no surgical emergency and could stay at home for some hours undisturbed. That is why we could write this letter . . .

Now what next. What shall we do? For the moment we have no choice, being the only doctors to serve Gulu. But after? Right now we are planning a long holiday starting next July with Dominique, our daughter (we have not seen her since January, and we were without new[s] of each other for more than two months). We think that we are not mentally & physically in condition to take decisions or make plans for the future. – Surely, for the first time in 18 years, on the 15 of May I was contemplating leaving Gulu forever and immediately . . . if that could have been possible! But that temptation did not last very long. Also it is worth to see what will happen with the new government.

To you all . . . we send our best regards, hoping to see you all sometimes in the near or far future.

Lucille

About the time she wrote this letter, Lucille operated on a patient infected with HIV. In 1985 she learned she had AIDS, yet continued to work in an outpatient clinic and to operate, wearing two pairs of gloves. She died in 1996. Lucille received the Order of Canada and the Ordre national du Québec as well as numerous other awards. She was buried on the grounds of St. Mary's-Lacor Hospital, which Piero continued to operate.

THE RIGHT STUFF

Michael Walker, who believes "the success of the wealthy is impor-
tant for the maintenance of the unfortunate," is executive director
of the Fraser Institute, established in Vancouver in 1974 as a research
and educational group espousing conservative ideas on public policy.
In this long letter to Mark Ungrin, a medical biophysicist at the
University of Toronto, Walker responded to Ungrin's detailed criti-
cism of free trade and the Fraser Institute's philosophy.

June 13, 2001

Dear Mr. Ungrin:

I have just gotten a copy of your comments on Economic Freedom
of the World from Michel Kelly-Gagnon who I guess had used
some of the results of our report in a CBC commentary. I would have
been happy to dispel some of the misimpressions you evidently gathered if you had been in touch with me . . .

. . . You imply that economic freedom is to a certain degree
implicitly anti-democratic because you believe that power derives
from wealth and you evidently believe that wealth is generally
acquired in some sort of illegitimate way.

First of all, considering the connection between economic freedom
and in particular the right to trade and democracy, I would point
you to two interesting propositions that you may find useful in puz-
zling this one through.

First of all there is the recent final "annuncio" of the departing president of Mexico, Mr. [Ernesto] Zedillo who noted that the unprece-
dented pluralism which had emerged in Mexican politics and the
unseating of the PRI by the PAN of [Vicente] Fox was the result of
the North American Free Trade Agreement. What he meant was that
the transparency and the due process which had been associated with
the adoption of the North American Free Trade Agreement and the
disciplines which it imposes on Mexico had created the circumstances
in which a pluralistic political outcome was now possible in Mexico.

A second example which may give you some thought with regard to the connection between economic freedom and in particular trade and democracy, was my own experience working in Latin America some twenty years ago when I discovered that in spite of the fact that it had no domestic industry to protect, Mexico nevertheless had import licenses on newsprint. Being a naive economist in those days I asked the question of my Mexican friends, "why does the government have tariffs on newsprint when there is no domestic industry to protect?" My friends didn't answer but simply left me hanging and dangling until finally it dawned on me that the reason why you want to have import controls on newsprint in a totalitarian regime is because you want to prevent the locals from engaging in freedom of the press.

Similar restrictions on the ability to own foreign currency, the right to exchange your currency, to hold foreign bank deposits, to engage in capital transactions with foreigners etc. etc. have [a] direct impact on the extent to which people can engage in democracy or any kind of civil or political freedom. It is for that reason that our research and that of others is beginning to discover that a prerequisite for real political freedom is to have economic freedom so that in the very most basic case one can import the paper and the ink to engage in the most primitive exercise of political freedom – free speech. So when we say that economic freedom is implicitly anti-democratic you will want to think through what the implications are, particularly with regard to your own feeling that free trade is not a good idea.

But there is another sense in which economic freedom is important in the establishment of political rights and it is a connection noted by Lord Acton who is most well known for his comment that power corrupts and absolute power corrupts absolutely. Lord Acton noted that in the development of British democracy it was the creation of small pockets of private wealth that effectively became the counterbalance to the power of the Crown and its ability to have its way with the populace. In turn, as has been well established, it was the right to engage in economic transactions without [the] permission of the

Crown which produced the private wealth which ultimately was the undoing of totalitarian power in Britain and indeed, as we observe, in most other countries around the world.

Point 3: Economic freedom per se is not shown to serve the general good. You return here to the notion of correlation not proving causality and you say that while there are problems in the social sciences with testing hypotheses, "this does not excuse economists' inability to provide proof of causation, that is all it is – an excuse." Well, of course, no scientist ever proved anything with data, no theory is ever "proved" . The whole edifice of science rests on theory which is continuously subject to tests to see whether it can be disproved. As Karl Popper has pointed out, the whole purpose of science is to find data which is not consistent with the maintained hypothesis.

So economists can't prove that free trade works to improve the standard of living of the general population but we can show the data which shows the relationship between, for example, free trade or higher levels of economic freedom and the associated levels of income. If we were to find instances where there are high levels of economic freedom and shrinking levels of income then this would constitute an example where the theory apparently does not work. It causes us to re-examine the theory in the same way that when we boil water on the top of Grouse Mountain we find that it does not boil at 100 degrees centigrade and this causes us to look for the reason why the theory that water boils at 100 degrees centigrade is not found to apply.

But the fact is that while there has been a lot of vituperation about the negative impact on the general population of free trade, no evidence of this general impact has been provided. On the contrary, the evidence is overwhelmingly in the other direction. This does not mean that certain individuals and certain industries which have enjoyed the privilege of being able to overcharge their fellow citizens for products which would be more cheaply provided if they had been freely traded will not lose once that privilege is withdrawn. But we must not mistake this effect of the withdrawal of protectionism on the beneficiaries of protectionism as an adverse consequence of free trade. This is an adverse consequence of protectionism. It simply becomes evident once it is withdrawn and consumers, once having the choice, no longer provide the higher prices to the domestic producer. Perhaps you could provide some illustrations of a general population which has been badly affected by a move towards freer trade. I have been researching the impact of freer trade for more than 30 years and don't know of a single instance myself . . .

All the foregoing notwithstanding, of course it is true that economic freedom is not the only factor which influences human development and it may be possible to produce better outcomes with any given level of economic freedom if there is a different attitude towards success, for example, or a different attitude towards work effort, or a different attitude towards social compacts as for example in the case of Sweden which seems to be able to tolerate lower levels of economic freedom and produce nevertheless higher economic outcomes than might otherwise be expected . . .

The Fraser Institute does not embrace the idea of "more wealth for the wealthy". It embraces the idea that people should be free to choose how they use their natural endowment. They should be free to set their own paths in life and that that path ought not to be interfered with by others through the power of government except to the minimal extent that is consistent with maintaining a safe and secure community. What we observe is that when governments permit their citizens to have economic freedom they generally become wealthier irrespective of where in the income distribution they find themselves . . .

Of course none of the foregoing means that, as a person who is obviously as opposed to free trade as you are, you need to just lie down and take it. You have the opportunity to provide evidence that free trade is bad for people. Provide this evidence. Show that free trade is bad for people. Argue your case and convince others that they should come around to your way of thinking and if you can get a majority, or even a plurality, of people to agree with your point of view then maybe in the next election you can change Canada's trade policy. Having looked at all of the evidence that I have over the past

30 years on the wonderful and powerful effects that free trade can have [in] ameliorating poverty and improving the standard of living of people, I sincerely hope that you shall not be successful but I would be perfectly happy to consider any evidence that you might bring to bear on this subject. Heaven knows, we have brought very considerable evidence to bear, most of which is available on our web site and I encourage you to peruse it.

I would be happy to respond to any evidence you might like to offer with regard to free trade.

Sincerely,
Michael Walker
Executive Director
The Fraser Institute

WRITERS AND ARTISTS

THE IDEAL OF ONESELF

"Writers are not a tribe," the expatriate Canadian writer Mavis Gallant once insisted – while maintaining a close long-distance friendship with fellow Montrealers Mordecai Richler and Brian Moore. Many of our writers have sought one another's company. Among them was **Archibald Lampman**, *postal clerk, federal civil servant, and the best (and most underappreciated) nature poet in 19th-century Canada. He wrote regularly to his friend, the Toronto Globe editorial writer Edward Thomson.*

P.O. Dept., Ottawa
11 Feby 1896

My dear Thomson,
I find myself for the first time in my life approaching a condition of philosophy. In a little while I shall no longer care whether people pay

any attention to me or not, whether those I love return my affection or not, whether publishers accept my books, or whether anyone reads them when they are published. When I have actually reached that point I believe I shall be happy. I have already well begun the process of self abnegation. I no longer grumble at the Civil Service, for I have given up for good and all the notion of writing any thing large and important. Hereafter I shall be well content to produce such things as the nature of my gift and the circumstances of my life permit.

All our troubles in reality proceed from nothing but vanity, if we track them to their source. We form an ideal of ourselves, and claim what seems to be due to that ideal. The ideal of myself is entitled to love and approbation from my fellow creatures; but the love and approbation does not appear, and I fret and abuse the constitution of things. To the ideal of myself money and power and practical success are no doubt due, but they do not come, and again I abuse the constitution of things.

It is necessary for every man when he reaches maturity of understanding to take himself carefully to pieces and ascertain with pitiless scientific accuracy just what he is; then he must adjust his attitude to life accordingly and adhere to it. If we would only do that we should have less conflict, and we should suffer infinitely less. That is what I am trying to do now . . .

[Yours affectionately]

[A. Lampman]

Lampman died three years later, at the age of thirty-seven.

A FLAVOUR OF OUR OWN

Robertson Davies, after acting at London's Old Vic and other English theatres, returned to Canada and in 1942 became editor of The Peterborough Examiner. *In the 1950s he began writing the novels that eventually won him international success. He discussed his third*

novel in these letters to a friend and a distinguished British novelist
and playwright, and replied to a Quebec woman who criticized him.

[August 11, 1958]

Dear Joan: Thanks for writing to me about <u>A Mixture of Frailties</u>,
& in such a kind strain . . . So a pattern of not making the grade
[movies] has asserted itself – if the movies are "the grade". I would
be glad enough of such success, because it would impress Canada,
and if that is a base ambition, I can't help it. I am sick of the Canadian
tendency to exalt the Monsarrats and Costains because they make a
great deal of money . . . It delights me that you & Graham both
think the book really Canadian. I don't know why I fuss so about
this, except that I am convinced that Canada <u>has</u> a flavour of its own,
& a subtle one, & I would like to be one of the earliest ones to
capture some of it & make it known to the outside world . . .

Love & thanks,

Rob

February 2, 1959

[To a critic]

Thank you for your letter of January 27th. Yes, I have read <u>The</u>
<u>Brothers Karamazov</u> and also the other novels of Dostoyevsky. Did
you know that he suffered lifelong remorse because he once raped a
child of seven, with the assistance of the child's governess. He refers
to this unpleasing incident indirectly in one of his novels, and at
considerable length in <u>Crime and Punishment</u>. I thought that you
might be interested in this detail from the life of a writer whose work
you admire.

As to the occurrence of sexual incident and reference in modern
novels, it is there because sex is an important element of life, and the
development of character requires some reference to it. If you read
the novels of early days with insight and understanding you will find
that it is there too. I do not know of any modern books which are so

frank about sex as Fielding's <u>Tom Jones</u>, or so thoroughly soaked in it as the works of Charlotte Bronte. If, as you tell me, the experience of reading novels is a fresh one for you, you may be interested to make some observations in this realm yourself.

Yours sincerely,
Robertson Davies

February 6, 1959

J.B.Priestley, Esq.,

B4 Albany

Piccadilly, W.1

London, England

The January 21st copy of <u>Punch</u> has made its slow way to Peterborough and I write to tell you how greatly I enjoyed your article on Snobbery in Literature. Particularly I was happy about what you said concerning Camus and Sartre, about whom I hear a great deal from the U.S.A., where they are extravagantly admired. Ionesco beats me completely; I have the worrying consciousness that something interesting is going on in his plays but I am quite unable to discover what it is; it is as though something about oneself were being said just out of earshot.

My last novel came out on this continent in September and has had a very pleasant degree of success. It appeared in England in December and fell like a stone, for no particular reason that I can discover, except that a very great number of novels were appearing at the same time and, understandably, two-thirds of them were generally overlooked. Under separate cover I am sending you a copy of the book and if you find time to read it I would be very happy to hear any criticism of it which you choose to offer. I think it is better than the last one, and it may be that the musical stuff in it will appeal to you. In this connection I would like to say how much I have enjoyed the musical passages in your own novels, and it was that enjoyment which moved me to attempt something of the sort myself.

With every good wish to yourself and Mrs. Priestley,

I am

Yours sincerely,

Robertson Davies

GUTS

Novelist, scriptwriter, and raconteur **W.O. Mitchell** *taught a wildly popular writing course for many years at The Banff Centre in Alberta. When one of his students, Lauri E. Nerman, wrote to thank him for his advice and encouragement – "As my grandmother would say (a real compliment) you have a jewish heart" – he replied with this letter.*

Nov. 24, 1982.

Dear Nerman:

Chicken soup is not as effective a remedy for everything that it has been cracked up to be. It will take care of neither writers' angst nor herpes. Writing from the heart works for the first of these. You are so able to write from the heart that you were hated last summer by both students and instructors. I include myself. To become a writer requires: a. Initial potential growing out of a born-with spectator-listening-caring quality. As the offensively commanding voice-over of the industrial safety adds orders: "You've got it. Use it!" People who write poems about seaweed, self-centred scavenger hunts, totem poles, logging camps, perfumed with the smell of Pacific salt and rotting kelp, win only the Canadian Authors' Association silver quill award. They are chi-chi and amateur performers and almost never loving hearted.

You will never run out of brick walls to beat your head against; if you do you are through as an artist of any sort. I see that I started out to list the recipe ingredients of a writer. This is b.: A sense of confusion relieved regularly by a lack of confidence followed by a conviction you're a phoney whom God never intended to be a writer – certainly not a person who would ever write anything which would stop strangers long enough to read what she had written. Only amateurs are sure enough of themselves to love what they have done in one lightning stroke of genius. This is the reason they never have to polish to improve to try again to learn a craft ten times more difficult than brain surgery. Continue to be unsure of your ability – as I am. If not – go ahead and study to be a licensed embalmer and funeral director or a Mary Kay sales person. You won't make it, because you haven't got the strong stomach required for either of these careers.

I think that c. is: Guts, whatever that is – stubborn consistency, the only answer to writers' block. I know this sounds like a locker room football coach and that is unfortunate, but forgive me for being male instead of female. No – you don't have to forgive me. The best humans and especially artists are androgynous.

Now – go to the showers and sluice the sweat off yourself and find another brick wall. Hit that type-writer.

Love
Mitchell

KNOWING THE UNKNOWABLE

*After **Carol Shields** was diagnosed with breast cancer in 1998, she remarked: "Complete strangers have sent me the most supportive letters." Her readers had long been writing her about her work, including the Pulitzer Prize–winning novel,* The Stone Diaries, *which* The New York Times *said "reminds us again why literature matters." When a British biographer confided in her, the author, then the chancellor of the University of Winnipeg, replied in kind.*

8 St Paul's Road
Cambridge
CB1 2EZ
[1997]

Carol Shields
c/o The Guardian
119 Farrington Road
London EC1R 3ER

Dear Carol Shields

On reading your article "Others" (Guardian, 25 August 1997), I experienced such a surge of personal recognition and relief that I felt compelled to make contact with you. Not only am I delighted but I feel personally validated in the knowledge that somebody else possesses the same curiosity about her fellow human beings as I; shares that 'voyeuristic' impulse that shapes my life.

I too, have always been fascinated by other people – but not everybody – just certain people who for some reason or other have caught my imagination and stirred my interest. Yet, as you correctly point out, in our society a curious nature is forced undercover: disapproval looms large . . .

. . . Peering into people's windows from passing trains, observing communities from coach windows, evokes some sort of wistfulness deep inside me for all the things I can imagine, but never really know, about the world around me.

What do I do with all this human information stored inside my brain? Well, I use it sometimes, selectively, to understand and shape my own life. In respect of your article, however, it will not surprise you to know that currently I am writing a biography: given official sanction, as you noted, to poke and pry into the distant past of somebody's life. Wonderful. And I don't have to make any of it up which is probably why I prefer biography to novel writing.

With very best wishes

Maureen Cressey-Hackett

Born Potters Bar. Age 41. Only daughter of divorced parents. Divorced, cohabiting, no children. Guardian reader, doing historical/

biographical PhD at Cambridge – if you need to know any more feel
free to contact me at above address . . .

CAROL SHIELDS

DEPARTMENT OF ENGLISH – UNIVERSITY OF MANITOBA

WINNIPEG, MANITOBA R3T 5V5

23 September 1997

Dear Maureen,
Your wonderful letter warmed my day. In fact, it MADE my day. So!
I am not alone.

I liked your analysis and felt comforted by it, the fact that we
only want to know about the unknowable world around us – such
an innocent motive really. And like you, I've learned to extract a
whole life situation from a glimpse into window or a piece of jewelry.
Still I hesitate to inquire directly. The last time I asked a woman what
her job was (1982) she informed me she had no job, then stared at
me coldly and said, "And I don't take courses either."

All best wishes in the safe world of biographical research.

Carol Shields

Born Oak Park, Illinois, aged 62, third child of conventional parents,
married 40 years, five children, no pets, don't believe in the prophetic
nature of dreams, don't believe in fortune cookie messages, extremely
doubtful about left brain/right brain theories, love conversation,
good food, Virginia Woolf, long walks.

*In the spring of 2002 Carol Shields observed: "I am now sixty-six,
live in Victoria, and not so committed to all my previous theories.
In fact, I've more or less renounced my old theories and I am
working toward a no-theory existence, taking everything at a one-
by-one basis."*

THE HORRORS OF LITERATURE

Robert Fulford – the Toronto-based magazine editor, literary critic, newspaper columnist, broadcaster, teacher – has helped set the course of Canadian writing for more than three decades. This letter was a response to Katherine Ashenburg, who was planning a CBC radio biography on one of Canada's literary icons.

Nov 1, 2000

Dear Katherine:

I regret that in the research for your documentary on Hugh MacLennan you didn't find my interviews with him in the CBC archives. The main reason, I suppose, is that I never did any.

But why not? You are about to peek into the horrors of Toronto Literature, circa 1960.

Believe it or not, there were exactly two novelists in Canada who mattered at that time, Morley Callaghan and MacLennan. Richler counted in a way, but he was always in England, and might never return – besides, he had written only one good book, Duddy. Others were peripheral, usually one-book people. In my recollection it seems that we admired people who managed somehow to write novels even though their names were neither Callaghan nor MacLennan; it was like Dr. Johnson and the woman preacher.

[Literary editor] Bob Weaver told us (in his diffident way) that we should read Ethel Wilson, but most of us didn't. Davies had written the Salterton novels, which I liked but did not take seriously. They were "comic novels," therefore not to be compared with the solemn moral thrashings of Callaghan's and MacLennan's characters. We didn't even realize that the greatest English writer of our time was Waugh, also a comic novelist, though we acknowledged that he wrote pretty good stuff.

As between Callaghan and MacLennan, it seems (again, I understand this only in retrospect) that we had to take sides. Callaghan was my guy. I loved his short stories. I loved several of the early novels. I lit a candle every night at the cathedral (well, metaphorically speaking) in the hope that God would give him back his talent, much of which He had cruelly snatched away, in the capricious manner for which He has justly become notorious.

But MacLennan? His prose was heavy, his intentions obvious, his ambitions overweening, etc., etc. There never was any talent.

Well, maybe a little. With The Watch That Ends the Night, I liked the early parts about the hero's boyhood, but after he turns into Norman Bethune I found it, to say the least, unsatisfactory. Communists hated the book because it seemed to say Bethune was not quite a Communist, or maybe a vague fellow traveller. Communists denied MacLennan the right to recreate his friend or acquaintance as a fictional character – they as Communists owned him, and didn't want his political identity fiddled with. Anti-Communists (I among others) didn't like to see an aura of non-partisan altruism being created around this Stalinist/Maoist. We of course had no idea that the kind of thing MacLennan was doing would eventually (with Chairman Mao's help) elevate Bethune into the pantheon of great Canadians, right up there with Louis Riel.

Then there's the long section in The Watch about the miracle-working woman (that's how I recall her) who was based on the first Mrs. MacLennan. I liked that even less.

By now, of course, I had long since read Two Solitudes and decided it was painfully over-explicit. And when I met MacLennan the man I found him a solemn bore. (Many years later, when it was disclosed that Marian Engel had been his stalker/groupie/student, I had a terrible thought: serves him right.)

Something else: MacLennan was tiresomely, relentlessly anti-American, and I was not. In fact, it seemed to me that anti-Americanism was a poison in the system of Canadian culture. It still is, but in a much smaller way, perhaps because there are so many other things to worry about. MacLennan's anti-Americanism took the form of looking down on America from a great height. He was one of those

Canadians of Vincent Massey's generation who unconsciously inherited (and felt entitled to) English snobbery toward America.

So I was anti-MacLennan on several grounds, not exclusively literary. And in 1967, when he wrote his novel about separatism, Return of the Sphinx, I found I believed not a single paragraph of it. My review was unfavorable. But the book got some good reviews in the U.S. (magazines like Commonweal) and a favorable letter from Edmund Wilson. I made a column of these and got a lovely letter from Hugh MacLennan praising me for reporting on all this even though I didn't like the book.

I showed this to a rather critical friend, who said: "Fulford! How the hell do you get away with it? First you beat up this poor old guy. Then you get a free column out of the American reviews and the Wilson letter – and then you get praised by MacLennan." I had to admit it sounded like trickery somewhere.

Love

Bob

THE INFORMING SPIRIT

Lawren S. Harris was a scion of the wealthy family that formed half of the giant Massey-Harris farm-implement company, but he shunned business for art. In the 1920s he and J.E.H. MacDonald were the moving forces behind the Group of Seven, whose paintings of northern Ontario landscapes became Canadian icons. Harris's own minimalist work became increasingly abstract and deeply philosophical through the 1930s – in a transformation he explains in one of the many encouraging letters he wrote to another of Canada's most accomplished artists, the ailing Emily Carr, of Victoria.

35 School St.
Hanover,
New Hampshire.
U.S.A.
April 15/37

Dear T'other Emily,

We <u>are</u> so glad to hear your health improves. After all the improvement is not <u>so</u> slow. Let's see, it not much over two months since you were laid low and with a heart condition such as you had to be up and around now is darn good . . .

You ask about our abstract endeavors. Well they are all different and yet alike – some more abstract than others – some verging on the representational – one never knows where the specific work in hand will lead. I try always to keep away from the representational however – for it seems the further I can keep away and into abstract idiom the more expressive the things become – yet one has in mind and heart the informing spirit of great Nature. This seems fundamental if one [wants?] to escape the mechanical. The things must live in conviction or they are hopeless. I must say that I become more and more convinced that non-representational painting contains the possibility of expressing everything. It takes the expression away from the specific, the incidental and can lift it into another place, where the experience is enhanced, clarified – and its great fun – there is so very much of adventure in it and an intensity of concentration that I like.

Your work is on the verge of what I mean. Sometime when you are painting again – take a definite feeling for nature and try to express it by rhythm, movement, relationships, intensity and difussion and yet keep away from the representational. It can be done . . . It is now a new language or idiom that adds to the range and scope of art. It does not replace any other phase – each has its expressive province – but it is to my mind the idiom of the near future . . .

I dont think there is anything that man cannot know about. I firmly believe the after Death states will become known and that this will be of very great benefit to mankind. Everything on earth and in heaven and every where else and in every state of being is man's province of knowledge. Nothing can be excluded and in milleniums to come man – the thinker, the perceiver, the ongoing enduring Spirit will know the universe of spirit and of matter and of all life completely and utterly – that surely is his job – the unfolding of his spiritual Nature can be but that – all wisdom and understanding – Well, one might say that Man would be a God when that occurs. Quite so. Man is a God. The kingdom of Heaven and all else that is High and Immortal, the spirit, God and all angels are <u>within</u> Man, not to be found anywhere else . . .

Well – what a slang whanging preacher I am . . .

Blessing to you,

Yours,

Lawren.

In 2000 Carr's "War Canoes, Alert Bay" set a western Canadian auction record, selling for $1.019 million, and in 2001 Harris's "Baffin Island" set a Canadian record, selling for $2.43 million.

IN PRAISE OF US

A LEGACY OF 9/11

When terrorists destroyed the World Trade Center and attacked the Pentagon, trans-Atlantic aircraft were diverted to Newfoundland's Gander International Airport. Suddenly a town of 10,300 residents had 6,500 unexpected visitors. Communities across the province rallied to house and feed, inform and entertain their guests in churches, schools, community centres, and private homes. Some people were stranded for two weeks as the tail end of a hurricane delayed flights out of the province. In the following weeks many of those visitors sent their Newfoundland hosts e-mails and letters of thanks, including this *one mailed to a church in Gander from **Dr. Douglas Gordon** of Yellow Springs, Ohio.*

September 16th, 2001

St. Pius X
Catholic Community
16 Smithville Crescent
St. John's, Newfoundland A1B 2V2
Dear Father Bolton and all the Parishioners of St. Pius X,
I was one of the thousands of air travelers who descended on St. John's urgently on September the 11th. We landed in a state of uncertainty and fear for our loved ones, not even fully aware of the nature and extent of the day's horrors. We had been nearly nineteen hours on the airplane when we finally emerged, disoriented and apprehensive, as refugees in your community, knowing that our numbers must be overwhelming.

We were met by the sympathetic and friendly faces of Red Cross and Salvation Army volunteers where we were registered and given nourishment, news, and access to free telephones so that we might contact our families. We were sent out by busses to various community centers already feeling the friendly warmth of the people of St. John's, not realizing this was only a hint of what was yet to come. It was thus that I came to St. Pius X.

You greeted us with much more than a sense of duty or a simple desire to do one's part in a time of crisis but rather with an open enthusiasm and empathy that can only come from profound goodness of spirit. It cannot be feigned nor simulated. You graciously provided us with not only all of our physical needs, but also with the only possible remedy for the sense of evil that enveloped us – your frank and honest good will. You have truly demonstrated the power of good over evil and I will hold all of you in my highest esteem for the remainder of my days.

Though I have enclosed a donation to St. Pius X with this letter, please rest assured that I understand that the only way I can repay my debt to you is by passing on your kindnesses to others and keeping your example with me forever. Please know that you have created with your goodness, ambassadors all over the world as each of us returns home with your message. I can only believe that there is no more powerful means to combat evil in our societies.

With my profound regards

Douglas A. Gordon, MD

ACKNOWLEDGMENTS

Compiling a broad collection of correspondence like this depends on the interest and enthusiasm of Canadians across the country, from those who sent us letters from their family records to those who so generously helped us find letters in public archives.

First and foremost, though, we would like to thank the efficient and untiring Julia McGowan, who transferred most of these letters, many of them with eccentric handwriting, to computer files; dear friend Penny Williams, who translated several French letters into English with her usual style and speed; and Frank Ianni, who was such a gracious host during our time in Ottawa and, as a bonus, let us browse through his wonderful library.

Archivists across Canada were vital collaborators in compiling this collection: Anne Goddard, Sophie Tellier, Daniel Dubé, and the many other helpful reference specialists at the National Archives; Jane Naisbitt and Carol Reid, who gave us such open access to the Canadian War Museum files; Doug Cass and his highly accommodating staff at the Glenbow Museum in Calgary; Apollonia Lang Steele and Marlys Chevrefils of the University of Calgary Library's Special Collections; Diane Lamoreux of the Provincial Archives of Alberta; Raymond Frogner of the University of Alberta Archives;

Mary Rae Shantz and Christine Mosser of the Toronto Reference Library's Special Collections; Harold Averill of the University of Toronto Archives and the Canadian Lesbian and Gay Archives; Gail Weir of the Queen Elizabeth II Library at Memorial University of Newfoundland; Stephen Lyons of the Canadian Pacific Railway Archives; Val Patenaude of the Maple Ridge (B.C.) Museum; Carol Haber and her welcoming staff at the City of Vancouver Archives; Twila Buttimer of the Provincial Archives of New Brunswick; Renu Barrett of the William Ready Division of Archives, McMaster University; and Graham Hill of the McMaster University Library.

We're particularly grateful to several old friends, including Anne Moon (and her friends Margaret Horsfield and Leona Taylor), who doggedly tracked down several letters; David Cobb and Loral Dean, who not only offered us letters from their personal files but also put us up in Toronto and provided some vital local contacts; the multifaceted George Fetherling, who inspired us in our search; and Marty O'Malley, who helped us make a key connection. Joan Bond kindly sent us a letter about letter-writing from which we have quoted.

People in the media embraced the project by publicizing our calls for letters from the public: Christine Langlois and her colleagues at *Canadian Living*; Chris Dafoe, a columnist with the *Winnipeg Free Press*; Rob Mills of *The Telegram*, St. John's; Cynthia deKluyver of *The New Brunswick Reader*; Bev Dauphinee of *The Herald*, Halifax; and the well-connected Jack McAndrew of Charlottetown, who publishes *Golden Times*.

The people of Macfarlane Walter & Ross – especially Gary Ross and Adrienne Guthrie – deserve special credit for quickly grasping the potential of the book and helping to bring it forth so painlessly. John Eerkes-Medrano was a highly sensitive, sharp-eyed, and endlessly patient copyeditor. And, as always, we want to thank our determined and delightful family literary agent, Carolyn Swayze.

At the following archives, museums, and libraries we obtained letters in the fonds or collections indicated or found letters from the people named. Publishers mentioned here gave us permission to reprint letters:

Archives of Ontario (Sir Sandford Fleming fonds);

Bowen Island Archives (Margaret Laurence and Earle Birney);

Canadian Lesbian and Gay Archives (Jack Pollock);

Canadian Pacific Railway Archives, RG-1, 8721 (James Ross);

Canadian War Museum (Ross Baker, Joseph Greenblatt, Horace Bishop);

Centre du Patrimoine, St. Boniface (Father Lacombe);

Centre for Newfoundland Studies Archives, Memorial University of Newfoundland and the Smallwood Family (Joseph Smallwood);

City of Vancouver Archives (Leon Ladner, John Deighton, Henry Clinton, *Komagata Maru* letters; Ernest T. Rea, Henry Cambie);

Gingko Press (Marshall McLuhan);

Glenbow Museum: Bob Edwards fonds; Monica Hopkins fonds; Harold Wigmore McGill and Emma Griffis McGill fonds; Richard Barrington Nevitt fonds; Susan B. Peters fonds; Emilio Picariello fonds; George and Norma Piper Pocaterra fonds; Abraham I. Shumiatcher fonds; John Ware fonds; Strong Buffalo to Jerry Potts (newspaper files)

Imperial Oil Limited Archives (Vern Hunter);

Maple Ridge (B.C.) Museum (Russell Bruce);

Museum at Campbell River (Roderick Haig-Brown and Ann Elmore);

National Archives of Canada: Ted Allan fonds (Norman Bethune letter); Emily Carr fonds (Lawren Harris letter); Frederick Temple Hamilton-Temple-Blackwood, 1st Marquess of Dufferin and Ava fonds; Robertson Davies fonds; Tommy Douglas fonds; Naomi Jackson Grove fonds (A.Y. Jackson letter); James Hargrave and Family fonds (Letitia Hargrave letters); Archibald Kains fonds (Pauline Johnson letters); Grey Owl fonds; Jacques and Raymonde Plante fonds; Talbot Mercer Papineau fonds; collection Louis Riel; Clifford Sifton fonds; John S.D. Thompson papers; Lucille Teasdale and Piero Corti fonds; Traill family collection (Catharine Parr Traill letters); Peter Varley–Frederick Horsman Varley collection; J.S. Woodsworth fonds;

National Library of Canada (Carol Shields);

Niagara-on-the-Lake Library (William Kirby collection);

Provincial Archives of British Columbia (Emily Murphy and D. McDougall);

Springhill Miners' Heritage Society (Con Embree);

Stephen Leacock Museum (Stephen Leacock);

The Champlain Society (Samuel Anderson);

Thomas Fisher Rare Book Library, University of Toronto (Frederick G. Banting papers);

Toronto Public Library (Maynard Grange);

University of Calgary Library Special Collections (W.O. Mitchell and Brian Moore);

University of New Brunswick (Charles G.D. Roberts);

University of Toronto Archives: Fraser Family papers, B1995-0044/ 010C10 (Edith Williams);

University of Toronto Library (J.B. Tyrrell);

University of Toronto Press (Eugene Forsey and John Sparrow David Thompson).

We thank these individuals who sent us the letters indicated or gave us permission to publish letters they had written.

Jack Anawak (to *Up Here*); Elizabeth McCurdy Armour (her correspondence with Douglas Armour); Jane Atkinson (to Ross Atkinson); Patty Beaver (Rick Beaver to her, with his permission); Susan Beresford (her letter to Frank Beresford); Fiona Bially (to Chris Bially); Esther Birney (Earle Birney to Einar Neilson); George Bowering (to *The Georgia Straight*); Amy Brannen (Robert H. Young to her, with his permission); Johanne Brodeur (Randolph Parker to her, with his permission); Rory Brown (Wallace Ross to Amelia Steele); Viola Buchanan (G.B. Buchanan to HMS *Princess Beatrix*); Stephanie Cameron (Eleanor Bone to her mother and father); Karen Candlish (Jack Patterson to Kay Hamilton); Judith Cardwell (William Herbert Griffiths to Elizabeth Ann Barrett); Robert Collins (F.W. Whelihan to Massey Company); Gillian Colton (William Brown to Lila Scott); Loral Dean (Jean Woodburn to Homer Dean); Evelyn Dickie (Walter Dickie to her); Joseph Dobbin (to *The Evening Telegram*); Julie Duncan (Tom Hunt and Mary Stinson); Shirley Douglas (T.C.

Douglas to R.L. Foster and F. Menzies); Vic Daradick (to Peter
Gzowski); Susan C. French (Joseph French to Winnifred French);
Margaret Fulford (John Harris to his father); Robert Fulford (to
Katherine Ashenburg); Anna Gibson (Donald Arthur Fawthrop
to her); Mary Gillis (Muriel Wetmore Teed to her); Beverly Gooding
(Percy John Brown to Ruth Ann Brown); Douglas A. Gordon (to
St. Pius X Catholic Community); Valerie Haig-Brown (Roderick
Haig-Brown and Ann Elmore); Ivan L. Head, O.C., Q.C. (to Justin
and Sacha Trudeau); Norma Hoeppner (Charles Spalding to Mary
Dyck); Gillian Howard (Peter Gzowski to *The Globe and Mail*);
Arthur Hughes (Charles G.D. Roberts to Kathleen Strathearn); Bob
Hunter (to Jim Bohlen); Mel Hurtig (to Jean Chrétien); Elinor
Kartzmark (Martin Kartzmark and George Camplin); Darlene
Kernot (Dan Hauck to her); Barbara Klippenstein (Charles Howatt
to Jennie Silcox); Margaret H. Knox (Lawren Harris to Emily Carr);
Jocelyn Laurence (Margaret Laurence to Muriel and Einar Neilson);
Ina Light (William Wight Robson to Harriet May Currie); Judith
Mader (Maude Estelle de Long to cousin); Wayne and Suzanne
Martel (to *The Ottawa Citizen*); John Masters (to Alf Powis);
Marilyn Michelson (Charles Michelson to her); Catherine Mitchell
(Frank Williams to her, with his permission); Orm Mitchell (W.O.
Mitchell to Merna Hirtle and to Lauri E. Nerman); Jack McClelland
(to Leonard Cohen and to John Fisher); Jean Moore (Brian Moore
to André Deutsch); Eric Nicol (to his parents); Kathy Norstrom (Kirk
Duncan to her, with his permission); Caroline Raymonde Plante
(Jacques Plante to her); Eileen Porteous (Erle Shakespeare to her);
Donna Ratz (Amasa Winger to Lorne Ratz); Tammy Richard (James
Walmsley to Maude and Jimmie Walmsley); Pauline Rowe (Richmond
Sands to Margaret Fraser); Mary Schnarr (Elizabeth Sutherland to
Mary Jackson); Vernon and Mary Scragg (Walter Scragg to Pearl
Scragg); Jeffrey Scouten (to Jacques Tremblay); Betsy Sheffield
(Edward Lordly to Montagu Medlen); Carol Shields (to Maureen
Cressey-Hackett); Katherine Stewart (J.B.Tyrrell to Edith Carey);
Jennifer Surridge (Robertson Davies to Joan, an unnamed woman,
and J.B. Priestley); Monique Teasdale (Lucille Teasdale to friends);

R.H. Thomson (George Stratford to John, Joe Stratford to mother); Elizabeth Thunstrom (W.D. Gunn to Joanna Gunn); Verna G. Tivy (Anna Leveridge to her mother); Phil Vogler (Alvah Chipman to his brother); Michael Walker (to Mark Ungrin); Rex Weyler (to his wife, Glenn); Susan Witton (Harry Witton to her); Alexander Wolfe (to *The Gazette*); Ingeborg Woodcock (George Woodcock to Herbert Read); Woods Family (Clarence McCuaig to his mother).

BIBLIOGRAPHY

Bagnell, Kenneth, *The Little Immigrants: The Orphans Who Came to Canada*. New ed. (Toronto: Dundurn Press, 2001).

Blassingame, John W., ed., *Slave Testimony: Two Centuries of Letters, Speeches, Interviews, and Autobiographies* (Baton Rouge: Louisiana State University Press, 1977).

Bliss, Michael, *Banting: A Biography* (Toronto: McClelland and Stewart, 1984).

Blondin, Robert, and Gilles LaMontagne, eds., *Chers nous autres: un siècle de correspondance québécoise* (Montréal: VLB Éditeur, 1978).

Caswell, Maryanne, *Pioneer Girl* (Toronto: McGraw-Hill, 1964).

Fischer, Doug, ed., *To the Editor: A Century of Letters* (Ottawa: The Ottawa Citizen, 2000).

Forsey, Eugene, *The Sound of One Voice: Eugene Forsey and His Letters to the Press*, ed. J. E. Hodgetts (Toronto: University of Toronto Press, 2000).

Fox, William Sherwood, ed., *Letters of William Davies: Toronto 1854-1861* (Toronto: The University of Toronto Press, 1945).

Ganzevoort, Herman, ed., *The Last Illusion: Letters from Dutch Immigrants in the "Land of Opportunity," 1924-1930*

(Calgary: University of Calgary Press, 1999). (Letter of Frans
van Waeterstadt).

Gibbon, John Murray, *Steel of Empire: The Romantic History of
the Canadian Pacific, the Northwest Passage of Today* (New
York: Bobbs-Merrill, 1935).

Haggart, Ron, and Aubrey E. Golden, *Rumours of War: Canada
and the Kidnap Crisis* (Toronto: New Press, 1971).

Harris, Joseph, and Samuel Anderson, *Letters from the 49th
Parallel, 1857-1873*, ed. C. Ian Jackson (Toronto: The
Champlain Society, 2000).

Hopkins, Monica, *Letters From a Lady Rancher* (Calgary:
Glenbow Museum, 1982).

Kapica, Jack, ed., *Shocked and Appalled: A Century of Letters to
The Globe and Mail* (Toronto: The Globe and Mail, 1985).

Kitagawa, Muriel, *This Is My Own: Letters to Wes And Other
Writings* (Vancouver: Talonbooks, 1985).

Laurier, Wilfrid, *Dearest Émilie: The Love-Letters of Sir Wilfrid
Laurier to Madame Lavergne* (Toronto: NC Press, 1989).

Lawrence, Margaret, *Love Letters to Baruch*, ed. Barnet M. Greene
(Toronto: Musson Book Co., 1973).

Lynn, Helen, ed., *An Annotated Edition of the Correspondence
Between Archibald Lampman and Edward William Thomson
(1890-1898)* (Ottawa: The Tecumseh Press, 1980).

Macdonald, John A., *Affectionately Yours: The Letters of Sir John
A. Macdonald and His Family*, ed. J.K. Johnson (Toronto:
Macmillan, 1969).

MacLeod, Margaret, ed., *Letters of Letitia Hargrave* (Toronto: The
Champlain Society, 1947).

Miller, Craig W., *Union of Opposites: Letters from Rit Svane
Wengel* (Canadian Plains Research Center, University of Regina,
1996).

Pettigrew, Eileen, *The Silent Enemy: Canada and the Deadly Flu of
1918* (Saskatoon: Western Producer Prairie Books, 1983).

Preston, Richard Arthur, ed., *For Friends at Home: A Scottish
Emigrant's Letters from Canada, California and the Cariboo*

1844-1864 (Montreal and London: McGill-Queen's University Press, 1974).

Smith, Goldwin, *The Empire: A Series of Letters Published in "The Daily News," 1862, 1863* (Oxford: J.H. & J. Parker, 1863).

Tuck, Robert C., ed., *Ned Harris: Letters from Mahone Bay* (Charlottetown: Maplewood Books, 2000).

Tuck, Robert C., ed., *The Island Family Harris: Letters of an Immigrant Family in British North America, 1856-1866* (Charlottetown: Ragweed Press, 1983).

Woodcock, George, *A George Woodcock Reader*, ed. Doug (George) Fetherling (Ottawa: Deneau & Greenberg, 1980).

Woods, James Parke, Dorothy Jean Woods, and Timothy Christopher Woods, *The Woods Family in Canada, 1824-1993* (Ottawa, 1993).

Index of Letter Writers

Affleck, Annie (Lady Thompson), 135
Anawak, Jack, 118
Anderson, Captain Samuel, 20
Armour, Douglas, 180
Armour, Libby McCurdy, 180
Arnold, Christina, 69
Baker, Ross, 82
Beaver, Rick, 190
Belaney, Archibald, 238
Beresford, Susan, 202
Bethune, Dr. Norman, 296
Bially, Fiona, 197
Bibb, Henry, 10
Birney, Earle, 259
Bishop, Horace, 59
Blackball, J.H.E., 71
Bone, Eleanor, 243
Bourassa, Robert, 109
Bowering, George, 103
Brown, Percy John, 183
Brown, William Seath, 161
Bruce, Russell, 237
Buchanan, Captain G.B., 80
Cambie, Henry J., 33
Camplin, George, 233
Caswell, Maryanne, 218
Chesson, F.W., 26
Chipman, Alvah, 54
Clinton, Henry Glynne Fiennes, 19
Cressey-Hackett, Maureen, 314
Crowfoot, 32
Currie, Harriet May, 149
Daradick, Vic, 105
Davies, Robertson, 309
Davies, William, 211
De Long, Maude Estelle, 224
Deighton, John, 18
Dickie, Walter, 186

Dobbin, Joseph, 270
Douglas, T.C. (Tommy), 100
Dufferin, Lord, 210
Duncan, Kirk, 195
Edwards, Bob, 228
Elmore, Ann, 168
Embree, Con, 93
Fawthrop, Donald Arthur, 184
Fleming, Jeanie, 208
Fleming, Sandford, 208
Ford, Mary, 25
Forsey, Eugene, 284
French, Sergeant Joseph Tye., Jr., 179
Fulford, Robert, 316
Gordon, Dr. Douglas, 321
Grange, Maynard, 48
Greenblatt, Captain Joseph, 84
Grey Owl, 238
Griffiths, William Herbert, 144
Gunn, Lieutenant Commander W.D., 73
Gzowski, Peter, 103
Haig-Brown, Roderick, 168
Hargrave, Letitia, 8
Harris, Lawren, 318
Harris, Major John L.W., 62
Harris, Reverend Ned, 214
Harris, Sarah Stretch, 13
Hauck, Dan, 194
Head, Ivan, 119
Hopkins, Monica, 226
Howatt, Charles William, 162
Hunt, Tom, 138
Hunter, Bob, 110
Hunter, Vern, 88
Hurtig, Mel, 115
Jackson, A.Y., 45
Johnson, Pauline, 141
Kartzmark, Martin, 233

Kirby, William, 276
Kitagawa, Muriel, 75
Lacombe, Father Albert, 16
Ladner, Leon, 221
Lafrance, Yolande, 188
Lampman, Archibald, 308
Langlois, Charles-Henri, 34
Laporte, Pierre, 107
Laurence, Margaret, 257
Laurier, Sir Wilfrid, 145
Lawrence, Margaret, 176
Leacock, Stephen, 216
Leveridge, Anna, 28
Lordly, Edward, 136
Macdonald, Sir John A., 14
Martel, Suzanne and Wayne, 117
Martin, Julien, 98
Masters, John, 268
McClelland, Jack, 95
McCuaig, Captain Clarence, 43
McDougall, Chief D., 231
McGill, Dr. Harold, 48
McLean, Jean E., 70
McLuhan, Marshall, 286
Me, 203
Michelson, Charles (Sonny), 94
Mitchell, W.O., 174, 312
Moore, Brian, 254
Murphy, Emily, 64
Nathalie, 97
Nevitt, Richard Barrington, 22
Nicol, Eric, 247
Papineau, Talbot, 278
Parker, Randolph, 200
Parsons, Ella, 61
Patterson, John, 66
Peters, Susan B., 262
Picariello, Emilio, 232
Piper, Norma, 240
Plante, Jacques, 189
Pollock, Jack, 113
Ram, Pohlo, 40
Rea, Ernest T., 60
Reid, Malcolm J.R., 41
Renault, Raymond, 129
Richardson, Jane, 192
Riel, Louis, 137
Roach, Edith, 165

Roberts, Sir Charles G.D., 167
Robson, William Wight, 149
Ross, James, 30
Ross, Wallace, 213
Sands, Dr. Richmond, 132
Savelieff, Pheodor, 39
Scouten, Jeffrey, 288
Scragg, Walter, 183
Shakespeare, Erle, 85
Shields, Carol, 313
Sifton, Clifford, 37
Singh, Bhan, 40
Smallwood, Joseph, 91
Smith, Goldwin, 274
Spalding, Charles, 155, 156
Stinson, Mary, 138
Stratford, George, 52
Stratford, Jack, 53
Stratford, Joe, 52
Strong Buffalo, 222
Sutherland, Elizabeth, 157
Teasdale, Dr. Lucille, 299
Teed, Muriel Wetmore, 72
Thompson, James, 130
Thompson, Sir John S.D., 134
Traill, Catharine Parr, 125
Trudeau, Pierre Elliott, 273
Tyrrell, Joseph Burr, 148
Van Waeterstadt, Frans, 234
Varley, Frederick Horsman, 159
Vigneault, Steve, 265
Vitzko, Mike, 38
Vogt, Mrs. William, 156
Walker, Michael, 304
Walmsley, James, 178
Ware, John, 225
Wengel, Rit, 246
Weyler, Rex, 112
Whelihan, F.W., 27
Williams, Dr. Edith Bickerton, 171
Williams, Frank, 204
Winger, Amasa, 164
Witton, Harry, 198
Wolfe, Alexander P., 121
Woodburn, Jean Blair, 172
Woodcock, George, 251
Woodsworth, J.S., 292
Young, Robert, 193

The text of this book was set in Sabon, Jan Tschichold's interpretation of Garamond, originally released in metal by Stempel in 1964 and later digitized by Adobe. Renaissance letter forms and large x-height make Sabon ideal for book setting.

Text design by Terri Nimmo